MAKING OUR PEACE
WITH THE
WARRI☾RS
OF THE
SAND

MAKING OUR PEACE
WITH THE
WARRIORS
OF THE
SAND

Dr. Jeffrey L. Seif & Dr. Ihab Griess

DEFENDER

CRANE, MISSOURI

Making Our Peace with the Warriors of the Sand
Defender
Crane, Missouri 65633
©2010 by Jeffrey L. Seif and Ihab Griess

ISBN-10: 0984061150
ISBN-13: 9780984061150

A CIP catalog record of this book is available from the Library
of Congress.

All Scripture references are taken from the King James Version.

DEDICATED TO MARK LEVITT

In appreciation for giving me the opportunity to walk in the footsteps of his father, the late Zola Levitt, whom Moishe Rosen, the founder of Jews for Jesus, appropriately eulogized as being the most beloved and best known Jewish believer in Jesus since the Apostle Paul.

—J. S.

CONTENTS

INTRODUCTION

Why Focus on the
Warriors of the Sand?

Should Israel-supporting Jews and Christians construe Arabs as "enemies," of a sort? Israel's being situated in a Middle Eastern world with sworn enemies round about, its precarious predicament is obvious to all. The Christian and Jewish response to the situation isn't so obvious, however, and begs us to ask some pertinent questions—foremost of which is the following: How can Bible believers reconcile the Bible's insistence that we love our enemies, on the one hand, with the legitimate need to protect ourselves from those bent on doing us harm, on the other?

Believing that traditional Christian communities and theologies have neither proffered nor modeled sufficient answers to the aforementioned personal and political questions, and that the need to come to terms with them is particularly acute these days, I applied myself to offer a Messianic Jewish reckoning. Mindful that the Arab-Jewish struggle is the Bible's oldest and greatest family feud, I perceive the perennial conflict between my Hebrew people and our estranged Arab cousins to be both spiritual and theological as much as it is economical, social, and political.

1

Biblical revelation extends the Arab-Israeli struggle backward to the very dawn of biblical revelation and then forward to the sunset of human history. Addressed in biblical history and prophecy as the Jewish-Arab struggle is, I believe those of us caught somewhere between the beginning of time and its termination would do well to consider it, as would those who simply want to learn what Scripture says about getting the better of difficult people and circumstances—the Jewish-Arab struggle being foremost.

Believing that a consideration of how we Judeo-Christian sorts might protect ourselves from nasty belligerents while somehow being graciously and appropriately "Torah-observant" and/or "Christ-like" toward them to be a question for our times, this book takes readers to and through some of today's geopolitical troubles and raises penetrating and provocative questions while so doing. Though the principal actors here are what I will call the "people of the sand," and though the stage upon which this drama of the centuries is played out over time is what we call the "Middle East," lessons learned through this Bible study go way beyond Israel and Arabia and have universal appeal and application to a host of political and personal challenges—not to mention an understanding of prophecy.

How Bible believers might reconcile the Scripture's insistence that we love our enemies with the legitimate need to protect ourselves from them speaks to the individual who dwells in a house with an extremely difficult spouse, much as it speaks to those who happen to work with a particularly hard-to-deal-with jerk. The thorny question of how to love those "others"—while protecting ourselves from some of those "others"—imposes itself upon many in other unique ways these days. It imposes itself upon post-9/11 Americans concerned with Islamic aggression and expansionism as much as it imposes itself upon any and all Israel-supporting individuals who, in the post-Holocaust era, are concerned with the Arabian intrigue that threatens Israel's existence, Jewish survival by association, and the West—not to mention that it does so all at the very same time.

Working to untie the perennial Middle Eastern knot and wrestling with conundrums associated with the peace-defying entanglements will help us better come to terms with some of the contentious peoples and geopolitical issues that have bearing on the times in which we live. Taking a fresh look at our estranged Arabian brother-from-another-mother at this particular time similarly holds out promise of also helping us come to terms with those with whom we may be presently estranged in our more immediate and personal webs of relationships. How biblically minded, conservative folks might be peacemakers when dealing with liberal, left-leaning, adversarial sorts is a question for our times as well, is it not?

With these social, political, and religious questions in mind, I ask: Can we do better than simply shake our fists at the devil and say: "Damn you and damn all those *other* people"? I surely think we must do better—especially if we want to attract more and more people to the Scripture's message. If we're to unpack its meaning in a Jewish light, we do well to consider that counter-raging with Bibles in hand may well help us vent frustration, but still, it simply is not the Jewish way—and it certainly is not Jesus' way.

In His famous Sermon on the Mount, Jesus extolled the problems, possibilities, and prospects of peacemaking and imposed upon His hearers the mandate to somehow be peacemakers in a conflicted world. If peacemaking is to be the biblically minded person's principal and principled business, the question of how we might attend to it is worthy of serious consideration, especially given all of the above. Must we simply "turn the other cheek," as instructed in the Sermon on the Mount? Some say so—though I believe this to be overly simplistic.

Jesus' premium—as with the Torah's—on blessing the disenfranchised "poor" (Matt. 5:3), on comforting disoriented "mourners" (v. 4), and on providing satisfaction to the "hungry" and "thirsty" (v. 6), coupled with His placing great value on being a "merciful" "peacemaker" on top (vv. 7, 9) must carry great stock in Bible believers' personal economies—if one is to be truly somehow "Messiah-like" or "Christian." In like manner, Rabbi/Apostle Paul's extolling the virtues of love, peace, kindness, goodness, and gentleness (Gal. 5:22–23) similarly commends a way of being that should endear itself to all of us with Judeo-Christian constitutions.

But what might these exhortations mean in the real world, where such lofty rhetoric needs to be lived out? Considering how we are to be as human beings, with the Bible's overarching preference for peacemaking and reconciling if and when possible, forces serious believers to come to terms with the estranged "other," whether we like it or not, does it not? That we are to interact positively with the broader culture—as with some of those disenfranchised in it and by it—is obvious; how we are to do so is not nearly as obvious. Thus the reason for this book.

Seeing the present-day nation-state of Israel as particularly strong and the ragtag Arab-Muslim resistance to it as rather weak, the tender side of Judeo-Christian virtue beckons good-hearted individuals to support the folks they construe as the unfortunate underdogs in the contest—the weaker. Thus minded, considering what the Gospel might compel us to do for the "poor," the weak and "mourning," and the disenfranchised who are "hungry and thirsty" imposes itself upon those of us who prefer "mercy" and "peacemaking," with the net result that biblical virtue typically inclines religious folk to take the case of the weaker—typically, the so-called Palestinians, in this case. Oftentimes, and for understandable reasons, Jews in Israel draw the short straw in public opinion, construed as they are as the conquerors and the victors, with the Arabs as having been conquered and now the molested victims. "What would Jesus do?" some wonder. "Jesus would obviously support the underdogs," they opine by way of response. Though this kindly disposed perspective may indeed be noble, it nevertheless is overly simplistic, much as the handy recounting and application of the Sermon on the Mount to the situation may be out of context.

Those of us who listen to the underdogs incessantly barking out their incendiary rhetoric and who take note how they consistently bite and devour others in conjunction with their incessant howling construe their vociferousness and dogged determination to "wipe Israel off the face of the earth" in another light—one that draws upon other sympathies and prompts other legitimate biblical responses. For us sorts, *Arab Muslim discontents are not seen as weak and unfortunate victims of Jewish perfidy as much as they are seen as foot soldiers in an ongoing battle against Judeo-Christian civilization.* Given that they are bent on taking the world for Allah, docile responses to such persons are deemed imprudent by those of us who prefer being more resolute—and I include myself in this particular list.

Though we may indeed want to be merciful, loving, and kindly disposed ourselves because some of us see Jesus' "turn-the-other-cheek" doctrine as an exhortation to gracefully and patiently bear up under petty insults for the Gospel's sake, *I do not think it's necessarily prudent to employ the passage as a guiding principle when responding to the perennial geopolitical troubles of our day*—ones that surface in the typically merciless and perennially incendiary clashes known to us as the ongoing Middle East conflict.

The upshot is that those of us who do not want to sheepishly bow to tyrants—as seems the habit in today's "politically correct" climate—and who are not inclined to give credence to the acquiescence and tolerance mantras that hold sway in the current social economy are feeling increasingly alienated and marginalized. In a world where more and more individuals are inclined to mindlessly and sheepishly offer less and less resistance to belligerents in the foolish hope of somehow placating them through gestures of docile acquiescence, those of us who resist the day's politically correct, acquiescent doctrines are seen as irreligious (according to the standards of others), as unreasonable, and as folk who hold to anachronistic ways of thinking and being—ways that supposedly disrupt facilitating progress and world peace. In the present culture, we "religious" folk are seen as bearers of the problem and not as carriers of the solution.

How tragic.

Wearied by devastating wars in the last century and unable to marshal independent national armies to hold invaders at bay in the present century, our dovish and conciliatory European friends are much less inclined to offer spirited responses to aggressors than in days past—as are we on the other side of the big pond. Possessing no serious military might to speak of, and thus having no viable means to hold aggressive belligerents at bay anyway, Europeans have placed their hopes in syrupy tolerance, in statecraft, in diplomacy, and in the hoped-for peacekeeping power of a federation of states called the European Union. They hope to make peace with the warriors of the sand simply by making room for them, by acquiescing to them, and by, in effect, surrendering their culture and their continent to them. I personally think this is ill-advised. What will become of the West?

Though personally appreciative of the need to be a peace-making conversationalist if and when at all possible, and though I place great stock in being a peacemaker, I see no value in sheepishly cowering to adversaries and surrendering our way of life piece by piece—as seems the case in Europe and even in sectors of Israel today. Though *I do not believe there is any real future in giving land for peace,* I do believe that *we need to give away some parcels of prejudice for peace* in the interest of facilitating peace, and that *we need to make some room for Arabs in our minds and hearts.*

In the interest of so doing, herein I will go far out of my way to be as fair, balanced, friendly, and accommodating to Arabs as I know to be. I do not advocate giving away anything, save the fact that I want to give Arab peoples the respect they deserve, and I want to offer Bible readers a much-needed corrective to the way we often misconstrue Arab peoples—peoples I am just now coming to know.

With no firsthand knowledge of Islam and the Arabian world to speak of, our shallow minds have typically had little more than Spartan fantasy images of flying carpets, cartoon depictions of genies in bottles, and romantic impressions left over from movies like *Lawrence of Arabia,* from which we get pictures of those "other" people over there, the Arabs. For most of us, Arabia has traditionally been the stuff of Disney animation. Even though we may have known that the Jewish people have been engaged in a conflict with the Arab people since Israel's inception, the truth is that most of us know precious little about "those people" over yonder, who live and breathe Arabian visions beyond our horizons. The few we do know are typically the sort we would call terrorists. That "other" and distant world was brought nearer to us after 9/11, however, with the result that we have been flooded by all sorts of images—ones that speak to our fears.

For some years now, to varying degrees, many of us have been prayerfully and carefully casting our gaze eastward toward the peoples of the sand. Caught up in the trend, I have looked at Scripture, read thousands of articles, traveled to the Middle East many times, been engaged in many conversations, and digested a variety of books written by well-attested scholars. In the wake and in the process of my so doing, I have begun articulating what I want to say and have weighed in on the issues of the day. This book contains some of the fruit of those labors.

Though I managed to birth and develop most of the volume you have in hand, I was ever mindful of my own personal and professional limitations. While working on the final draft, I asked a former student and old friend from Egypt, Dr. Ihab Griess, if he would assist me. Ihab is a Bible scholar with expertise in Arabic, Hebrew, and Greek. He has understanding of the Scripture and a firsthand knowledge of Muslim peoples and cultures. He is an expert in the history of the Middle East, the very place of his birth. In what follows, and by way of further introduction, I'll introduce you to him—and to myself—thinking the information might help you see what's unique about our individual and combined perspectives and how the synergy stimulates interpretive impulses that prompt new perspectives on current Middle East dilemmas. After a few words about the messengers, I'll go on to inform how the message will be unpacked.

THE AUTHORS

I first met Ihab Griess when he came from Egypt to study at
Christ for the Nations Institute (CFNI), Dallas, where I have
served as an instructor for more than twenty years. Though a
pharmacist by education and vocation, Ihab had an itch for theological studies, which prompted him to come to the States to
pursue his theological education and ministry ambitions.

His first stop was in Dallas, where he became a student of
mine at CFNI and where, for a short time, he attended the
congregation I pastored. I got to know him both as a professor
and as a pastor, and soon became impressed by his insightful-
ness and gentle ways. Feeling called to graduate school, Ihab
told me he wanted to move on and study at Regent University.
I heartily recommended him to Regent, where he went on to
take an M.A. in Old Testament. After finishing that program,
Ihab then went to Trinity Evangelical Divinity School to take
his Ph.D. Unfortunately, after finishing his coursework, fund-
ing dried up with the result that he couldn't complete his studies there. Determined as he was, Ihab went to Southern Baptist
Theological Seminary in Louisville, Kentucky, where he started
his course work over and eventually finished his Ph.D. in Old
Testament in December 2006.

Informed as my Egyptian friend is in biblical literature, with
experience in Islamic language and culture, and with expertise
in Islamic history and studies, I was anxious to pitch my book
proposal and manuscript to him, hoping he would take a liking
to my thesis and the overall intellectual package. Growing up in
Egypt in a Coptic Christian family, Dr. Griess experienced anti-
Christian prejudice firsthand. Thrown on his heels as he was by
"those people" as I knew him to be, I wondered if he'd be able

to marshal the necessary internal resources to contribute to my vision even if he saw merit in it. Happily for me—and for you, I believe—he caught the vision.

In addition to helping with the draft he had in hand, Dr. Griess was able to improve upon it. He was particularly helpful in papering up the section on helping us see how we might build bridges to Muslim peoples. Mindful of historic Islamic encroachment as I am (as you'll see in my section on heterology), I was anxious for Dr. Griess to add some needed counter-balance there, which he did in his closing section on bridge-building.

Unlike Dr. Griess, I—Jeffrey Seif—am not from the Middle East and have no firsthand knowledge of the people, the language, or the culture, except for my many, many experiences in Israel. I was born in the States into a German-Jewish family on November 9, 1955, and was raised in a typical American-Jewish household, save the fact that I was sent off to a yeshiva—an Orthodox Jewish training school. Though raised with a "traditional" American-Jewish upbringing, I eventually came to a saving faith in Jesus (whom I personally prefer calling "Yeshua"), subsequent to which I experienced a "call" into vocational gospel ministry. I eventually went to school to prepare for the ministerial vocation at Moody Bible Institute, Trinity College, the Graduate Theological Foundation, and then the theological seminary at Southern Methodist University, where I took both a master's degree and a doctorate. I am an extremely proud graduate of the North Texas Regional Police Academy as well, retain an active police commission, and serve as a reserve police detective in a good-sized police department—where I also serve as a police chaplain. My law enforcement interests aside, professional ministry assignments include serving as a staff member with the American Board of Missions to the Jews and holding professorships, pastorates, and other professorial posts for well over twenty-six years. My principal employment is with Zola Levitt Ministries, a nationally syndicated television concern through which I teach on the Christian faith's Jewish roots and more. I keep active traveling and ministering in various foreign countries and American cities when invited to speak.

I understand myself to be of conservative ilk theologically, in addition to which I am decidedly pro-Israel and very, *very* pro-Jewish.[1] I believe that the Bible is God's Word and am inclined to take it both seriously and literally. Given to taking its challenge to love all people seriously, as noted above, I nevertheless do *not* understand myself to be anti-Arab—though some may mistakenly think me so.

Though I am critical of Islam, this book isn't full of hate. *Herein, I am more minded to extend a hand to my Arab cousins than I am to take them on.* Based on the assumption that to love our enemies beckons us to consider how to build bridges, I see no other first option for God-fearing sorts.[2] If forced to defend ourselves, then defend ourselves we must.[3] My willingness to *fight*, however, should not be confused with a willingness to *hate*[4]—a non-option, for the aforementioned reason.

I believe that many Arabs under Islam's sway are socialized into disdaining Jews from the womb, much as Christians and Jews now are similarly and understandably predisposed to dislike Arabs and keep them at arm's length. Harmful social proclivities aside—because I do not construe Arab people as enemies of Jews, in Scripture and by nature, as enemies of Americans, as enemies of Christians, or as particular enemies of God (any more than any other person)—I have no intention of casting them as such and pushing them away from me here. What then? I'll explain my positions and approaches in that which follows.

THE BOOK'S ESSENCE, STRUCTURE, AND TITLE

As stated, I believe the thorny Arab-Israeli conflict dates backward to the very dawn of biblical revelation with Abraham, Sarah, and Hagar, and extends forward to the dusk of human history and to the much-dreaded, climactic Battle of Armageddon—dreadfully referred to in the book of Revelation. Mindful of this, I observe that *seemingly intractable Arab-related, Jewish-related, and Christian-related problems serve as bookends in the biblical narrative*, with the rest of the biblical story played out in between. The story is thus the story of the ages—and not just the story of our times. An examination of it should take into account that the problem covers a vast expanse of time and extends out to what Scripture refers to as the "end of time."

Between the Sacred Text's beginning and end, readers are introduced to social unrest, interpersonal conflict, and Arabian intrigue. Mideast tensions surface in early Genesis, and thorny geopolitical problems are noted throughout biblical literature—as with people problems generally. Readers of Israel's sacred story are thus beckoned to consider the place of mysterious Arabian peoples and lands in the unfolding human drama that's central to the Bible's story. Given that "paradise lost" was lost in the Middle East, I am inclined to think that we'd do well to see if the secrets to its recovery might be found there as well.

It is.

As much as human catastrophe is said to have originated in Eden, at the other end of the Bible, Revelation informs that human misery will be terminated from there, when it culminates in a climactic and cataclysmic final showdown. The exact location of Eden aside, *in no uncertain terms could it be said that the Bible's story is a Middle Eastern story*. Scripture predicts that forces marshaled in proximity to ancient Eden will one day stealthily slither into the Holy Land and, like a python, wrap themselves around a reconstituted nation-state of Israel. The relentless and merciless assault upon humankind that began in and/or around ancient Iraq (where Eden may have once been located) and that moved to and through Israel proper will manifest and move aggressively to and through the Holy Land—to be stopped there finally and fully at day's end. The "serpent of old who is the devil and Satan" will be defeated and "bound," according to Revelation 20:2, after which the once-lost, Edenic paradise will soon be restored. With the Kingdom's eventual inauguration comes a cessation of global hostility. Peace at last!

Though this is how I see it, this book is much more than a rehash of the aforementioned prophetic story line made popular in recent days by other authors. With secular and sacred eyes looking intently at the Middle East today, as noted above, I believe that a fresh biblical assessment of the Bible's protological and eschatological intrigues is in order[5]—*one that pays more deliberate attention to the Arab peoples.* This book endeavors to answer that need and is thus distinguished from many of the garden-variety prophecy and theology books on the subject.

While the Old Testament is principally focused on Jews, most do not realize that the Old Testament is *not* just about Jews and that the New Testament is *not* just about Christians. While the Old Testament does indeed focus upon Abraham's literal Hebrew descendants (my people by birth), and while the New Testament does indeed focus upon Jesus and make faith applications to Gentile folk descended from Abraham in a spiritual sense, Scriptures also speak of Abraham's *other* children—a group I'll refer to as the *mysterious* "warriors of the sand." Examining what Scripture says about Jews and Israel is good, as is considering the

Hebrew Bible's applications to Jesus and the Christian experience, generally. While keeping these concerns in view, *a consideration of the Arab question is similarly valuable*—and is long overdue, in my estimation. Believing that *all* lands and peoples of the Middle East are deemed significant in God's eyes—and that the interplay is quite bewildering—I humbly offer some of the fruits of my labor on the above.⁶

For me, Arabs themselves are not unwanted and vanquished castaways in the biblical economy. They are not a subclass of lesser beings destined merely to serve as cannon fodder for God's armies at the Battle of Armageddon. Scripture indicates that they possess abiding covenant promises. Abraham's other descendants are not omitted from the pale of biblical graces and forever banished to the backwaters of divine disfavor. Believing this to be true, permit me to press you by asking the following questions:

Do you think Bible-believing, European types are obliged to disdain Arab peoples and cultures? Does Israel-loving oblige us to be Arab-hating? If so, why? If not, what then? How are Judeo-Christians to be toward Arabs in a world set on edge since 9/11? What do you think it means to be a "peacemaker" in the current economy, where Islamic-inspired angst is ubiquitous and where Judeo-Christian sorts are understandably and appropriately disconcerted? At a time when Israel is making its bid to survive and thrive in its biblical homeland and when America is still embroiled in wars and rumors of wars with Arab-related folks, how are we to love these "other" people? If we are, in fact, to love these "others"—as I believe we somehow are—might we do well to better understand them in light of biblical perspectives and principles? In the process of trying to come to terms with them, might we be well-served to come to terms with ourselves in relation to them? With these and other questions in view, we will take a reasonably long stare in the direction of the mysterious people of the East: the "warriors of the sand."

"Staring" speaks of fixing one's wide-open gaze upon a particular person or object. "Staring someone down," by association, speaks of boldly fixing one's gaze on another human being, until such time as that "other" person feels obliged to lower his or her eyes and/or turn away entirely in submission. "Staring someone in the eye," by contrast, speaks of setting one's fixed gaze upon someone. This expression is divested of the negative connotation of endeavoring to force one into a subordinate position, and denotes respect. It harks back to the daring of the one doing the staring—and no more. In this book, I "stare at" Abraham's estranged son Ishmael and his offspring—in a deliberately *non*-condescending fashion—and do not let him and his progeny out of sight till the book's end. *Making Our Peace with the Warriors of the Sand* doesn't "stare down" Ishmael and his kin—easy as it is for me to do (and easier still for Israelis); it "stares at" him—better, at his descendants, the Arabs. As pro-Israel and basically anti-Islamic as I admittedly am, *I still endeavor to look affectionately and admirably at my marginalized Arab cousins* and, as best as I can, I labor to give a fair and balanced accounting of the place in Scripture given to Arabs who have dwelt in proximity to Israel's daunting shadow[7] from time immemorial.

I deem the resurrection and establishment of a sovereign Jewish nation-state, located smack in the heart of the Arab world, to be providential—not accidental.[8] *Making Our Peace with the Warriors of the Sand* construes that the resurrected Jewish nation-state's existing in proximity to Ishmael's estates has, does, and will factor significantly into God's divine program, and that the concomitant Islamic-inspired, Arab-related angst that seems to nip at the heels of Israel—and the world!—forever is really only to be expected. Speaking of expectations, this book informs that the present-day tensions are themselves preludes to cataclysmic wars yet to come, battles presaged in Scriptures millennia ago—and are thus to be expected, for that reason. *Making Our Peace with the Warriors of the Sand* understands that present-day tensions are birth pangs for a new day and will come to an end on a future day, at the beckoning of a Prince of Peace yet to come, who will bring about the cessation of global hostilities with the arrival of His Kingdom.

This study "stares down" negative attitudes, unchecked critical assumptions, and brazenly anti-Arab dispositions—all of which are deemed to be racist proclivities the Prince of Peace most certainly would *not* approve of. I challenge assumptions that these other grandchildren of Abraham are degenerated subhuman souls made of lesser stock and worth less in the Maker's eye as a result. I posit that Arabs—as with Jews like myself—have inherent and enduring worth, and are not merely demon-inspired, subhuman sorts parading around in human form, destined to be disposed of when God's Judeo-Christian forces oppose and destroy them in an end-time war.

Making Our Peace with the Warriors of the Sand thus "stares down" disrespect and shows how we can respect our estranged Arab friends without relinquishing biblically required support for full Jewish sovereignty in her God-given ancestral homeland. *I demonstrate that we can love and respect Arab neighbors without disrespecting or compromising conservative and evangelical theological convictions*, based on literal understandings of sacred Scripture. I believe, as well, that we—and Israel—do well to protect ourselves from criminals when assaulted. It's in that sense that I have come to terms with the legitimacy of armed responses to Islamic belligerents (or belligerents of any sort), construing as I do that a state's right of self-defense and the necessity of its prosecuting criminal offenders affronts no religion.

Though I am as kindly disposed toward Arabs as I know to be, the following chapters don't shy away from addressing challenges posed by Islamic-inspired Arabic theology, political ideology, and aggression. *However, I, deliberately differentiate between Arab peoples, political dispositions, and radical Islamic persuasions,* and thus, by means of so doing, endeavor to offer a fair and balanced assessment of these "other" Abrahamic people—individuals whom many women and men mistakenly assume to have been banished to the backwaters of divine favor in preference for European Christians and Jews.[9]

Some may slight me for wanting to be Arab-friendly, based on their perception that I am "hopping into bed with the devil." I'll risk that and absorb whatever scorn I get because of it, based on a deep-felt belief that it is simply unacceptable to say, "Damn those people!" Were I to adopt an anti-Arab disposition *carte blanche* and disparage an entire group of humanity based on a race theory that consigns it to an inferior status, I'd be hard-pressed to see how I would be any better than a Nazi theorist in World War II. Blanket hatred of this sort is patently offensive to me, as both a Jew, and one with affections for the world's greatest Jew—Jesus.

More given to pity and compassion than to hatred, I think those predisposed to outright disdain Arab peoples and/or Muslims who dwell within the Islamic world should consider that most of these unfortunate souls are almost completely cut off from modern thought and experience. At the risk of sounding like a dispassionate social scientist, let me point out that many are of illiterate, peasant stock, and are essentially a slave caste being used and pressed under the weight of totalitarian regimes. Because they have little to no exposure to others' ways of thinking and being, the better part of virtue should incline us to be more compassionate than adversarial—though contend we must when pressed. Given the chance, were the option available, I am sure that many Muslims would flee their oppressive worlds for better possibilities elsewhere—as indeed many are already doing. Though compassionate, given that there exists a violent strain within the religion that drives many in the center, I believe we should be guarded still—and thus be "wise as serpents" on the one hand while still being "innocent as doves" on the other.

In the process of wrestling with who these people are and how we are to deal with them and/or ourselves in relation to them, this volume takes readers through a whirlwind study of biblical literature, ancient Near Eastern history,[10] and biblical eschatology. Looking through an optimistic biblical lens all the while, we look at Arabs in the past, in the present, and in the future, and raise questions about ourselves in relation to them all the while.

Though I went with the name *Making Our Peace with the Warriors of the Sand*, I personally preferred an esoteric title: *Arabiology in Protology, Heterology, Eschatology, and Soteriology*. After consulting with a publisher, I opted for the simpler title on the basis of the fact that the other one was deemed too hard to grasp. (Duh?) I dropped it—so as not to scare people away from the book before they had a chance to actually read it. Of the five odd-sounding words in the original—"arabiology," "protology," "heterology," "eschatology," and "soteriology"—only "eschatology" is generally known in some aspects of our culture.[11] Herein, I retain the classifications in the book's subtitles. Because I do so, a word about them is in order here.

"Eschatology," as typically and correctly construed, is a theological term denoting end-time events. It has enjoyed some measured circulation and utility in religious circles for some time now—despite its having been suggested that churchgoing people would be best served to avoid eschatology outright, on the basis of a belief that there isn't much of a future in trying to understand the future. For me, countering the objection seems a good starting point, so I'll "stare it down" here at the outset and by way of introduction.

Warning about "end-times fever" and describing the interest in eschatology as "unfortunate," "dangerous," and "destructive," Dr. Kai Kjaer-Hansen offered a negative assessment of the field. Speaking at a coordinating committee for the Lausanne Conference on Evangelism, Kjaer-Hansen proffered, "Believers would do themselves and the rest of us an enormous favor if they dissociated themselves from speculative prophecy," and then he opined that "eschatological pressure may very well be the greatest danger to the movement."

The Lausanne Conference gathers together the world's most significant mission organizations, professors of missions, and practitioners in the fields of evangelistic outreach. Academic papers are presented there, mission executives network there, and mission strategies are cultivated there. It was there where one of our movement's greatest minds postulated that "there isn't much of a future in looking at the future."

Given the significance of the conference and the brilliance of Dr. Kjaer-Hansen, his taking prophecy teaching to task warrants a response. Because I am asked to give an accounting of prophecy—among other things—in local churches, at conferences, via articles, and through nationally syndicated television productions, I figured I might as well do so here.

First of all, let me say that—at one level—I agree with Dr. Kjaer-Hansen, as with others whom he employs in proffering his critique. I sincerely respect Kai and, with him, note that there are

lots of eccentric "crazies" in the end-of-the-world teaching industry. I don't want to be one of them myself, but I imagine that
some will lump me in with the "nuts." Irrespective, my response
to Dr. Kjaer-Hansen's censure comes not in the form of a defensive question, but in the form of an offensive question: *If responsible theologians shy away from addressing eschatology, don't we give
exclusive teaching rights to the "crazies" by default?*

I think we do.

With Kjaer-Hansen, I am mindful that many creative individuals let their imaginations loose onto biblical literature and come
up with all sorts of "inspirations." Intoxicated by how their biblical assessments allegedly correlate in modern history, they present
their idiosyncratic work-products to the world. Not knowing better, people not only buy their books, but they also buy into their
assumptions and expose themselves to ridicule when giving voice
to them. While conceding with Kjaer-Hansen that there indeed
is a problem, I say that *shutting down prophecy teaching altogether
hardly seems the solution.*

I remember sitting down and discussing this issue with my
mentor and former doctoral advisor, Professor William "Billy"
Abraham. Billy took his doctorate from Oxford University and,
with Dr. Kjaer-Hansen, has an abiding preference for responsible
scholarship. Once, when I was complaining about the prophecy
field and giving voice to my aversion to engaging it personally,
Billy challenged me, saying in effect: "If you don't like it as it is,
why don't you get in there and do a better job—as a more responsible theologian?"

Billy's challenge resonated with me then, as now.

Realizing that dedicated and intelligent people want to learn
prophecy, I believe that I—a Jewish believer in Jesus who is a for-
mally trained theologian—have both the mandate and a respon-

sibility to weigh in on the heavy issues associated with it, and not run away from ancillary burdens that result.

The legitimate interest in prophecy is precipitated by the incredible corpse of modern Israel emerging from the grave after centuries of death, dismemberment, and decay. Providence seems not only to have guided the biblically based nation both to and through its re-emergence, but also to have given the state assistance in its myriad recurrent national emergencies since inception. Israel's presence among nations—and against all odds—raises a host of sociological, philosophical, and theological questions, not to mention biblical questions related to prophecy particularly. These need to be assessed and addressed.

With the material nation's rise has come the providential spiritual rise of the Messianic Jewish movement—comprising multiple hundreds of thousands of Jews who are, in fact, now for Jesus. I am one of them.

The nearly simultaneous recreations of both—particularly the nation's miraculous emergence—produced a starburst of enthusiasm and a legitimate interest in connecting the ancient Jewish Bible with the modern world, one where Jews are making a fresh bid to survive and thrive in the ancestral homeland. As we know, Israel's emergence likewise stimulated the angst of regional powers, which in various ways and on various days vented their fury by fomenting "wars and rumors of wars."

How mysterious.

What a social and theological marvel to behold in our day! Refusing biblical commentary on the modern miracle and its attendant possibilities and problems not only denies the miracle unfolding before our very eyes, but by refusing to come to terms with the world and the Word, the myriad theologians who disengage from offering perspective on Middle East events surrender their prerogatives to offer a responsible telling to others. A Bible school professor of twenty years myself, I prefer weighing in on the issues and—with formal experience and education—assume I have earned the right to do that, the objections from detractors aside.

I am not lumping Kjaer-Hansen—an expert on the past and present—with everyone in the discontented lot. I am saying, though, that his presentation motivates me to say that erudite Bible teachers have no right to complain about the state of the teaching field if they walk away from it. Why is that? It's because the disarray in the prophecy field stems, in part, from many having surrendered their mandates to be responsible Bible teachers and to offer timely accountings of what God is doing in the world.

Yes, there is a future in considering the future. I say: Let's seize the day while it is day and give voice to the dawning tomorrow!

So much for "staring down" critics and speaking directly to the issue of eschatology—future events. What of "arabiology," "protology," and the rest of the "-ologies" noted previously? Before letting you out of my lengthy introduction, a word on these is in order.

As much as eschatology speaks of "last things," protology speaks of "first things"—as in the word "prototype." Just as the book of Revelation looks ahead to things to come and is thus arguably eschatological in nature, Genesis looks backward to things that once were, and is thus partly protological. I don't want to make much of it here, at the outset. Know, though, that in this volume I will demonstrate how *history's endgame is theologically unintelligible without understanding the Bible's telling of its first game*—both of which present with mysterious Arab-related issues. Knowing you'll see how that is the case shortly, I'll move beyond protology to discuss a word I pretty much invented for this book: "arabiology." [12]

Most Christians—and many American Jews, for that matter—knew little to nothing about Arabs prior to 9/11. Arabia was
a fantasy world replete with mythic flying carpets and genies in
bottles, and, thanks to *Lawrence of Arabia*, was the stuff of movie
lore. Arabia—and Islam, by association—invoked the imaginations of screenwriters and Disney animators, not of church folks,
theologians, soldiers, and politicians—never mind the general
public. America knew nothing.[13] Israeli Jews weren't afforded the
luxury of maintaining the distance, however.

Annexed as Jewish Israel had been by Islamic-inspired Arabian
conquerors from AD 634–1072, by Seljuk from AD 1072–1099,
by the Mameluk Muslims from AD 1291–1517, and by the
Turkish Muslims from AD 1517–1917, the modern Muslim
descendants of these affiliated peoples demonstrated time and
time again that they were displeased by Israel's fresh emergence as
a Jewish nation-state, and were doggedly determined to destroy
it. Though Westerners are just now being confronted with Islamic
and Arabian political unrest and intrigue, Jewish Israel has been
wrestling with it for decades. Set on edge as we have been by news
of and experience with Arab nation-states and belligerent terrorist groups at the present, we are naturally inclined to outright
demonize Arabian peoples and the religion that inspires so many
of them. Though critical, I want to caution against this—tempt-
ing as it is to fall into it myself.

Pictures of America being attacked by commandeered air-
planes are indelibly marked upon our psyche. In addition to those
shots that were imprinted on our mind's eye are pictures of U.S.
troops on the ground in the Middle East. Not only have the "dogs
of war" been unleashed in our exterior world, but interior to us
is an unchecked assumption that all of those Muslim people over
there are a horribly bad lot by nature. It is likewise believed that

their innate "badness" will facilitate their coming into their own as a condemned race, as a miserable people destined to lead the world to the brink of a final and climactic struggle, one that will have its resolution at the coming of the Christ at the Battle of Armageddon. Thus construed, *Arabs become either depersonalized or are personalized as incarnated demons, little more.* It's bad either way, is it not? If this is the operative assumption—and I believe it is the assumption many people work with and from, whether noted tacitly or explicitly—then, on the basis of its being loaded with lots of theological baggage, I think it is prudent for a theologian to examine these and related assumptions, and see if the Scriptures fully support the assessment.

Dr. Griess concurred, so off we go to begin our assessment of Holy Writ.

Jeffrey L. Seif

Dallas, Texas

2010

ARABIAN PEOPLE IN SACRED SCRIPTURE

Arabiology: Arabs and Jews
at the Dawn of Sacred Time

Situated as Israel is at the southwestern part of the Fertile Crescent, and perched precariously at the major overland crossroads connecting Africa, Asia, and Europe, the fact that war would come to the land over and again is only to be expected. While Scripture records the various skirmishes and wars with the people of the East (our "warriors of the sand"), it similarly attests to Abraham being the father of *both* Arab peoples and Jewish peoples, and thus frames some of the conflict in the context of a family feud. That tensions and troubles are dually noted is only to be expected; what is unexpected, by my reckoning, is how the Jewish Bible nevertheless goes way out of its way to show God's love for Arab peoples, even so.

Given the influence biblical literature has had upon many, the biblical story of the interrelationship between Abraham, Ishmael, and Isaac is reasonably well known in our culture's lore—improperly nuanced though it often is. Believing that since all the biblical roads lead back to our "father" Abraham, we would do well to start with him—and begin by exploring the mysterious and

affectionate interplay between the Jewish and Arabian peoples in
the Sacred Writ. The following story will start off slowly. The
pace will pick up, however, and you'll be left breathless before you
get out of the chapter.

ABRAHAM

In Genesis 11:29–30, Moses matter-of-factly told his readers that
Abram (referred to later as "Abraham") took a wife who was "barren" and thus had "no child." A seminal promise of peoples to
come was then noted in 12:1–3, where it was stated that Abram
would eventually be a "great nation" and a great people, and that
the "families of the earth" would be blessed through his yet non-
existent progeny. This must have surely seemed odd to him, given
the fact that Abraham had no children at the time and the prospects of his having them were diminishing with time.

Strange start, is it not?

Bible readers hear Abraham and Sarai (referred to later as
"Sarah") expressing frustration in the biblical record, given Sarah's
ineptness. For example, in response to a later assurance that God
is Abraham's "shield, and...reward" (15:1), Abraham retorted:
"LORD GOD, what wilt thou give me, seeing I go childless, and the
heir of my house is this Eliezer of Damascus?" (v. 2). In essence,
the frustrated man was saying: "Why are you promising what
you have yet to deliver?" That it indeed weighed heavy upon him
is evidenced by the fact that his concern was repeated twice: In
verse 3, Abraham responded again, not with a question but with
a seemingly superfluous follow-up: "Look, You have given me no
offspring...!" He obviously was not a happy camper.

The frustration oozing out in and from the text attests to the fact that the problem had been bothering[14] Abraham for years. That aside, the promise of future generations was affirmed later in an ancient covenant-making ceremony in Genesis 15:7–11, after which the Lord affirmed the covenant afresh, noting more particulars: "Unto thy seed have I given this land, from the river of Egypt unto the great river, the river Euphrates: [as with] The Kenites, and the Kenizzites, and the Kadmonites, And the Hittites, and the Perizzites, and the the Rephaim, And the Amorites, and the Canaanites, and the Girgashites, and the Jebusites" (Gen. 15:18b–21). Though no doubt himself touched by the aforementioned moving "religious" experience, for her part, a perhaps more practically minded Sarah was ever so cognizant of her inability to contribute and was given to considering the means by which her husband's destiny might be fulfilled.

In 16:1a, Moses repeated what he'd already said twice: "Now Sarai, Abram's wife, bore him no children." This time, however, he noted that Sarai's Egyptian maidservant, Hagar, was nearby (v. 1b), and then he proceeded to inform why that was significant: "And Sarai said unto Abram, 'Behold now, the Lord hath restrained me from bearing: I pray thee, go in unto my maid; it may be that I may obtain children by her.' And Abram hearkened to the voice of Sarai" (v. 2). Moses reported that this arguably young domestic worker was then taken and given to Abram by Sarai (v. 3), and that she eventually conceived a child (v. 4).

Tensions between the "first lady," Sarai, and the younger, "other lady," Hagar, came to the surface immediately in the text—much as they seem to have been coming to the surface ever since. In verse 4, Moses noted that Hagar "despised" Sarai, a disposition known to Sarai, who then flew off the handle at Abram with: "The wrong done me be upon thee: I have given my maid into thy bosom; and when she saw that she had conceived,

I was despised in her eyes" (v. 5). Here, Sarai was arguably giving expression to sentiments she had carried with her for some time: feelings that turned to actions—as is often the case with the passage of time.

There is no evidence that the likely teenaged Hagar had any interest in marrying Abraham—a man well advanced in age by this time. Something of a disempowered domestic worker herself, Hagar seems to have been simply pawned off on this elderly fellow. For all we know, she might have loved a younger field hand, and may well have had hopes of securing a life with him—if she had any personal hopes at all. It was not to be, however. Sarah commandeered her in the service of her own interests, and then, according to verse 6b, she "dealt hardly" with Hagar, with the result that much younger and less powerful Hagar fled from her presence. The Lord visited the young Egyptian girl after she had taken flight, and exhorted her to "return...and submit" to her mistress, Sarai (v. 9). Additionally, and more importantly for our purposes here, Hagar was told that she'd bear a son named "Ishmael," that he'd be a strong and "wild man," that he'd be neither domesticated nor shackled by confines of forced submission, and that he'd "dwell" in proximity to the rest of "his brethren" (vv. 11–12). Good news indeed!

Though word of his being a strong and "wild man" seems a negative connotation at first blush, it would arguably have been welcome news to the subservient Hagar, who though forever acted upon by forces beyond her control now learned that her son would not be so shackled.

In time, providence had it that intermediaries came to Abraham with news of a coming breakthrough—a soon-coming heir. In Genesis 18:10, a few heavenly messengers came, saying: "Lo, Sarah, thy wife, shall have a son." Moses noted that Sarah was eavesdropping on the conversation (v. 10b) and that she had passed the age of child bearing (v. 11b). Thus noted, Sarah's cynical voice was interjected into the narrative with, "After I have become old shall I have pleasure, my lord being old also?" in verse 12. The answer was "yes," though she barely believed it herself (vv. 12, 15). Notwithstanding, in due time, "the LORD visited Sarah as He had said, and the LORD did unto Sarah as He had spoken" (Genesis 21:1). She "conceived, and bore Abraham a son in his old age" (v. 2), and when he was one hundred years old, "his son, Isaac, was born to him" (v. 5).

That there was no love between Abraham's two principal ladies—the best-known mothers of the Arab and Jewish peoples—is evidenced by the fact that "on the same day that Isaac was weaned" from Sarah's breast (v. 8), Sarah turned and "said unto Abraham, 'Cast out this bondwoman and her son; for the son of this bondwoman shall not be heir with my son, even with Isaac'" (v. 10). Sounds harsh, does it not?

Time and time again, Sarah strikes me as being particularly culpable in the narrative. She set up Hagar, agitated her, opted to displace her, and then forcefully drove her away when her own son arrived. Moses said the exploding contention was particularly "grievous in Abraham's sight because of his son" (v. 11). Though Abraham deeply loved his son Ishmael (v. 11) and was minded to be kindly disposed toward his Egyptian wife Hagar, the Lord visited him and told Abraham: "In all that Sarah has said to unto thee, hearken unto her voice; for in Isaac shall thy seed be called. And also of the son of the bondwoman will I make a nation, because he is thy seed" (vv. 12b–13). Then, in verse 18, He said that Ishmael would be a "great nation." God is represented as loving Ishmael, as promising a future for him and the Arab peoples generally, and as only tolerating Sarah's flagrant and unkind disregard.

Casual readers of the texts note obvious tensions between Sarah and Hagar, and that Abraham's principal land inheritance went to Sarah's son Isaac. Though marginalized, and despite the fact that Hagar and Ishmael eventually moved away, God's graces are still evident upon them and their descendants, with promises that they would likewise be strong and successful—more so than Hagar was in her day.

Abraham was little more than a petty tribal chief at this time and had barely secured a toehold in Canaan. Given that he himself was little better than a stranger in a foreign and hostile land, his sending away Hagar and Ishmael to confront uncertainties should not be construed as brazen disregard for them. Truth is, all parties were beset with uncertainties. His descendants through Isaac would themselves be forced to eke out their own livings in an uncertain and precarious world. What was certain for all parties, however, was a promise of *blessings*—each in their own way. That this indeed has proven to be the case down to this day is amply attested in history. What's often unremembered, however, is the place for Hagar vouchsafed in that history.

It is likely that the heavenly being that spoke to Hagar in Genesis 16 was the Creator God Himself, for in verse 10, He stated that He would greatly increase her offspring. Assuming that creating is a prerogative of God alone forces the conclusion. It is noteworthy that Ishmael's name was divinely inspired and that the name given was not Hagar's innovation (cf. Gen. 16:11). This is profoundly important! The name "Ishmael" in and of itself is loaded with prophetic significance. Ishmael means "God hears." The *name is impregnated with a prophetic anticipation that God will hear Ishmael and his descendants—the Ishmaelites, by association.*

Later, in Genesis 21:17, when Hagar was dismissed from

Abraham's household and was wandering around the desert with her child dying under a shrub, the biblical text twice states clearly that God *heard* the cry of the child, Ishmael: "God heard the voice of the lad; and the angel of God called to Hagar out of heaven, and said unto her, 'What aileth thee, Hagar? Fear not; for *God hath heard the voice of the lad* where he is.'"

Does God still hear his cries? *Yes He does!*

Does God abandon Ishmael? *No He does not!*

These two passages signify some sort of a developing relationship between Ishmael and his descendants on one hand, and with God on the other hand. Though not exactly a covenant relationship like Isaac's (and, by association, with the Hebrews to come), where there is in fact a covenantal relationship, there is still something worth noting and remembering. Those minded to disparage and dismiss Ishmael and his descendants would do well to keep this in mind.

Hagar—the mother of Arab peoples—took the liberty of addressing God in person, calling Him in Genesis 16:13 "El-Roi," which means "You are the One that sees" (a commonly circulating Semitic expression). In this regard, Hagar—again the Egyptian-born mother of future Arab peoples—stands out as the only person in the entire Bible who confers a name on Yahweh, the God of Israel.

Hagar proceeded in 16:14 to call the well *Beer Lahai Roi*, which means "the well of the 'Living One that Sees.'" It is noteworthy that calling places after God's name was a practice hardly ever found outside of the patriarchal circle. This graces Hagar—the mother of the Arabs—with a special place in sacred history, as much as the noting that God both sees and hears Arabs should mark itself on our memories, lest we be too inclined to minimize those whom God wants to maximize.

The aforementioned well became the dwelling place of Isaac. We're told that Isaac settled near Beer-lahai-roi (Gen. 25:11). That there is no mention of any conflict whatsoever between Ishmael and Isaac by the well of Ishmael's mother is telling, and speaks of peaceful days in the past. Would that they returned in the present!

The promise Hagar received in Genesis 16:10—that God would greatly increase her offspring, and that they would be too many to count—is similar to that received by Abraham in Genesis 13:16, where the text says: "I will make thy seed as the dust of the earth, so that if a man can number the dust of the earth, then shall thy seed also be numbered." In this regard, Hagar—as with Sarah, Rachel, and others—stands in the circle of the few women in biblical history promised the multiplication of offspring, and some special offspring at that.

"Kings shall come out of thee [Ishmael]" is the promise noted in Genesis 17:6. This forceful biblical promise elevates Ishmael and his children to a higher plane. Abraham's saying "Oh, that Ishmael might live before Thee" in Genesis 17:18 similarly lends credence to the notion that the father of the Arabs was loved with an abiding love. In Genesis 17:20, Scripture says, "As for Ishmael, I have heard thee: behold, I have blessed him, and will make him fruitful, and will multiply him exceedingly; twelve princes shall he beget, and I will make him a great nation."

God promised Abraham that He'd bless his son Ishmael, make him fruitful, and greatly increase him in number. In fact, God proceeded to give Ishmael a parallel of Abraham's promise of making a "great nation" out of him.

Being part of Abraham's household, Ishmael accepted circumcision in his flesh as the sign of the covenant—as was the case with the Hebrews. In fact, the biblical text makes an interesting point in this regard. Genesis 17:24 points out Abraham's acceptance of the sign in his flesh, along with a record of his age at the time of the event: "Abraham was ninety years old and nine, when he was circumcised in the flesh of his foreskin." Genesis 17:25 does the very same thing with Ishmael: "And Ishmael, his son, was thirteen years old, when he was circumcised in the flesh of his foreskin." Scripture says: "In the very same day was Abraham circumcised, and Ishmael, his son" (Gen. 17:26). The main purpose of putting 17:26 the way it is (against the background of vv. 24 and 25) is to highlight once again the *special connection between Abraham and Ishmael*, a bond that should prompt reflection on the relationship between Ishmael and Isaac and their respective descendants.

The boys eventually separated, of course, and went their individual ways. Nevertheless, the promise of making a great nation out of Ishmael elsewhere is reaffirmed later in the narrative, but this time to Hagar: "Arise, lift up the lad, and hold him in thine hand; for I will make him a great nation" (Gen. 21:18). Finally, Genesis 21:20 bears testimony that God would not abandon the lad: "God was with the lad; and he grew, and dwelt in the wilderness, and became an archer."

About seventy-two years later, a peaceful family reunion occurred between the two elderly brothers—Isaac and Ishmael. The brothers-from-other-mothers met to bury their then-deceased father, Abraham: "His sons Isaac and Ishmael buried him in the cave of Machpelah" (Gen. 25:9). It is noteworthy here that the event went peacefully, with the Bible bearing no testimony of past grudges revisited. Would that the spirit of mutual respect prevail today!

Moving on, we note that the dwelling places of Ishmael's swelling descendants were not confined to the Arab Peninsula alone (contemporary Saudi Arabia), though this was their primary locale. According to Genesis 25:18, their habitations extended from north of the Arabian Peninsula to the eastern strip of Sinai, and northeastwards across the Jordan River to the western side of the Euphrates in what is called the Syro-Arabian desert: "They dwelt from Havilah unto Shur, that is before Egypt, as thou goest toward Assyria." They camped alongside all their kinsmen, we're told. This expanse of land that literally surrounds Israel from the south, east, and northeast explains the biblical statement that their dwelling was alongside their brethren, as Genesis 25:18 states. This geographical allocation explains why there were later instances of intermarriage. Esau—Isaac's other son—married an Ishmaelite woman (Gen. 28:9). These related kin dwelt near enough and offered marital options for the burgeoning clans. Their extended geographical allocation also helps explain the inadvertent role the descendants of Ishmael played in the life of the nation of Israel through Joseph, and via their trade associations—a role that eventually rescued Jacob's clan from premature extinction, as we shall see later.

Speaking of proximity, the Hebrew phrase in Genesis 16:12c (וְעַל־פְּנֵי כָל־אֶחָיו יִשְׁכֹּן) literally means "before the face of" or "in front of." Grammatically speaking, this is an adverbial phrase with a type of adverb conventionally known to linguistics as an adverb of place/placement. The verb (יִשְׁכֹּן) speaks not only of dwelling, but also insinuates an atmosphere of *serenity*.[15] The context of the whole passage of Genesis 16:10 and 14 is that of vision, provision, blessedness, and peace. This phrase is repeated in Genesis 25:18 with a slight change of the verb (עַל־פְּנֵי כָל־אֶחָיו נָפָל), which is translated as "they camped *alongside* their kinsmen," and thus they lived in peace. The beginning of the verse explores all the actual locales included under "in front of," as follows: "And they dwelt from Havilah unto Shur, that is before Egypt, as thou goest toward

Assyria." On one hand, this confirms the fact that Genesis 16:12c
(וְעַל־פְּנֵי כָל־אֶחָיו יִשְׁכֹּן) should be understood and translated as an
adverbial phrase of place and not of a state of affairs. Consequently,
this does away with any possibility of a notion of hostility. On the
other hand, naming the locales gives this misconceived statement
of Genesis 16:12c (וְעַל־פְּנֵי כָל־אֶחָיו יִשְׁכֹּן) a panoramic background
that refutes all the more any notion of hostility intended to be
communicated by the biblical text.

*There is simply no biblical evidence that Ishmael was inherently
evil and/or was destined to make others miserable.* If you have trouble getting the point on the basis of the aforementioned textual
evidence, you'll surely pick it up as you read on. The Bible com-
municates that Ishmael's kin would live all the way around the
sons of Isaac. Further, the biblical historical evidence repeatedly
shows that Ishmael and Isaac were *fraternally bonded—not only
biologically bonded*—and that they dwelt peacefully side by side
along the banks of the Jordan River.

Given the high regard in which Ishmael was held in Abraham's
estimation, *there is absolutely no merit in disparaging Ishmael's
descendants* on the basis of an alleged biblical bias. Construing
Arabs as forgotten outcasts says more about the bias of some biblical interpreters than it does about any bias in the Sacred Text. It
is hardly reflective of Abraham's own sentiments and, as we shall
see, *carte-blanche* disdain for Arabian peoples was hardly the perspective of others in the Bible's unfolding drama.

ARABS, ARAB-CONFEDERATES, AND JOSEPH

Though not ethnically Arabians or even Semites, the Egyptians,
along with the Hebrews, were the progenitors of the Arab race—

with the principal protagonists in the biblical telling of the story being Abraham, Hagar, and Ishmael. Though perhaps the most popular, the Abraham-Hagar marriage was not the only incident of Egyptian-Hebrew intermarriage. When thinking of another significant occasion of Egyptian-Hebrew intermarriage, the amazing story of Joseph comes to mind.

Bible readers learn that though Joseph was not appreciated by his own Hebrew brethren, the neighboring Egyptians came to respect and honor him to the point that he ascended to be second to Pharaoh in the kingdom. Genesis 41:40–44 states that the Egyptian Pharaoh said and did the following:

> "Thou shalt be over my house, and according unto thy word shall all my people be ruled: only in the throne will I be greater than thou." And Pharaoh said unto Joseph, "See, I have set thee over all the land of Egypt." And Pharaoh took off his ring from his hand, and put it upon Joseph's hand, and arrayed him in vestures of fine linen, and put a gold chain about his neck; And he made him to ride in the second chariot which he had; and they cried before him, "Bow the knee," and he made him ruler over all the land of Egypt. And Pharaoh said unto Joseph, "I am Pharaoh, and without thee shall no man lift up his hand or foot in all the land of Egypt."

Impressive, is it not?

Imagine a citizen of a neighboring country becoming the vice president of your own, long before the world knew anything about globalization. That Joseph went on to marry a politically positioned Egyptian woman (not an Israelite!) and produced two boys with her—Manasseh and Ephraim—is but another example both of intermarriage and of the interconnections between the neighboring and related peoples and lands. The latter, Ephraim (who was basically a biracial son with half of his blood Hebrew and the other half Egyptian), eventually acquired presidency over ten of Israel's twelve tribes and became a counterpart of Judah, did he not? Israel has never had a tribe under the name of Joseph. Joseph's inheritance within the chosen race was split between his two biracial sons whom Jacob eventually claimed to be his own: "An angel who redeemed me from all evil, bless the lads; and let my name be named on them, and the name of my fathers, Abraham and Isaac; and let them grow into a multitude in the midst of the earth" (Gen. 48:16). The last patriarch called his name, as well as the names of Abraham and Isaac, upon the two lads who were half-Egyptian half-Hebraic, and invoked the blessing of multiplicity.

Summarized above is interplay between the sons of Isaac and their lifelong neighbors, the Egyptians. This interplay would not have been transacted without the significant contribution of the Ishmaelites, themselves the fruit of Egyptian-Hebrew intermarriage.

MOSES

The name "Moses" is Egyptian in origin (akin, for example, to the famous kings Ramses and Thutmose [i.e., Ra-*moses* and Tut-*moses*]). While Abraham is credited with being the father of the Hebrew *race*, in biblical literature Moses is credited as being the father of the Hebrew people's *religion*—now called Judaism. Moses' person and writings can be likened to a shining sun, with the various Old Testament prophets revolving around that sun and, to varying degrees and in various ways, reflecting that light's rays onto different planets in the solar system. Jesus Christ Himself credited Moses as being Israel's principal lawgiver. He went on record lending credence by saying that "the Law was given by Moses" (John 1:17). Jesus referred to Moses as the decisive authority later, with: "For had ye believed Moses, ye would have believed Me" (5:39–47, esp. v. 46). Given contributions noted in Genesis, Exodus, Leviticus, Numbers, and Deuteronomy, Moses really needs no introduction and would have stood out just fine had Jesus not given him the endorsement. His wife, on the other hand, needs to be reintroduced—particularly because, as you shall see, *she was in effect a non-Jewish Arab.* Let's revisit the story of Judaism's most well-respected sage and pay attention to his family.

Moses made his entrance onto the stage of the human drama in troubled times. The story is clearly noted in Exodus 1:8–22, where, wanting to regulate the growth of Hebrew slave stock, Egyptians had Israelite boys put to death after birth (vv. 15–22). Not wishing such a fate for their child, a couple bent on defying the policy built a little boat and placed the newborn in it. Hoping providence might shine upon him and spare him the fate that awaited the children of parents who were less proactive (2:1–4), they trusted God amidst their precarious circumstances. Fortuitously—better, providentially!—one of Pharaoh's daughters was bathing in the Nile (v. 5a) and happened upon the little ark. She noticed the child therein (v. 6a), and though she knew he was a Hebrew, she "had compassion on him" (v. 6b), made arrangements for his upbringing (vv. 7–9), and adopted Moses as her own royal son (v. 10).

Despite Sarah's not being previously minded to be kindly disposed toward a disempowered Egyptian woman named Hagar, here, a young Egyptian woman of significant standing is represented as being kindly disposed toward Moses—to date, Abraham's most significant son. If an Egyptian can have compassion on a Hebrew, one wonders if a Jew (and/or a "grafted-in" Christian) might do well to develop an aptitude to be a bit more compassionate toward Egyptians—as with others. That reasonable question aside, we note in the narrative that Moses eventually had a falling-out with the Egyptians, with the result that he was banished from the realm (Exodus 2:11–15a), as Hagar and Ishmael had been beforehand. It seems that pushing people to the borders is an intrinsic part of the unfolding story.

While on the run and alone in the world—as Hagar and Ishmael are said to have been previously—Moses went and "dwelt in the land of Midian; and he sat down by a well" (v. 15b). While there, seven Midianite girls came to water their flock. Though they were there first and thus had first rights at the well, some local shepherd boys figured they could get the better of the weaker girls and had no compunction about driving them away from the well and tending to their livestock first (v. 17a). Moses didn't personally know the girls, and he didn't know the boys and thus had no stake in any argument over watering rights, yet he still knew right from wrong and that the weaker shouldn't be molested by the stronger. Exodus 2:17b says that Moses "stood up and helped them, and watered their flock" for them. Moses is on record as forcefully defending weaker Midianite women, is he not?

As one might well imagine, the young Midianite women wanted to know who the new guy was in town. After offering a telling of the fortuitous event to their father (vv. 18–19), believing that the good deed should not go unrewarded, the girls' father invited Moses over to the house. Moses stopped by and stayed. He eventually married into the family and took the Midianite woman Zipporah to be his wife (v. 21). Who was she? Worth noting is the fact that *Moses did not marry a Hebrew woman*, but was involved in an interracial marriage to a Midianite. Where was Midian in Moses' day? Those who consult an atlas to ascertain where Midian was located will discover that Midian was in—you guessed it—*Arabia*.

Moses married an Arab woman! Could it really be?

Before delving into this point further, let's clarify that the Midianites came from Abraham's wife Keturah and the Arabs came from Hagar. While in part distinguished, they are still related since both came from Abraham's two other wives. In fact, historical records establish that the names "Ishmaelites" and "Arabs" became synonymous—not only because they originated from Abraham, but also because of their intermarriage. In this regard, Professor James Charlesworth at Princeton wrote:

> And he [Abraham] gave to Ishmael and to his sons, and to the sons of Keturah, gifts, and sent them away from Isaac his son, and he gave everything to Isaac his son. And Ishmael and his sons, the sons of Keturah and their sons, went together and dwelt from Paran to the entering of Babylon in all the land which towards the East facing the desert. And these mingled with each other, and their name was called Arabs, and Ishmaelites.[16]

If no less than the likes of Moses can love an Arab woman, one wonders if other "children of the book" would not do well to develop an aptitude to be a bit more kindly disposed toward the Arab people—and Arab peoples with Hebrews. Unabashedly pro-Israel as I am, this is not an easy assignment for me—much as it would be a stretch for many of my non-Arab associates.

Nevertheless, worth noting and enforcing is the fact that Arabs are Abraham's people by birth, much as the Midianites are Abraham's descendants. The interrelationships should prompt reflection and reconsideration. Those who have trouble coming to terms with this assignment are not alone, for as we shall see, Moses' sister Miriam was unable to come to terms with her sister-in-law, whom she apparently utterly disdained. An assessment of this story will prove helpful here.

In Numbers 12:1, Miriam and Aaron are cast in a less than favorable light because they "spoke against...the Cushite woman whom he had married." Because Cush in antiquity is Ethiopia in modernity, one can surmise that Moses' wife not only was from a different culture, but she also had a darker skin color on top.[17] For her part, Miriam simply did not like this dark-skinned, Midianitish woman and, like big sisters are known to do, she had no problem voicing her concerns with other family members and drawing them into her downward-spiraling vortex.

That hers was a racial issue is evident by the superfluity in the text: She "spoke against Moses because of the Cushite woman whom he had married; for he had married a woman of Cush" (12:1). Note how it's repeated twice, and back to back. God noted it. In verses 4 through 8, the Lord called them all out, descended upon them in a cloud, and had a little family chat to straighten out Miriam's consternation over Moses' having married a dark-skinned, Midianite woman. The text continues: "And the cloud departed...behold, Miriam became leprous, white as snow...and, behold, she was leprous" (v. 10). Here again, the text is superfluous, twice noting that she "became leprous" and "behold, she was leprous." Since Miriam apparently had a problem with dark-skinned women, God basically said: "Fair enough, Miriam. Since you prefer light skin over dark skin, how about Me lightening you up a bit yourself?" She became a leper—white as snow! She got the point. Do we?

Moses cried out to God to heal her in verses 12–13, and He did. In verses 14–15, however, God required that she be "shut out from the camp" for a season. Her seasonal estrangement reminds that there is to be no place in the camp for racist attitudes, and that we are particularly well-served to note that we should not be prejudiced against a family that Moses married into—a family faring originally from what would be northwest Saudi Arabia today, and one with North African connections on top.

RUTH

When it comes to ethnic divides, people can be "ruthless," can't they?

The rhetorical question is raised here not just because it is true, but because it truly provides an introductory pathway for considering one of the most beautiful stories in the Hebrew Bible. The following romantic tale is not only significant because of its portrayal of love and devotion, but it is particularly meaningful in salvation history because it introduces the family of Israel's greatest king, David, and because it facilitates the dynastic line that eventually brought Israel's greatest Son—the Messiah—into the world. Additionally, and more important for our specific purposes here, is that the Bible's greatest love story, the one that tells of *the Bible's greatest woman and the great, great grandmother of the Jewish Bible's greatest king (David), was a Gentile woman, and was from the despised country of Moab—which is part of the Arabian world today.*

Ruth the Moabitess left such an indelible mark upon biblical literature and virtue that to be without virtue is described as being "ruthless." To her story we will now attend.

The breaking out of a relentless famine in Judah precipitated a certain Jewish family's decision to leave the ancestral Israelite homeland and reside in the East, in Moab (Ruth 1:1). The reasonably hospitable Moabites not only welcomed the impoverished Jewish family, but allowed them to intermarry with their own. The Hebrew Bible informs that two daughters-in-law married in: Ruth and Orpah (v. 4). Tragically, however, over a ten-year period, the intermarried Jewish family's misfortunes seem to have continued: All the men died off—old and young alike—with the result that only the mother-in-law, Naomi, was left with her two daughters-in-law.

After coming to terms with what she would have construed as justly deserved, providential misfortune, Naomi opted to return to her ancestral homeland and throw herself upon the welfare system in place there to help destitute folks like her (v. 6). Minded to leave things as they were and leave as she was, Naomi forcefully dismissed the young women, saying: "Go, return each to her mother's house; the LORD deal kindly with you, as you have dealt with the dead, and with me" (v. 8). The girls refused, saying, "Surely we will return with thee unto thy people" (v. 10). Tearfully, no doubt, Naomi pressed them further, saying in effect: "I have nothing for you girls…no sons, no future—nothing! Go! You are young and beautiful. Providence may indeed shine upon you. As for me, I cannot guarantee you anything, and insist that you make your bid for success in life elsewhere" (1:12–14).

Ruth deeply loved Naomi, however, and was not to be dissuaded by her teary and forceful remonstrations.

Ruth said, "Entreat me not to leave thee, or to turn away from following after thee; for where thou goest, I will go; and where thou lodgest, I will lodge: thy people shall be my people, and thy God [shall be] my God. Where thou diest, will I die, and there will I be buried; the LORD do so to me, and more also, if anything but death parts thee and me." (Ruth 1:16–17)

She was doggedly determined. In verse 18, Naomi noted that Ruth was not to be dissuaded, and said nothing more. Together, she and Ruth walked into an uncertain future, and the rest is history (1:19–22).

Providence is said to have shined upon both. The Moabitess' sterling character surfaced and caught the attention of others in the new world—and of one man in particular. She fortuitously found a protector, and with him longed for love and hope. She subsequently married into a prominent family and became a mother in a family line that went through David all the way to Jesus (4:13–18).

The unyielding resolve and virtue of one descended from what's now an Arab land and race stands as a paragon of loyalty and faithfulness, does it not? That it was a non-Jewish woman who captured the fancy of the Old Testament's author—as had Hagar and others—has not escaped my attention, and I want to commend it to yours.

When one factors that: the Hebrew Bible's most famous woman was a non-Jewish Moabitess; the Old Testament lawgiver's wife was a Midianitess (with Cushite lineage); and the Hebrew race's father's first child, Ishmael, was born through an Egyptian wife (and that Jews and Arabs are thus joined together in a bloodline through him), one is better able to appreciate that the "people of the book"—i.e., Christians and Jews—*have more in common with our Arab friends than we may have previously realized.*

Does this mean that presently estranged cousins should just mindlessly throw arms around each other and make like there has been no bad blood over the last thirty-five hundred years? No. It does, however, mean that the uncritically accepted notion that Arabs are a despised and vanquished people in the biblical economy needs to be reassessed and abandoned.

DAVID AND THE ARABS

No matter how much time passed or how many protagonists appear on the stage of the biblical narrative, David—the "sweet psalmist of Israel"—remains the most prominent king of Israel, the actual progenitor of Israel's royal lineage, and the grandfather of the Messiah Himself.[18] Just before, during, and after David, Israel came into its own as a state and not just a loose tribal confederacy. This is amply attested in the Sacred Text through the development of its administrative apparatus (royalty), through its upwardly evolving military, and through its more sophisticated Temple facility and practice. As the culture was ramping up, in the midst of all of this glory, power, and escalating spirituality (particularly manifested in the restoration of the Ark of the Covenant and David's bringing it back to settle permanently in Jerusalem), *we find astonishing Arab-friendly threads running along the main line of the story*—and particularly with David himself.

One of King David's sisters—Abigail (who is distinct from his wife)—was given in marriage to Jether the Ishmaelite—one of the descendants of Ishmael. He was an Arab. "Abigail bore Amasa; and the father of Amasa was Jether, the Ishmaelite," according to

1 Chronicles 2:17. Noteworthy is the fact that we did not hear any screams or remonstrations on any ground from either clan. Pause and consider this: *An Arab was incorporated through marriage into the royal family of Israel in the zenith of its glory!* This is not the end of the story.

It was to the son of this interracial marriage—an Arab named Amasa—that David uttered one of his most sincere statements: "You are my brother, ye are my bones and my flesh," he said in 2 Samuel 19:12. This statement is an ultimate verbal expression of fraternity, is it not? In fact, it was to this particular son of an interracial marriage, to an Arab, that David swore he'd give command of Israel's army. "And say ye to Amasa, 'Art thou not of my bone, and of my flesh? God do so to me, and more also, if thou be not captain of the host before me continually in the place of Joab'" (2 Sam. 19:13).

David, the great warrior king, gave charge of his Jewish army to an Arab! That David would hand his and his nation's security over to the son of an Arab is significant though not altogether surprising, considering that David's administration did not lack Arabs. In 1 Chronicles 27:30, for example, we find out that "Obil the Ishmaelite" was placed in charge of the camel herds, while "Jaziz the Hagrite" was placed in charge of the flocks (27:31). Apparently, the biblical texts do not indicate or even insinuate any sense of exclusivity or racism here on any ground, with Arabs placed high in David's army, as in commerce and industry. The implications are striking.

SOLOMON AND THE ARABS

When it came to politics, intertribal relationships, and global connections, David's son and successor Solomon invested himself in a wider spectrum of relationships than even his father—a move that was both the source of his strength and of his undoing, though not because of Arabs.

In 1 Kings 10, we are told of a royal visitation paid to Solomon in his homeland by a female royal, the famed Queen of Sheba. Yesterday's Sheba is today's Yemen. It was from there that one of the oldest civilizations in the world arose. This part of the world—one that extends to the southern end of the Arabian Peninsula—is and always has been part of the Arab world. It was from this very place in the Arab world that the famed visitor emerged and engaged the great King Solomon.

The biblical text relates that at the end of her visit, the Arab queen blessed the Lord God of Israel. She pointed to God's everlasting love for Israel, demonstrated by the placement of Solomon as a king. "Blessed be the LORD thy God," said she, "who delighted in thee, to set thee on the throne of Israel. Because the LORD loved Israel forever, therefore made He thee king" (1 Kings 10:9). That the tone is graceful is telling; it is evidence that Israel was not at odds with Arabs round about at the time. The same chapter indicates that the communication between Solomon and the Arab world there and then was not confined to this peculiar incident with the Queen of Sheba.

Beyond recognition and mutual affections, 1 Kings 10:15 speaks of abundant trade, with mention of revenues from "the spice merchants, and of all the kings of Arabia, and of the governors of the country." For all the kings of Arabia to send their gifts of gold to Solomon attests to strong bonds and alliances born out of friendship and necessity. The reliable biblical record indirectly provides no historical evidence to suggest the existence of any level or sense of rivalry or hostility between the Arabs and the Jews at that time. Exchanging gifts on the international level testifies to the mutual recognition of the involved parties. Evidently, there was no denial of each other's right to live in peace and in proximity on pieces of property they each called home. So, why the denial now? Does it have to be that way?

The influence of the Arabic culture stepped beyond international affairs into Solomon's household itself. It is eye-catching that one of Solomon's daughters was given an Arabic name: "Basemath." First Kings 4:15 speaks of "Ahimaaz in Naphtali," and states that he married "Basemath the daughter of Solomon." This name has no roots in Hebrew altogether. Its root and meaning can only be found in Arabic, and it means "smile." In fact, this feminine proper name is still circulating at this time. Would that Jews and Arabs smile upon one another today!

KING HIRAM OF TYRE AND THE HOUSE OF DAVID

From the south of Lebanon came an exceptional king by the name of Hiram. He made a permanent record for himself in the biblical story by establishing a remarkably strong relationship with the house of David. This he did for a time span long enough to cover the reigns of both David and his successor, Solomon. The friendship that tied King Hiram of Tyre with David and Solomon was unmatched in international relationships. The story goes like this: After a long struggle with the house of Saul, David eventually secured his hold as the king of Israel. This accomplishment culminated with the capture of the fortress of Zion, which was to be—and still is to be!—the capital of Israel: Jerusalem. Right after, King Hiram of Tyre—acknowledged as the richest monarch in the region at the time—offered to build a royal palace for the new king of Israel. In so doing, he "sent messengers to David," along with "cedar trees, and carpenters, and masons; and they built David a house" (2 Sam. 5:11). Using contemporary language, this was tacit recognition of David's legitimacy as a king over Judah and Israel in much the same way as countries today recognize each other by establishing diplomatic relationships and by firming the acknowledgement with state gifts. After so much internal struggle with Hebrew brothers, a sign of requisite recognition and a salutary gift came from a powerful and friendly Arab-related neighbor.

The biblical testimony of the Hiram-David relationship had no match on the international level back then. First Kings 5:1 speaks of Hiram's sincere love for David, saying: "For Hiram was ever a lover of David." We need more of this today, do we not?

The role Hiram played did not stop at David, however, but extended even to his son Solomon. The Hiram-Solomon relationship developed even further than that with David. Hiram's role was again affirmative, later to Solomon's installation on the throne. He rejoiced when he learned of Solomon's plan to build the Temple, and in response said, "Blessed be the LORD this day, who hath given unto David a wise son over this great people" (1 Kings 5:7). This particular praise from an Arab-related king is reminiscent of that uttered by the Arab Queen of Sheba elsewhere: Both praised Yahweh, the God of Israel, for installing Solomon as king over His inheritance.

All the wood Solomon used to build the Temple came from south Lebanon, under the able administration of King Hiram. In response to Solomon's request for wood, Hiram said:

I will do all thy desire concerning timber of cedar, and concerning timber of fir. My servants shall bring them

down from Lebanon unto the sea. And I will convey them
by sea in floats unto the place that thou shalt appoint, and
will cause them to be discharged there, and thou shalt
receive them. (1 Kings 5:8–9)

First Kings 5:18 additionally states: "And Solomon's builders and Hiram's builders did hew them, and the men of Gebal;
so they prepared timber and stones to build the house." In brief,
it is safe enough to say that Solomon's Temple was built with
Phoenician supplies and with the help of their master craftsmen
working alongside Hebrew workmen.

These wonderful interactions were on the state level, with
personal levels of interaction being greater yet. First Kings 5:12
states: "And there was peace between Hiram and Solomon, and
they two made a [*covenant*] together." This is probably one of the
very few instances when an Israeli king made a covenant with a
foreign counterpart, who in this case is Arab-related. Notice that
this was not a "treaty," as some translations put it, but a "covenant," which is by far much stronger and indissoluble—evidence
of bonds that are, sadly, pretty much nonexistent today.

ARABS IN SOLOMON'S PROVERBS

Beyond the diplomatic and commercial ties noted above, some
intellectual traditions from the Arabs are noted in the Hebrew Bible.
Let's examine the book of Proverbs to cite but one example.

In 1 Kings 4:30, we read: "And Solomon's wisdom excelled
the wisdom of all the children of the east country, and all the
wisdom of Egypt." Syntactically speaking, this is a comparative
statement noting that there was a wisdom tradition in the "East."

Obviously, no one can compare two items without bringing them side by side. That there was also some exchange of wisdom back and forth appears indirectly in the event of the Queen of Sheba, who endured the pains of a long journey across the Arabian desert to "test him with hard questions" (1 Kings 10:1). Further, the influence of Egyptian wisdom on the book of Proverbs has been attested to by biblical scholarship beyond any shadow of doubt.

In Middle Eastern culture—in both the past and the present—heads of state, high-profile figures, and prominent people come together and exchange ideas, thoughts, and oracles in what can be described in modern terms as summits. There is no clearer evidence of this notion than in the events of the book of Job, when Job's friends came to see him and exchange extended oracles with him. In the same way, the "sons of the East" (which, by the way, is a coined phrase that includes all the surrounding Arabs and Arab-related people groups) were summoned to Solomon on different occasions to exchange wisdom. As evidence thereof, 1 Kings 10:24 notes: "And all the earth consulted Solomon, to hear his wisdom, which God had put in his heart." In such a wonderful atmosphere of openness and exchange, Solomon—as self-confident as he was—did not have any problem borrowing the oracles of Agur (the man of Massa) of Ithiel and Ucal (Prov. 30:1), as with those of Lemuel (King of Massa), delivered to him by his mother (Prov. 31:1). If you wonder who or what Massa was, biblically speaking, he was one of Ishmael's sons (cf. Gen. 25:14 and 1 Chron. 1:30) who developed into an Arab tribe.

That there are Arab influences in Hebrew wisdom literature is irrefutable. It seems that the wisest man who ever lived—our famed King Solomon—allowed himself to be influenced by women and eat at the intellectual table of the Arabs. Would that that mutual respect be restored in our day!

ARABS AND SOLOMON'S TEMPLE

According to the Jewish historian Josephus, whether it was Solomon's (first) Temple or Zerubbabel or Herod's (second) Temple, the incense supply for the Golden Altar and other Temple uses came primarily from Arabia.[19] This is actually part of a broader context of commerce between Jews and Arabs in which "a great quantity of spices, precious stones, and gold is brought into the country [of Israel] by the Arabs,"[20] as noted elsewhere in this volume. It is actually fair to add that this list is not all-inclusive, and one should expect some of the Temple's sacrificial animals to have come from Arabia as well, since the Arabs were herdsmen. Without these historical records and the serious academic research that corroborates them, no one would have ever imagined that the incense burned on the Golden Altar before Yahweh, the God of Israel, as with some of the animals sacrificed before Him in His Temple, had been brought in from Arabia by Arab kinsmen supplying Hebrews with their needs.

It is to be observed, particularly during the time of Solomon, that there existed positive interactions, mutual recognition and respect, collaboration, and exchanges of knowledge and goods between the sons of Isaac and the sons of Ishmael. Arab kings and queens visited Solomon, established diplomatic relationships with him, gave him precious gifts, praised the God of Israel because of him, collaborated with him on his colossal architectural projects, exchanged wisdom and material goods, provided animals and incense for the Temple's ritual service, and went even as far as making personal covenants. The sons of Isaac and sons of Ishmael and Keturah were widely involved in economic, literary, religious, and cultural exchanges. This means the relationship between the Hebrew and Arab brothers was quite normal. Can we have those days back?

JONAH AND THE ARABS

Jonah was an actual prophet, not merely a mythic personality. That he was an imperfect prophet is amply attested in the biblical narrative. Thinking that we might derive some profit from this prophet's foibles, let's consider how he was something of a racist with no abiding affections for his Arab cousins.[21]

Before God sent Paul to Israel's eastern territories to check on the kinfolk and reach out to them (as we will discuss later), He sent this unwilling messenger, our Jonah. The major difference between Jonah and Paul is that Jonah did not have a mind to reach out to these estranged kinfolk in order to spread the Kingdom of the God to them. As evidence thereof, when commissioned to go eastward to Nineveh, Jonah sailed westward—the very opposite direction.

Nineveh was the capital of Assyria in the eighth century BC. Assyria was located in the northern part of contemporary Iraq, and was the Ancient Middle East's most dominant power at the time of Jonah. Something of a racist, Jonah didn't care about these people, these cruel outsiders. God did, however. In Jonah 1:2, we read God's command: "Arise, go to Nineveh, that great city, and cry against it; for their wickedness is come up before me." Why did God want to salvage the people of Ninevah? Why did He trouble the Hebrew nationalist prophet Jonah by sending him across the borders to them on an unprecedented mission? They were Israel's kinfolk, that's why! Part of Abraham's biological descendants, they needed to hear God's Word. Notice, by contrast, that this was not the case with Sodom and Gomorrah. The people of Sodom and Gomorrah were Canaanites and existed when Abraham did not yet have any progeny. This comparison and contrast, all by itself, builds a strong case for Israel's kinfolk, the Arabs, and underscores that they were the object of God's love, too.

Not only were these kinfolk objects of God's love, but oddly, so was the city. Notice what Jonah says in 3:3: (עִיר־גְּדוֹלָה֙ לֵֽאלֹהִ֔ים וְנִֽינְוֵ֖ה הָיְתָ֥ה) "And Nineveh was a great city *unto God*." The phrase in italics is curiously missing in most of the English translations, though it exists in the Hebrew text as shown above. This surprising phrase simply claims God's ownership of Nineveh, if you can imagine that: even Nineveh.

Imagine the biggest and most fortified city in the world back then, one with a population of about one hundred twenty thousand people living inside its walls. Then one day, a Hebrew foreigner shows up, tours the city, and cries aloud with one statement: "Forty days more, and Nineveh shall be overturned!" Did those eastern Arab-related kinfolk respond to Jonah, the Israeli prophet? With no earlier record of Jonah's establishing any credibility in Nineveh, and without even having a formal diplomatic introduction, the Assyrians believed him in a surprising way—and their response was overwhelming. The Bible says in Jonah 3:5–9:

> So the people of Nineveh believed God, and proclaimed
> a fast, and put on sackcloth, from the greatest of them
> even to the least of them. For word came unto the king
> of Nineveh, and he arose from his throne, and he laid
> his robe from him, and covered himself with sackcloth,
> and sat in ashes. And he caused it to be proclaimed and
> published through Nineveh by the decree of the king and

his nobles, saying, "Let neither man nor beast, herd, nor flock taste anything; let them not feed, nor drink water. But let man and beast be covered with sackcloth, and cry mightily unto God; yea, let them turn every one from his evil way, and from the violence that is in their hands. Who can tell if God will turn and repent, and turn away from this fierce anger, that we perish not?"

Arabs, Arab-related people, and Arab-confederates are not far from God's heart, love, or compassion. His wanting them reached and spared is here attested.

ARABS, ARAB-CONFEDERATES, AND ELIJAH

No one has ever doubted the paramount status of Elijah in the sacred history. His significance extends beyond his own day and time, and extends up and out to the end of time. By making his appearance on the glorious stage of Mt. Harmon during Jesus' transfiguration, Elijah imposed himself upon readers' imaginations and expanded his undying role beyond his days.

New Testament references aside, it is well known from the Old Testament that at the beginning of the Elijah-Ahab conflict and after the prophetic command of sealing up the heavens from raining, Elijah was commanded by God to "get thee from here [Israel], and turn thee eastward, and hide thyself by the brook, [the Valley of] Cherith, which is before the Jordan [River]" (1 Kings 17:3). The ultimate representative of the Hebrew non-writing prophets was thus commended to the East, where the Arab ancestry lived, and to the care and custody of Ammonite kinfolk.

Later, when the brook of Wadi Cherith dried up, Elijah was once more commanded to make a ninety-degree northwestward turn around Israel's borderline to the southern territory of what is known in modernity as the Arab state of Lebanon. "Arise, get thee to Zarephath, which belongeth to Sidon, and dwell there; behold, I have commanded a widow there to sustain thee," was his instruction in 1 Kings 17:9. Jesus made an insightful comment on this command of 1 Kings 17:9 that runs along the theme of this volume. In Luke 4:25–26, He said:

> But I tell you of a truth, many widows were in Israel in the days of Elijah, when the heaven was shut up three years and six months, when great famine was throughout all the land; But unto none of them was Elijah sent, but only unto Zarephath, a city of Sidon, unto a woman that was a widow.

According to Jesus' review of the historical account of 1 Kings 17:9 and from His matchless vantage point, worth noting is that it was a trustworthy Lebanese widow who was entrusted with the life and the subsequent ministry of Israel's most prominent non-writing prophet, Elijah.

JEREMIAH AND THE ARABS

Jeremiah was one of the most influential writing Hebrew prophets and is sometimes underestimated. He was aroused to his ministry in one of Judah's most dire times, when the country was under a series of ungodly and unwise kings—men who brought the country to its momentary demise at the hands of the Babylonians under the lead of King Nebuchadnezzar.

The episodes of Jeremiah's suffering at the hands of his own people were, to say the least, unbelievably cruel. For example, one time, the priest (who was also the chief officer of the Temple) had Jeremiah beaten and put in the stocks. "Pashhur, the son of Immer the priest, who was also chief governor in the House of the LORD, heard that Jeremiah prophesied these things. Then Pashhur smote Jeremiah, the prophet, and put him in the stocks that were in the high gate of Benjamin, which was by the house of the LORD," is the word in Jeremiah 20:1–2. This torture was done publicly, accompanied by public humiliation and mockery. "I am in derision daily, every one mocketh me," said Jeremiah in 20:7. In an attempt to kill Jeremiah, his foes secured King Zedekiah's permission to throw the prophet into an empty cistern covered with a thick layer of mud at the bottom, then to finish him off.

> Then Zedekiah, the king, said, "Behold, he is in your hand; for the king is not he who can do any thing against you." Then took they Jeremiah, and cast him into the dungeon of Malchiah…that was in the court of the prison; and they let down Jeremiah with cords. And in the dungeon there was no water, but mire; so Jeremiah sank in the mire. (Jer. 38:5–6)

His was not an easy life!

Against the background of this pitch darkness came a kinsman to shed some brightness. Was he a Hebrew prophet? No. This time it was the least-expected figure who came and showed mercy to the Judean prophet. It is the person of the invading and marauding conqueror himself, the pagan one, King Nebuchadnezzar. In the aftermath of the fall of Jerusalem in 586 BC, the biblical text narrates something beyond one's wildest imaginations:

> Now Nebuchadnezzar, king of Babylon, gave charge concerning Jeremiah to Nebuzaradan, the captain of the guard, saying, "Take him [Jeremiah], and *look well to him, and do him no harm,* but do unto him even as he shall say unto thee.". . . Even they sent, and took Jeremiah out of the court of the prison, and committed him unto him to Gedaliah. . . that he should carry him home; so, he dwelt among the people. (Jer. 39:11, 12 and 14, emphasis added)

The Babylonian was his redeemer, was he not?

We would do well to pay attention to the emphasized words in italics to see how kindly disposed Nebuchadnezzar, the Iraqi kin and king, was toward Jeremiah, the Jewish prophet. His performance stands in marked contrast to that of the ungodly Judean kings who had abused him. They sought to kill him, whereas Nebuchadnezzar saved Jeremiah by granting him his freedom back.

DANIEL AND THE ARABS

Daniel was another Hebrew writing prophet, one of the most recognized and highly esteemed prophets of the Old Testament. Not only was he a writing prophet as Jeremiah was, but he also ministered contemporaneously to Jeremiah, though he experienced a calling to the eastern kinfolk. While Jeremiah had a brief contact with the Iraqi kinsman, King Nebuchadnezzar, Daniel lived under his auspices, worked under his jurisdiction, and operated within the royal palace complex. Unlike Jeremiah, Daniel did not suffer at the hands of his own people. This, however, may be because he was deported to Babylon (in contemporary Iraq) while he was a lad, before he matriculated from his prophetic ministry.

Reading Daniel 1:8–16, one cannot help but notice the special treatment the chief officer of the royal court officials had given to some young Jewish men—Daniel and his companions. If you know enough about the etiquette and politics of any royal court, you will quickly realize that what the chief officer (equivalent to today's chief of staff) did was no less than violate the king's commands for the sake of some foreigners who were basically under his custodianship—a dangerous move, to be sure. This is why at first he responded negatively to Daniel, saying: "I fear my lord, the king, who hath appointed your food and your drink; for why should he see your face worse looking than the youths who are of your age? *Then shall ye make me endanger my head with the king*" (Dan. 1:10, emphasis added). The kind of violation the chief officer committed for the sake of the Hebrew young men could have been penalized by execution, by beheading. That he stuck his neck out for Daniel is telling.

Daniel hadn't established himself yet. Daniel's special gifting was not manifested yet. Despite that Daniel and his companions were no more than statistics among many other captives from different nations, the Iraqi chief officer, who had the authority and ability to impose the king's menu, showed mercy and kindly conceded to the young men's request. This goes to show that God has His people in all sorts of places and from all sorts of backgrounds.

JESUS AND THE ARABS

In his Gospel, Matthew explicitly notes how Jesus descended from Ruth (Matt. 1:5). Luke, for his part, notes that Jesus came through her husband, Boaz (Luke 3:32). Clear in either case is that the Messiah's great, great grandmother—Ruth—was herself of non-Jewish extract. This gives an initial clue about Matthew's intentions and orientation that will help us decipher the code of his version of the nativity.

Of the four Gospels, only Matthew and Luke offer any sort of "Christmas" narrative. Mark begins with John the Baptist's serving as a harbinger for the adult Jesus (1:1–13), with nothing said of the early Christ child. In John, a weighty theological prologue is offered first, in 1:1–18. Then John does much the same as Mark, highlighting John the Baptist's welcome and endorsement of the adult Jesus (1:19–34). Mark and John have no infancy narratives. Though Matthew and Luke offer "baby Jesus" stories, they differ in what they draw attention to.

To illustrate, in Luke's Gospel, Jesus' arrival is attended by a considerable number of angelic visitations (1:5–25, 26–45; 2:8–9) and prophetic pronouncements (1:46–56, 67–79; 2:8–14, 28–32). Though not without his divine encounters and announcements, as in Matthew 1:18–23, Matthew is clearly much more on the ground, and is given to rooting Jesus' arrival in the day and time in which he lived—Jewish days and Jewish times particularly. For Matthew, individuals inspired by starbursts of prophetic unction play a back seat to how the Old Testament predicted the life and times of the Messiah. It is for this reason that Matthew, more than any other Gospel writer, checkers his narrative with proof texts, saying in effect, "This event of Jesus fulfills what was written by the prophet," over and again buttressing Jesus' story with "that it might be fulfilled what was written by the prophet" (cf. 1:22; 2:5, 15, 17, 23; 3:3; 4:14). The days and times of Jesus' arrival were marked by social unrest and political intrigue; against that backdrop, faithful and watchful Hebrews were looking for heaven's help for earthly dilemmas—as were others.

A non-Jewish Idumaean/Edomite had stealthily worked his way into the throne of Judah under the banner of the Herodian dynasty. "When Herod the king" heard about the birth of an alleged Messiah—someone he knew would be construed as a more legitimate "king of the Jews" than he—Matthew says he was "troubled" (2:3), and was given to finding the child, ostensibly to "worship" Him. That such was not his intention, however, is amply noted in the New Testament. Herod's stealthy consternation was stimulated by "wise men from the east [who came] to Jerusalem" (2:1), guided by "His [bright] star in the east" (1:2). Herod inquired about the timing of the great light's appearance (1:7 and 9), and Matthew said, "The star, which they saw in the east, went before them, till it came and stood over where the young child was." He continued, noting that, "When they saw the [bright] star, they rejoiced with exceedingly great joy" (1:10), after which they entered the house and "presented unto Him gifts: gold, and frankincense, and myrrh" (1:11). That business attended to, they made haste to return to the East from whence they came, albeit by another way for fear of Herod (1:12), who was obviously up to no good.

Despite its having worked its way into popular lore, the text never says there were "three" wise men or astrologers. Over and over again, though, it does note that these men were from the East and that they were guided to Israel by a star. Though the number of these eastern astrologers has been the object of fanciful speculation, the question of exactly who the first Gentile worshippers of Jesus were can be ascertained with a much greater measure of certainty: *The first non-Jews to worship Jesus were Arabs.*

First, we have already acknowledged the fact that "sons of the East" is a biblical phrase referring to what lies immediately to the east of Israel and its natural borderline, the Jordan River, in what looks like a crescent-shaped cluster of territories. These territories include the Syro-Arabian desert to the northeast and the Transjordan area, Negev, to the northern Arab Peninsula—inhabited by an ethnic amalgam of Arabs and Ishmaelites.

Second, worth noting is that from ancient times the regional spice trade was Arabian in origin. You may recall, for example, that when the Queen of Sheba (southern Arabia) visited Solomon, she brought with her *spices* and gold (1 Kings 10:2). These were the very types of gifts later presented to the divine infant Jesus—a descendant of Solomon. This, in fact, reflects a regional tradition of the type of honorary gifts presented to royalties and dignitaries in the ancient world.

Third, Justin Martyr, a church father who grew up within the territories of Israel, in his debate with a Jew named Trypho around AD 135, referred to the Magi a few times as being from Arabia:

> For, at the time of His birth, the Magi *came from Arabia* and worshipped Him, after they had met Herod, then the king of your country, whom Scriptures calls king of Assyria because of his wicked ungodliness...at the time when *the Magi from Arabia* came to King Herod and said.... Now, *these Magi from Arabia* came to Bethlehem, worshipped the Child, and presented to Him gifts of gold, frankincense, and myrrh.... There the *Arabian Magi* found Him.... Now when the *Arabian Magi* failed to return to Herod.... (emphasis added)[22]

Fourth, the Hebrew prophet Isaiah—who, by the way, is the most oft-employed Old Testament writer in the New Testament—saw the coming of Israel's Redeemer and voiced it in various ways. In 60:1, Isaiah encouraged folks with, "Arise, shine; for thy light is come, and the glory of the LORD is risen upon thee." Though deep "darkness" is said to have engulfed the people, there was a promise that "the LORD shall arise upon thee, and His glory shall be seen upon thee" (60:2). Seen by whom? In 60:3, Isaiah said, "The nations [Gentiles] shall come to thy light," and then in 60:5b, he noted, "The forces [wealth] of the nations [Gentiles] shall come unto thee." Interesting as the correlation between Isaiah's "Gentiles" coming to Israel's "light" with "wealth" in hand is, it's the prophet's mention of exactly who these "Gentiles" were that's particularly striking. Solomon once said that "there is no new thing under the sun" (Ecc. 1:9). Here, the aforementioned event with Solomon is revisited in this interaction with Jesus. As in the past, Arabian elite came bearing gifts; this time, they crossed the border carrying their wealth and gave it to One who was greater than Solomon.

In 60:6–7, Isaiah went on describing the gift-bearers, noting that, "The multitude of camels shall cover thee, the dromedaries of Midian and Ephah; they all from Sheba shall come; they shall bring gold and incense, and they shall show forth the praises of the LORD."

As with Isaac and his descendants, Midian was himself a legitimate son of Abraham, though in his case he came by Keturah—whom Abraham married after the death of Sarah (Gen. 25:1–2). In Genesis 25:6, Moses informed that "Abraham gave gifts" to him and his other brothers, and "sent them away from Isaac, his son, while he yet lived, eastward, unto the east country," as with Ishmael previously. Worthy of special note is Isaiah's mention that the first Gentiles to come and acknowledge Jesus will be returning Arab peoples—another unexpected piece of Arab-related trivia in the biblical narrative.

Is Matthew's noting that sons from the East will come bearing gifts indicative of some sort of family reunion to come? If so, I find that delightful. That question can be left open for now. What definitely needs opened now is the realization that Matthew's "Gentiles" coming to Jesus first were some of the Jewish people's estranged Arab relatives. Located northeast, eastward, and southward in Arabia, Midian is mentioned first in Isaiah 60:6. Ephah follows immediately in the text. Who was Ephah? He was actually the son of Midian and likewise descended from Abraham by his wife Keturah (Gen. 25:4; 1 Chron.1:33).

"Sheba" follows in Isaiah 60:6, which says, "they all from Sheba shall come." Sheba was similarly a son of Abraham, mentioned in conjunction with Dedan in Genesis 25:3. On the basis of their being mentioned together and as being Cushites in Genesis 10:7, one can conclude that there were migrations to Ethiopia. That their descendants were more firmly entrenched in Southern Arabia is evident by the places named after them in Southern Arabia. The people of Sheba—or Sabeans, as they are known—were noted in the Bible as traders of gold and spices. The famous Queen of Sheba once came to Solomon bearing "spices, and very much gold, and precious stones" (1 Kings 10:1–2, 10).[23] Jeremiah noted frankincense that was coming "from Sheba" in Jeremiah 6:20. In 27:22, Ezekiel spoke of "merchants of Sheba," informing that they traded in the "best of all spices...and gold."

That Arabs were the first to acknowledge Jesus is striking. Their doing so gets more interesting yet.

How and why a star guided them from the East has been

the object of considerable speculation. Amongst Jews, there is a long-standing tradition connecting a star with deliverance and salvation. In the second century AD, when some of Judaism's endorsed rabbis thought the Messiah had come, they named a pretender "Bar Kochba" as the promised one. His name means "son of the star." They were so serious that they even minted coins with his name and this image. Similarly, in the twentieth century, when modern Jews were looking for a symbol of deliverance and national hope, Jews chose a star and even placed the Star of David on the national flag.

The employment of a star to denote political salvation not only has a long-standing tradition in Hebrew lore, but it is even rooted in the Hebrew Bible. In Numbers 24:17–19, a very significant prophecy goes: "There shall come a Star out of Jacob, and a Scepter shall rise out of Israel, and shall smite the corners of Moab, and destroy all the children of Sheth.… Out of Jacob One shall he come who shall have dominion." Taken together, "Star out of Jacob," "Scepter," "smit[ing] the corners of Moab," "destroy[ing] the children of Sheth," and having consequential "dominion" all conjure an image of a strong and triumphant warrior-king. Little wonder that the Hebrew people got utility from the prophetic image of a bright rising light appearing and displacing prevailing darkness.

The prophesied and immortalized star that has left its indelible mark on ancient Jewish faith and practice, the Jewish religious psyche, and is even emblazoned on modern Israel's national flag, was not a prophecy that came from a Jewish person. Though Moses reports it in Numbers 24:17–19, he is also crystal clear about its not having come from him or any Jew, but rather from the mouth of a non-Jewish sage—a wise man from the East

(Num. 22:1–24:25). Balaam came from Pethor, an ancient city in Mesopotamia. He fared from a land known today as Iraq, and from what would have essentially been from the northernmost rim of the Arabian Peninsula.

In sum, Arabs coming to acknowledge the One known as the "King of the Jews" was predicted by Isaiah. Their taking note of a star was envisioned by an eastern wise man from the environs of what would be modern Iraq today. Wise men, rich men from the East bearing gold, frankincense, and myrrh—what a story! Though the story of early first worshippers is well attested in the Scripture and in the church, *buried beneath the storytelling and religious traditions is the truth that these fine men were Arabs.*

PAUL'S ARABIAN CONNECTIONS

Personally coming to Jesus and worshipping Him for a short season is one thing; taking Him to others over an extended period of years is another. Though Jesus is on record exhorting individuals to go into all the world and preach the Gospel (Matt. 28:19–20), what's interesting in the historical record is the fact that many of His Jewish followers did not seem to fancy going.

Peter is appropriately construed as the principal shepherd of the apostolic flock. His being particularly sheepish about engaging folks outside the Jewish flock (i.e., Gentiles), however, is amply attested in the New Testament. In Acts 10:9–16, for example, the thought of eating Gentile foods caused him to shudder and utter objections over and over again. Similarly, in Galatians 2:11–21, Peter's discomfort with Gentiles—people now, and not just food staples—is noted. In this case, though, it is not only made apparent, but it becomes for Bible readers an object lesson of insincerity and disloyalty because of Paul of Tarsus' stern rebuke of him.

Though commissioned by Jesus to go forth and tell the story, the New Testament goes on to tell of the earliest faith community's lackluster resolve to get the story out, evidenced above by their principal leader's inability to get comfortable with the mandate, as with people generally. What is likewise clear in the New Testament is the fact that the Gospel's chief advocate for going beyond Israel's borders was someone who was not part of the original apostolic community. Not only was Paul not an original disciple, but he himself was hell-bent on destroying that group particularly—till confronted by the Lord one day while on the road to Damascus, where he was going to go and get them (Acts 9:1ff).[24]

Though He picked up followers in other places, Jesus' first disciples were Israelis from Galilee in northern Israel. Paul, by contrast, was not an Israeli Jew. He was from Tarsus, a principal city in Asia Minor, which is what would be modern Islam-controlled Turkey today. Though Paul was Jewish, unlike the others with more legitimate claims to apostleship (based on firsthand experience with Jesus), he would not have carried an Israeli passport. A seemingly proud Roman citizen on top, it could be said that Paul was a "man of the world."

That he was a man of the Arab world will now be noted. In his Acts of the Apostle, Paul's non-Jewish associate Luke tells his readers that a then-infamous Pharisaic rabbi named Paul was en route to Damascus—in Syria!—when he had a very radical and life-changing encounter with the Lord (Acts 9:2–6). After gathering his composure and coming to terms with what had happened, Luke says, "He was strengthened. Then was Saul certain days with the disciples who were at Damascus" (Acts 9:19b). During those first days in Syria, continues Luke, "he preached Christ in the synagogues, that He is the Son of God" (9:20), and then "confounded the Jews who dwelt at Damascus, proving that this is [the] very Christ" (v. 22). After a word of a consequential plot to kill Paul was made known to him, he was snuck out of the Syrian city by night (9:23–25).

We need to consider where he went. Before we do, however, some historical background on the Nabataeans is necessary in order to furnish readers with the necessary historical and geographical setting of Jesus and Paul's time in history.

The origin of the Nabataeans is something of a riddle because they left behind only a few scraps of writings—in itself one of the enigmatic features of their history. The abnormality of their decision appears clearly against the backdrop of people groups around them who did write. The Egyptians wrote on walls, the Babylonians on clay tables, and the Jews on scrolls. The Nabataeans, however, seem to have made a decision not to write anything of their history, and so we must proceed cautiously, given the lack of data.

It seems that they lived in tents, preferring the nomadic lifestyle with its frequent moving about. They were spotted almost everywhere from the Euphrates to the Red Sea and from the Persian Gulf to the borders of Egypt. That they moved about is clear; their exact origin is still ambiguous, however. Because of their infiltration into various Arab groups scattered throughout the same geographical expanse, they were identified with Arabs.[25]

The *Bibliotheca Historica* of the Greek historian Diodorus Siculus of Sicily (first century BC) indicates that the Nabataeans and other Arab tribes settled in the eastern region of what he called "Arabia," showing that the Nabataeans formed only one element in the broader family of Arabic tribes resident there:

The land of the Arabs called Nabataeans…indicating that
in his eyes there were also other Arabs not Nabataeans.
Later in his survey (XIX, 94, 4), he clearly distinguished
between Nabataeans and what he called "other Arab
tribes," and even distinguished them from the others by
indicating their wealth. Later (XIX, 94, 10), he again dis-
tinguishes between them and "other Arab tribes," several
of whom were farmers and had customs similar to those
of the "Syrians," apart from the fact that they did not live
in permanent houses.

Because later Islamic literature dealt with them as two quasi-
distinguished groups (Nabat al-Iraq and Nabat al-Sham [of
Damascus]), it is believed that the northern area of the Fertile
Crescent is their place of provenance. But important for our purposes here is that the Nabataeans of Damascus actually controlled
Damascus during the time and ministry of the Apostle Paul,
according to the *Encyclopedia of Islam*, volume VII.[26] The Bible,
for its part, is in agreement with this notion.

In his extraordinarily moving chapter of 2 Corinthians 11—
labeled as "Paul's [un]foolish boasting"—Paul reveals many personal experiences along the road of his in-many-ways outstanding
ministry. In concluding the list of his sufferings and perils, he
says, "In Damascus the governor under *Aretas,* the king, kept the
city of the Damascenes with a garrison, desirous to apprehend
me, And through a window in a basket was I let down by the wall,
and escaped his hands" (2 Cor. 11:32–33 emphasis added). The
proper name "Aretas" is not a Greek name at all, and is definitely
Arabic, with roots and meaning only in Arabic. This comes as
further confirmation that Damascus was under the Nabataean
Arabs during Paul's time. This, in and by itself, gives much more

credibility to the notion that Paul's first evangelistic target was the neighboring Arabs. In fact, this comes as a practical fulfillment of Jesus' expansive evangelistic agenda. Jesus' program appears like ripples in a pond with Jerusalem in the center, followed by Judea, Samaria, and to the end of the earth—wider, wider, and wider still (cf. Acts 1:8).

Despite the biblical and extra-biblical support showing Nabataean control over Damascus during Paul's time, historians regard Edom as the heart of the Nabataeans' empire. Were the Nabataeans Edomites, then? No. After Nebuchadnezzar's sweeping conquest over the entire Middle East and the consequential compulsory deportations, many lands and countries were abandoned and left empty. The nomads, who escaped the wrath of Nebuchadnezzar (whose actions were vented against fortified cities in the sixth century BC), had the freedom to move around, relocate, and occupy whatever land they pleased. This was the case with the Nabataeans. The Nabataeans dominated the landscape and their culture gradually replaced the Edomites to the immediate east of Israel.

This was a brief sketch of their history. Now we'll consider their relationship with their immediate neighbors across the river: the Jews. It seems that the Nabataean-Jewish relationship was predominantly friendly, based on the fact that the Nabataeans were not hostile to any people group around them. For example, during the Maccabean revolt against Antiochus Epiphanes, Judas and Jonathan Maccabeus fled Judea, crossed the Jordan River, journeyed for three days in the desert until "they encountered the Nabataeans who met them peaceably," and helped them throughout their revolt against Antiochus Epiphanes (cf. 1 Macc. 5:24–28 and 2 Macc. 12:10–12). In fact, 1 Maccabees 9:35 continues, "Jonathan sent his brother as leader of the multitude and begged the Nabataeans, *who were his friends,* for permission to store with them the great amount of baggage which they had" (emphasis added).

Paul took refuge with Nabataean cousins as well. Paul recalled his flight from Damascus in 2 Corinthians 11:32–33, much as he reflected upon it when waxing autobiographical in his Galatians correspondence. It was in the latter document that he said, "When it pleased God…To reveal His Son in me…[I did not go]…up to Jerusalem to them who were apostles before me, but *I went into Arabia, and returned again unto Damascus*" (1:15–17, emphasis added). In Acts, Luke noted that a previous scattering of Jewish believers similarly sent emissaries into southern Phoenicia and coastal cities, as with other places bordering Israel. At Judea's doorstep, Nabataean Arabia was constituted by Gentiles with the closest Jewish ties—Arabs. Since the earlier Maccabean period, distant blood-related Judeans and Nabataean Arabs engaged in a variety of political and economic exchanges. The fact that both enjoyed common bonds through associations and traditions with Abraham and Moses afforded the intrepid Apostle to the Gentiles (Paul) an opportunity to speak to his first class of Jewish-friendly and Jewish-related Gentiles: *The Apostle to the Gentiles "cut his teeth" ministering to Arabs.* That both peoples laid siege to the Sinai experience gave him a good theological beginning point.

In Galatians 1:17, Paul said he went to Arabia, and in 4:25 he further stated that "Mount Sinai" is "in Arabia." Based on Pauline statements in his Galatians epistle, one view sees that this perspective on Mount Sinai's location gives credence to the notion that the present-day pilgrimage site of Mount Sinai—in the Egyptian-controlled Sinai Peninsula—may well be misplaced. Others still hold to the traditional site based on the ancient historians' testimonies—like those of Strabo and Herodotus[27]—who understood ancient Arabia to extend from the Nile to the Persian Gulf.[28] This is hotly debated, however, and is by no means a foregone conclusion.[29]

Commenting on Genesis 20:1, where it is noted that "Abraham journeyed [south] from there toward the Negev, and dwelt between Kadesh and Shur, and sojourned in Gerar," ancient authoritative Jewish manuscripts (Targum Onkelos and Jerushalmi I) attest that Abraham settled in the Nabataean lands—i.e., Arabia. In fact, the appendix to the book of Job in Judaism's authorized Greek translation of the Old Testament (the Septuagint) goes so far as to refer to a "king after Abraham over the territories of…Arabia."

Should that prevail in our thinking—as I am inclined to think it should—then Paul's going to Arabia to get revelation on the essence and substance of the New Covenant, as he said he did in Galatians 1:15–17, is much akin to Moses and Abraham having done so in their day. Worth noting as well is that he who was arguably the Old Testament's greatest non-writing prophet, Elijah, similarly went to Arabia to recover his equilibrium and hear from God at "Horeb, the mount of God," in the wake of his flight from Jezebel (1 Kings 19:1–18, esp. v. 8). If this perspective prevails in our thinking, then Arabia is the place where God first called Moses, and the place where Moses returned to following the Exodus to receive the divine revelation. It is similarly the place where Elijah—who, in effect, is the harbinger of the Messiah— went to get his instructions, much as, based on his own words, Arabia must be construed as Paul's spiritual breeding ground.

Let us stop and reflect on this for a minute. Rabbi Paul was from Tarsus (*in modern Turkey*). He was on his way to Damascus (*in modern Syria*) when he encountered the Lord. He then resided in

Damascus and spent considerable time in *Arabia*. Worthy of note is the fact that *the greatest apostolic evangelist in the New Testament "cut his teeth" in Arabia*—prior to his ever even going to Jerusalem to meet the other apostles. The implications are profound.

In Galatians 1:18, Paul informed, *"After three years,* I went up to Jerusalem to see Peter, and abode with him [only] fifteen days" (emphasis added). In the first three years of his new life, Paul stated that he spent all but two weeks of it in what we would call Arab-controlled lands today—in Tarsus, Syria, and Arabia. In 2:1, Paul then said, "Then fourteen years after, I went up again to Jerusalem," further informing that after his brief two-week stint in Jerusalem, which came after the first three years of his new life, he went to and then left Jerusalem, and only returned to the ancestral Jewish homeland ten years later. After Paul's initial experience in Judea, three years after his Damascus road encounter, he returned to Tarsus (in modern Turkey) and ministered in obscurity there. In Acts 11:19–21, Luke reported that there was a revival in Antioch, Syria, and that the "tidings of these things came unto the ears of the church which was in Jerusalem" (11:22a). Barnabas was subsequently dispatched to assist the fledgling community in Syria (11:22b). After assessing the situation in Syria, "then departed Barnabas to Tarsus, to seek Saul" (11:25). He sought him, he found him, he brought him back to Syria; it was from there that Paul's apostolic ministry was launched (13:1ff).

Worthy of note for our purposes is the fact that the New Testament's greatest missionary apostle was a cosmopolitan, Arabian-loving, Messianic Jewish rabbi. This, coupled with the rest, should open up the possibility that it is okay for we Judeo-Christian sorts to be kindly disposed toward Arab people.

ARABS IN EXTRA-BIBLICAL,
PSEUDEPIGRAPHICAL, JEWISH LITERATURE

As much as the Hebrew and Christian Bibles show evidence of being kindly disposed toward Arabian lands and peoples outside and inside Israel, Jewish interpreters of Israel's Sacred Text were likewise reasonably gracious in their assessment of the people of the sands. Some examples of this Arab-friendly tendency follow.

Artapanus was a historian who lived in Alexandria, Egypt, in the second century BC. He wrote a history of the Jewish people, parts of which have been preserved in the writings of ancient churchmen. In his *Præparatio Evangelica* ("Preparation for the Gospel"), Eusebius, the famous fourth-century AD church historian, passed along some of Artapanus' interesting glosses, which are revealing on the basis of their giving a window into how some biblical commentators perceived Jews in relation to Arabs in proximity to the time of the Messiah Yeshua, whom folks call Jesus Christ.[30]

Commenting on the Genesis story of Joseph and his estranged brothers, and while noting their having been given to killing Joseph, in his writings[31] Artapanus gives an interesting twist to the story line. Let us begin here and hear him out.

> "Joseph," said he, "obtained prior knowledge of the conspiracy and requested the neighboring Arabs to convey him to Egypt. They complied with the request, for the kings of the Arabs were descendants of Israel, sons of Abraham, and brothers of Isaac." (23:1)

This account differs some from the biblical narrative. In Genesis 37:23–28, the story is recounted. We are told there that Joseph's brothers "took him, and cast him into a pit" (v. 24) and later observed "a company of Ishmaelites, coming...with their camels, bearing spices, balm, and myrrh" (v. 25)—like the wise men noted previously. Judah responded, "Let us sell him to the Ishmaelites" (v. 27). Moses then continued, noting, "Then there passed by Midianites, merchantmen; and they drew and lifted up Joseph out of the pit, and sold Joseph to the Ishmaelites" (v. 28).

Remembering that they were kinsmen, Artapanus said Joseph figured he would fare better with his Arab relatives than with his own biological brothers. On that basis and for that reason, he arranged for his "conveyance" with them. That Artapanus' reckoning is not exactly how the biblical account reads is not as problematic as it is revealing. While granting that we all would do well to not add to or subtract from the biblical record, for our purposes here, the embellishment is telling. Joseph's request to be handed over to the Arabs for "conveyance" to Egypt could well suggest a certain comfort level with them, a comfort that is essentially non-existent in modernity.

Similarly, Eusebius passed on another of Artapanus' extra-biblical embellishments that is worthy of some note. Commenting in this case on Moses' plight in and flight from Egypt, Artapanus conjectured that Moses "invented boats, devices for stone construction, Egyptian arms, implements for drawing water and for warfare and [advanced] philosophy" in the land of Egypt (27:4). As a result, he said, Moses was deeply "loved by the [Egyptian] masses and was deemed worthy of honor" by them (27:6). When the king saw the favor that Moses enjoyed, he was "envious of him and sought to destroy him" (27:7). "One of the [Egyptian] conspirators" is said to have "informed Moses of the plot" (27:16), as did his brother Aaron, who summarily "advised his brother to flee to Arabia" (27:17). Moses complied and "fled to Arabia and lived with the ruler of the region" (27:19).

In this story, the flight to Arabia and the marrying into a well-positioned family is congruent with the biblical account (cf. Ex. 3:15–21). The biblical narrative does not credit Moses with all the entrepreneurial developments noted by the aforementioned author, however. In any case, the matter-of-fact way the author notes his brother Aaron's advising him to *flee to the Arabs for refuge* serves as another example of the relative lack of tension between the kindred peoples.

In both cases, when pressed amidst the turbulence of trying times, Joseph and Moses were commended to Arab hands and lands.

The *Book of Jubilees* contains fanciful Jewish inter-testamental commentary on the book of Genesis, and is said to have been an accounting of the things communicated to Moses while he spent forty days on Mount Sinai. As with the above, we are not as interested in accepting the non-biblical assumptions as much as we want to farm the non-canonical narrative to see what, if anything, it betrays about the relationship between ancient Jews and Arabs.

As much as the previous accounts seem friendly enough, here too the *Jubilees* text keeps the peace. Commenting on Abraham's blessings to his sons, the Jewish author says:

> And he gave gifts to Ishmael and his sons…and he sent them away from Isaac, and he gave everything to Isaac his sons. And Ishmael and his sons…went together and dwelt from Paran to the entrance to Babylon in all of the land which faces the east opposite the desert. And these mixed with each other, and they are called "Arabs" or "Ishmaelites." (20:11–13)

For its part, the Genesis counterpart—as we shall see later—reads that "Abraham gave all that he had unto Isaac" (Gen. 25:5–6) with a follow-up that he "gave gifts" to the others and "sent them away from Isaac, his son, while he yet lived, eastward, unto the east country" (25:6). *Jubilees* states that Ishmaelite tribes blended and extended, and are said to have taken residence in the vast expanse between Paran and Babylon. The Wilderness of Paran is said to be the place where Abraham's wife Hagar took Ishmael (Gen. 21). Mapmakers note that it's just north of the Gulf of Aqaba.[32] Babylon, of course, harks back to ancient Mesopotamia, the lands between the Tigris and Euphrates rivers.

Jubilees notes the parcel given to Isaac, and then goes on to denote that a massive inheritance was given to Ishmael as well. It reads as a friendly "Last Will and Testament," as opposed to being a story in which a disenfranchised Arab son is banished from his father's presence with instructions that he should be marked with disdain by the legitimate members of the family thereafter.

If one accepts this book's gloss on the biblical testimonies of Abraham, Moses, Ruth, the wise men, Paul, and others, and if one accepts that early commentators were reasonably kindly disposed toward Arab peoples as well, the following question is worth asking: *What happened?*

In short, *Islam happened*—but we will get to that later.

SUMMARY

What have we learned here—if anything? Hopefully, we have learned that the father of the Jewish people, Abraham, was also the father of Arab peoples, whom he loved and blessed. We learned that Moses was married to a non-Jewish, dark-skinned woman whose kin fared from what would be a part of Saudi Arabia today. We learned that the great, great grandmother of King David was a non-Jewish Moabite woman from what would be Arab Jordan today. We learned that the first non-Jews to acknowledge and adore Jesus were Arab wise men and traders, and we learned that the New Testament's greatest missionary advocate, Paul, cut his ministry teeth in Arabia and not Judea. We finished up by briefly stepping outside of the canonical literature and noted that Jewish commentators with biblical texts in view were reasonably Arab-friendly.

The aforementioned assessment does not consider the accounts in the biblical text where and when the warriors of the sand acted treacherously and, by so doing, invoked God's ire. Similarly, this incomplete accounting doesn't consider various non-biblical and post-biblical records of the same—nor is it meant to. Treacherous, Islamic-inspired perfidy and expansionism will be considered later. My principal purpose here is to disparage race-hate, and to impose upon the minds' eyes of my readers the fact that we have a brother-from-another-mother.

Anti-Arab sentiment—*or blanket race-hate in any form,* for that matter—cannot be granted on biblical grounds. We may well be angry—and deservedly so, for a variety of good reasons. Still, worth noting is the fact that Scripture does not go out of its way to cast Arabs in unfriendly light. In fact, I find evidence of it casting these long-lost relatives in respectful light. In the interest of better understanding the Arabian peoples and their interrelationship with others in the biblical drama, we will explore more of what Scripture says of their origin and development.

ARABIAN PEOPLE AND LANDS AT THE BEGINNING OF SACRED TIME

Protology: Arabia at the Jagged Start of Time

Though we briefly considered the biblical account of Ishmael's descent from Abraham in the previous chapter, precious little was actually developed thereinafter. Given that Jacob's brother Esau is a major Arabian player in the biblical narrative, as are Lot's sons Moab and Ammon and others, we do well to not oversimplify the Scripture's accounting of the origin of the people of the sand and to expand our search for the biblical accounting of the origin of the Arabian peoples—as with some interrelated others, peoples that have bearing upon the prophetic record.

In the interest of offering a fuller and decidedly biblical answer to the question of the origin and development of what we call the Arabian peoples of the sands, I will now introduce readers to what Scripture says about people and nations that formed in the ancient world at the beginning of time—thus "protology." I will offer a survey that will sweep us back up on the shores of Arabian intrigue. Given my interest in coming to terms later with "eschatology"—end times, that is—I will likewise pay attention to nations and Arabian-related peoples that arguably factor into world events at the ragged edge of time. Though incomplete, the section will hopefully serve as a worthy introduction—as with the book on the whole.[33]

Gog, Magog, Rosh, Meshech, Tubal, Persia, Ethiopia, Greece, Hebrews, Arabs, Canaanites, Sumerians, Philistines, Egyptians, Babylonians, and more will be considered herein—briefly. Offered will be an abbreviated biblical telling of the origin of human beings, of the start of federated tribal associations, and of the more complex and significant civilizations—constituted by various families and persons—that have bearing upon the biblical drama. Though a comprehensive telling of the above is impossible in this small and introductory volume—not to mention its being beyond my skill sets to offer such an accounting—we can consider the emergence of persons and tribes in and around the Fertile Crescent, where the biblical drama was first played out yesterday, where an unfolding drama is being played out today, and where it will arguably be played out tomorrow.

THE ORIGIN OF HUMAN COMMUNITY

According to Scripture, humankind began with the glorious creation of Adam and Eve (Gen. 1:26–30; 2:15–25), who in turn "begot" Cain (4:1), Abel (4:2), and Seth (4:25–26). Brief stories of their families' inglorious backslidings are subsequently told in Genesis 3:1–5:31, with evidence in the narrative that the world "went bad" at the start.

According to Genesis, sin entered the garden paradise called "Eden." Though often construed as having once been in Iraq, there is a cogent argument that the original Eden was in Israel— or possibly even a bit farther south in Arabia.[34]

Eden's placement at four riverheads is mentioned in Genesis 2:10. The river Pishon is referred to in verse 11, with the river Gihon following in verse 13; the Tigris is then noted in verse 14, as is the Euphrates in the very same verse. Factoring topographical changes in the region since the Great Flood—as with cataclysms at Sodom and Gomorrah—by connecting the Gihon with the Nile and the Pishon with perhaps what we would call the Jordan River today (that runs along a rift), with the Tigris and Euphrates rivers eastward, Eden would have been in the land of Israel—the glorious Promised Land!—located right in the middle of these rivers. If this perspective prevails in one's thinking, then Adam and Eve moved away from paradise/Israel east to Iraq when they were expunged from the garden.[35] As much as mankind was kicked out of Eden at the start, at history's close a refocus on Eden/Israel would seem all the more meaningful, would it not?

Irrespective of Eden's original location, Bible readers are told that sin made its entrance onto the stage of the human drama, rendering the perfectly made human race violated and imperfect. Though made in God's "image" and "likeness" (Gen. 1:26; 5:1), humanity descended into an ugly quagmire—from which it has yet to fully emerge. Moses would have us imagine that.

While assessing the ongoing deteriorating situation, God said, "My Spirit shall not always strive with man" (Gen. 6:3). He then went on record that He was sorry "that He made man on the earth" (6:6), and He rendered the following resultant judgment: "I will destroy man whom I have created" (6:7). It could be said that humanity's "dark ages" actually began at the dawn of time—and not during what some call the "Middle Ages." Humankind's descent into its abyss had nothing to do with Arabs, and everything to do with sin.

All was not lost, however; Noah "found grace in the eyes of

the LORD" (6:8). God expressed pleasure over Noah (6:9), whose sons we're told He noted by name—Shem, Ham, and Japheth (6:10). Afterward, the text goes on to decry the ubiquitous injustice that prevailed upon the earth (6:10–11), and represents God as giving instructions for the manufacture of an ark to save a small but righteous remnant (6:13–22). In 7:1–3, Noah was beckoned to enter the vessel. A one-hundred-and-fifty-day flood was then noted (7:4–24), after which a telling of the waters receding is offered, along with incidentals in 7:2–22.

Minded to start afresh, in Genesis 9:1, Noah was commanded: "Be fruitful, and multiply, and fill the earth," after which he was reminded of his supremacy over creation (9:2–3), as Adam had been previously (cf. 1:28–30). With Adam's other progeny now wiped out, Noah emerged not only as a survivor himself, but as the principal hope for the earth's future survival, a hope for replenishment that would be accomplished through his sons— the aforementioned Shem, Ham, and Japheth (10:1).

Though introduced twice already in the order of Shem, Ham, and Japheth (10:1; 6:10), the order was interestingly reversed when the details were added. Most Bible readers pass over genealogies or read through them swiftly. Let us slow down the action a bit, read the Genesis accounting, and with it in view, consider what Scripture says about the origin of the ancient world. We will now consider 10:1–5a, note the names, and consider if any sound remotely familiar—and they should.

¹Now these are the generations of the sons of Noah: Shem, Ham, and Japheth; and unto them were sons born after the flood. ²The sons of Japheth: Gomer, and Magog, and Madai, and Javan, and Tubal, and Meshech, and

Tiras. ³The sons of Gomer: Ashkenaz, and Riphath, and Togarmah. ⁴And the sons of Javan: Elishah, and Tarshish, Kittim, and Dodanim. ⁵From these the coastland peoples of the Gentiles were separated into their lands, everyone according to his language, according to their families, into their nations.

Noah's son Japheth was remembered at the start of this list, where he is credited with fathering Gomer, from whom came the inhabitants of ancient Turkey, the Cimmerians and the Scythians. His sons Magog, Rosh, Meshech, and Tubal—noted in conjunction with the world's last-days war (see below)—are related to those who became known for settling in southern Russia; Madai will later be identified with the Medes east of Assyria in Persia—another last-days warrior nation; Javon, being the general word for the Hellenic race, is identified with Greece—and with the Ionians of western Asia Minor; Tiras is associated with Italy—given an association with the seafaring Pelasgians along the Aegean coasts. Togarmah is noted with Armenia; Tarshish is usually associated with Spain; and lastly, Kittim is identified with Cyprus. After briefly introducing these individuals and associated tribes, Moses then said, "By these were the borders of the nations divided in their lands" (10:5a), a summary that lends further credence to the notion that these sons ventured out into the Mediterranean world by way of the sea.

For his part, in Genesis 10:6–20, Noah's son Ham was the progenitor of a variety of land-based peoples in Africa and the eastern and southern peoples of Mesopotamia, of which more will be said later. As before, let us read through the sacred record and then unpack some of its particulars.

[6]And the sons of Ham: Cush, and Mizraim, and Put, and Canaan. [7]And the sons of Cush: Seba, and Havilah, and Sabtah, and Raamah, and Sabtechah. And the sons of Raamah: Sheba, and Dedan. [8]And Cush begot Nimrod; he began to be a mighty one in the earth. [9]He was a mighty hunter before the LORD: wherefore it is said, "Even as Nimrod the mighty hunter before the LORD." [10]And the beginning of his kingdom was Babel, and Erech, and Accad, and Calneh, in the land of Shinar. [11]Out of that land went forth Asshur, and builded Nineveh, and the city Rehoboth, and Calah, [12]And Resen between Nineveh and Calah; the same is a great city. [13]And Mizraim begot Ludim, and Anamim, and Lehabim, and Naphtuhim, [14]And Pathrusim, and Casluhim (out of whom came the [Philistines]), and Caphtorim.

[15]And Canaan begot Sidon, his firstborn, and Heth, [16]And the Jebusite, and the Amorite, and the Girgashite; [17]And the Hivite, and the Arkite, and the Sinite, [18]And the Arvadite, and the Zemarite, and the Hamathite: and afterward the families of the Canaanites spread abroad. [19]And the border of the Canaanites was from Sidon, as thou comest to Gerar, unto Gaza; as thou goest, unto Sodom, and Gomorrah, and Admah, and Zeboiim, even unto Lasha. [20]These are the sons of Ham, after their families, after their tongues, in their countries, and in their nations.

Noah's son Cush is referred to in 10:6, and is noted as bearing descendants who eventually settled in south Arabia, Egypt, Sudan, and part of Ethiopia. Cushites mingled with other peoples and thus spilled over into other bloodlines. The text's Seba (10:7) is associated with upper Egypt; Havilah (10:7; i.e., "sand-land") could refer to northern and/or eastern Arabia or Ethiopia; Sabtah, in 10:7 also, is associated with the western shore of the Persian Gulf; and Raamah and Sebtecah are associated with southern Arabia. Sheba—known well through the story of the Queen of Sheba (1 Kings 10:1–13)— was in southwest Arabia (and possibly extending east from there into western Africa), with Dedan being in the north.

From another of Ham's sons, Mizraim (10:6), came the Egyptians, who developed into tribes that extended beyond Egypt proper, through northern Africa and into the Mediterranean Sea. Through another son, Phut (or simply Put), in 10:6 also, came the Africans, generally. Lastly, his fourth son, Canaan, fathered the Canaanites (in the land later called Israel), with Nimrod going farther eastward and fathering the Babylonians and Assyrians. Others are noted in 10:15–19. Sidon, in 10:15, is the progenitor of the Phoenicians, and Heth is the progenitor of the Hitties. The original inhabitants of Jerusalem, prior to David's conquest, were the Jebusi, descended from Jebus, noted in 10:16. The Pilistim in 10:13–14 are descended from Ham's son, as is Sin, the possible founder of the Oriental peoples in China, India, and Japan. Though more could be said, let it suffice to say that unlike the previous summary statement that refers to the "sea," this small subsection closes noting that "these are the sons of Ham, after their families…in their countries, and in their nations" (10:20).

After offering a telling of the conquests and habitation of northern African lands, the Mediterranean Sea (and world), and the lands of the Fertile Crescent (i.e., Mesopotamia), Moses then focused on the son who was previously noted first—Shem:

> [21]Unto Shem also, the father of all the children of Eber, the brother of Japheth, the elder, even to him were children born. [22]The children of Shem: Elam, and Asshur,

and Arpachshad, and Lud, and Aram. [23]And the children of Aram: Uz, and Hul, and Gether, and Mash. [24]And Arpachshad begot Shelah; and Shelah begot Eber. [25]And unto Eber were born two sons: the name of one was Peleg; for in his days was the earth divided; and his brother's name was Joktan. [26]And Joktan begot Almodad, and Sheleph, and Hazarmaveth, and Jerah, [27]And Hadoram, and Uzal, and Diklah, [28]And Obal, and Abimael, and Sheba, [29]And Ophir, and Havilah, and Jobab; all these were the sons of Joktan. [30]And their dwelling was from Mesha, as thou goest unto Sephar, a mount of the east. [31]These are the sons of Shem, after their families, after their tongues, in their lands, after their nations.

[32]These are the families of the sons of Noah, after their generations, in their nations: and by these were the nations divided in the earth after the flood. (Gen. 10:21–32)

Shem's son Elam is noted at the start, in 10:22. Elam's descendants dwelt in the highlands east of Babylonia—the once-dreaded Elamites. Asshur (also in 10:22), from whom the terrifying Assyrians are named, followed. Arphaxad and Lud—likewise associated with ancient Assyria—came next, followed by Aram, who was known for having established himself finally as the father of the Arameans in the Mesopotamian steppes. Notice that "in his days was the earth divided" (10:25) is not incidental. This notation—associated with the births of Shem's grandsons, Peleg and Joktan—presages the division that is about to come with the Tower of Babel (11:1–9), which facilitates the earth's ultimate super-fracture. The reference to Joktan's progeny in 10:25–29 beckons readers to over a dozen desert tribes who dwelt in the

Arabian Peninsula. These Arabian Shemites—called Semites today—can be divided into three categories: (1) extinct peoples, (2) northern Arabian peoples, and (3) southern Arabian peoples. These will be noted momentarily.

In 10:31–32, Moses summarized Noah's sons' families and turned his momentary attention to the story of Babel in 11:1–26, which we will now consider with some attendant details before looking more deliberately at the origin of the Hebrew people.

> [1]And the whole earth was of one language, and of one speech. [2]And it came to pass, as they journeyed from the east, that they found a plain in the land of Shinar; and they dwelt there. [3]And they said one to another, "Go to, let us make brick, and burn them thoroughly." And they had brick for stone, and slime had they for morter. [4]And they said, "Go to, let us build us a city and a tower, whose top may reach unto heaven; and let us make us a name, lest we be scattered abroad upon the face of the whole earth."
>
> [5]And the LORD came down to see the city and the tower, which the children of men builded. [6]And the LORD said, "Behold, the people is one, and they have all one language; and this they begin to do: and now nothing will be restrained from them, which they have imagined to do. [7]Go to, let us go down, and there confound their language, that they may not understand one another's speech." [8]So the LORD scattered them abroad from thence upon the face of all the earth: and they left off to build the city. [9]Therefore is the name of it called Babel; because the LORD did there confound the language of all the earth: and from thence did the LORD scatter them abroad upon the face of all the earth.

[10]These are the generations of Shem: Shem was an hundred years old, and begat Arphaxad two years after the flood: [11]And Shem lived after he begat Arphaxad five hundred years, and begat sons and daughters. [12]And Arphaxad lived five and thirty years, and begat Salah: [13]And Arphaxad lived after he begat Salah four hundred and three years, and begat sons and daughters. [14]And Salah lived thirty years, and begat Eber: [15]And Salah lived after he begat Eber four hundred and three years, and begat sons and daughters. [16]And Eber lived four and thirty years, and begat Peleg: [17]And Eber lived after he begat Peleg four hundred and thirty years, and begat sons and daughters. [18]And Peleg lived thirty years, and begat Reu: [19]And Peleg lived after he begat Reu two hundred and nine years, and begat sons and daughters. [20]And Reu lived two and thirty years, and begat Serug: [21]And Reu lived after he begat Serug two hundred and seven years, and begat sons and daughters. [22]And Serug lived thirty years, and begat Nahor: [23]And Serug lived after he begat Nahor two hundred years, and begat sons and daughters. [24]And Nahor lived nine and twenty years, and begat Terah: [25]And Nahor lived after he begat Terah an hundred and nineteen years, and begat sons and daughters. [26]And Terah lived seventy years, and begat Abram, Nahor, and Haran.

After noting that "the LORD scattered them abroad over the face of the earth" (11:8), Moses picked up with the seemingly pedantic nature of the family histories. In 11:10, Shem is again noted as having "begotten" Arphaxad. Arphaxad then "begot" Salah (11:12–13), who in turn "begot" Eber (11:14–16). Eber

then "begot" Peleg (11:16), who then "begot" Reu (11:18–19).
Reu "begot" one named Serug (11:20–21), who then "begot" a
fellow named Nahor (11:22–23). Nahor, in turn, fathered Terah
(11:24), who was the father of Abram, Nahor, and Haran (11:25–
27). Here readers are getting into better-known territory. Let us
briefly consider the principal text, unpack it some, and then wrap
up this section.

> [27]Now these are the generations of Terah: Terah begat
> Abram, Nahor, and Haran; and Haran begat Lot. [28]And
> Haran died before his father Terah in the land of his
> nativity, in Ur of the Chaldees. [29]And Abram and Nahor
> took them wives: the name of Abram's wife was Sarai; and
> the name of Nahor's wife, Milcah, the daughter of Haran,
> the father of Milcah, and the father of Iscah. [30]But Sarai
> was barren; she had no child. [31]And Terah took Abram
> his son, and Lot the son of Haran his son's son, and Sarai
> his daughter in law, his son Abram's wife; and they went
> forth with them from Ur of the Chaldees, to go into the
> land of Canaan; and they came unto Haran, and dwelt
> there. [32]And the days of Terah were two hundred and five
> years: and Terah died in Haran.

Of Terah's three sons, Haran is said to have died early in the
land of Ur of the Chaldeans (11:28). The surviving brothers,
Abram and Nahor, are noted with their taking wives. Sarah is mentioned first among them, with a seemingly superfluous double-
mention of her being "barren" and having "no child" (11:30).
Milcah is noted in 11:29, subsequent to which the father-in-law,
Terah, appears on record, pressing both Abram and his deceased
brother's son, Lot, to venture forth from Ur and settle in Haran

(our modern Syria), after which Terah is noted as having died (11:31–32).

So, what do we have here? In Genesis chapters 1–11, readers are exposed to the creation account and the rise of mankind, as with humankind's demise. Though Noah and his sons were spared the destruction that befell the rest, the decimating sin-plague that got the better of humankind is evidenced as having lived on—in and through Noah and his sons. Forgoing this theological consideration for the moment, what is important here for our very introductory purposes is to note the beginnings of human beings, of families, and of the rise of federated nation-states. In this biblical survey of the origin of human families, we hear names that occur later in end-time texts—names like Magog, Meshech, Tubal, and others that we will recall in a bit.

To narrow our focus to peoples and places that have a more direct bearing upon Arab-related considerations, at this juncture we will go on to offer more biblical-related accounting of the origin of the Hebrews, Arabs, Philistines, Canaanites, Egyptians, Akkadians, Sumerians, Babylonians, Assyrians, Persians, Greeks, and Romans.[36]

Given that Israel occupied space in the only landbridge connecting Africa, Asia, and Europe, like it or not, the sacred real estate was always forced to play host to major world powers given to traversing the region for reasons of their own. Because the various wars, treaties, political alliances, and intrigues are forever a factor in the biblical texts—as with history generally—students need to be at least aware of them, as with how these other non-Israelite nations factored into the Israelite prophets' divine pronouncements. Here, some of these ancient nations will be considered in the interest of coming to terms with the effect that Arabian peoples and nations had upon Israel—beginning with the Hebrews.

After considering the effect they once had, and after observing the effect they are having, we will then be better able to perceive the effect they will have—at the ragged edge of human history.

THE ORIGIN OF THE JEWISH AND ARAB PEOPLES

The word "Hebrew" comes from the ancient Aramaic *i-b-ray*, an expression said to mean "from beyond/across the river." Abraham and his family earned the appellation because they ventured forth from the Tigris and Euphrates valley area and made their way westward—and thus "beyond" those rivers. Though the story was presented in the previous chapter, a brief retelling fits here. On the basis of its being often offered up as biblical proof of the Arab peoples' innate, uncivil disposition, the need to rebuff the classical interpretation warrants the following reiteration—superfluous though it may seem at first.

Our story begins as follows.

Immediately on the heels of his father's death in Genesis 12:1, Abram was beckoned to finish the journey to Israel: "Get thee out of thy country, and from thy kindred, and from thy father's house, unto a land that I will show thee," said the Lord. With the promise of greatness to follow in 12:2–3, Abram departed Haran with his family and possessions and walked off toward an uncertain future with his barren wife, Sarah, in 12:4 and following.

With Sarah's ineptness amply noted in sacred literature and lore, little will be made of it here. With my principal interest in underscoring Ishmael's emergence and importance in view over and against Isaac's esteem and estate (culminating in the ultimate promise of the land to him and his descendants), let it here suffice that Sarah's restlessness is said to have prompted her to seek an alternate route to motherhood and nationhood—through an Egyptian handmaiden named Hagar (16:1–3). The biblical story follows.

> [1]Now Sarai Abram's wife bare him no children: and she had an handmaid, an Egyptian, whose name was Hagar. [2]And Sarai said unto Abram, Behold now, the LORD hath restrained me from bearing: I pray thee, go in unto my maid; it may be that I may obtain children by her. And Abram hearkened to the voice of Sarai.
>
> [3]And Sarai Abram's wife took Hagar her maid the Egyptian, after Abram had dwelt ten years in the land of Canaan, and gave her to her husband Abram to be his wife. [4]And he went in unto Hagar, and she conceived: and when she saw that she had conceived, her mistress was despised in her eyes.
>
> [5]And Sarai said unto Abram, "My wrong be upon thee: I have given my maid into thy bosom; and when she saw that she had conceived, I was despised in her eyes: the LORD judge between me and thee." [6]But Abram said unto Sarai, "Behold, thy maid is in thine hand; do to her as it pleaseth thee." And when Sarai dealt hardly with her, she fled from her face.
>
> [7]And the angel of the LORD found her by a fountain of water in the wilderness, by the fountain in the way to Shur. [8]And he said, "Hagar, Sarai's maid, whence camest thou? and whither wilt thou go?" And she said, "I flee from the face of my mistress Sarai." [9]And the angel of the LORD said unto her, "Return to thy mistress, and submit thyself under her hands."

[10]And the angel of the LORD said unto her, "I will multiply thy seed exceedingly, that it shall not be numbered for multitude." [11]And the angel of the LORD said unto her, "Behold, thou art with child and shalt bear a son, and shalt call his name Ishmael; because the LORD hath heard thy affliction. [12]And he will be a wild man; his hand will be against every man, and every man's hand against him; and he shall dwell in the presence of all his brethren."

[13]And she called the name of the LORD that spake unto her, Thou God seest me: for she said, Have I also here looked after him that seeth me? [14]Wherefore the well was called Beerlahairoi; behold, it is between Kadesh and Bered. [15]And Hagar bare Abram a son: and Abram called his son's name, which Hagar bare, Ishmael. [16]And Abram was fourscore and six years old, when Hagar bare Ishmael to Abram.

After being pawned off on Abraham, owing to Sarah's inability to birth a child, Hagar "conceived," after which her mistress, Sarah, "became despised in her eyes" (16:4). Though Hagar was carrying the heir apparent, Sarah still commanded more clout and made life absolutely miserable for her servant (16:6). Troubled as she was by the incessant bullying, Hagar fled to the wilderness, where she was visited by the Lord (16:7–8). She was instructed to return to Sarah (16:9) for the time being, and was comforted with an extremely significant, seminal promise (16:10–12):

"I will multiply thy seed exceedingly…. Behold, thou art with child, and shalt bear a son, and shalt call his name Ishmael; because the LORD hath heard thy affliction. And he will be a wild man; his hand will be against every man, and every man's hand against him; and he shall dwell in the presence of all his brethren."

Though this passage about Ishmael being "wild" is typically offered as proof of the horribly unruly nature of the Arab peoples whom Ishmael went on to later sire, as noted previously, we would do well to pause and consider this interpretation and reflect upon whether this inclination says more about our own inclinations than it does the text itself. While granting that he is indeed called a "wild man" (16:12), we would do well to consider that the strong, free-spirited essence of the term would be good news indeed for this Egyptian maiden, who has been acted upon by forces too strong for her. The text, thus, reads like more of a testament to God's love for her than a blanket condemnation of her offspring—whom He would later go on to bless in no uncertain terms.

I know neither the circumstances that forced Hagar into a subservient status under Abraham's employ, nor what her feelings might have been about being pawned off on this older man to birth his other wife's child. I am sure she was aware that her life was not her own, represented as she is as being little more than an object to serve her mistress' pleasures and treasures. God's abiding love for her personally and for her son specifically is forcefully attested, and would have been good news for her indeed. Would not this disempowered domestic worker who just recently was forced to mother a child through a man she may not have desired have construed the promise of a strong and free-spirited son, one who will not be domesticated by others and of whom others will not easily get the better of, as good news indeed? I think so.

In either case, should one opt for the traditional construal of "wild" as a disparaging term for his particularly unmanageable nature, we would still do well to remember that he was hardly unique, and was in very good company. Adam and Eve's son, unmanageable Cain, slew Abel (Gen. 4:8b). "Wild," don't you think? That Noah's son, wild Ham, was irreverent toward his father and invoked divine condemnation in response is well noted, too (Gen. 9:21–25). Lot—who later scandalously sired the Moabites and Ammonites with his very own daughters—was a "wild" sort who disrespected and disregarded his uncle Abraham (Gen. 13:1–18). Isaac's sons, Jacob and Esau, fought "wildly" from the womb (Gen. 25:19–26) and incessantly thereafter (25:29ff). Jacob's unruly sons were themselves minded to kill Joseph—an inclination that was only satisfied when they opted to give him up as a slave (Gen. 37:12–36). These examples demonstrate that when it comes to being "wild," one can hardly lay the inclination at the feet of Ishmael alone and single him out as a particularly dastardly sort. These considerations aside, Abraham's actual love for Ishmael and his other brothers—who father Arabian peoples—is amply noted in the Genesis 25:1–18 and should put to bed any inclinations that he thought the lesser of brothers from other mothers.

¹Then again Abraham took a wife, and her name was Keturah. ²And she bare him Zimran, and Jokshan, and Medan, and Midian, and Ishbak, and Shuah. ³And Jokshan begat Sheba, and Dedan. And the sons of Dedan were Asshurim, and Letushim, and Leummim. ⁴And the sons of Midian; Ephah, and Epher, and Hanoch, and Abidah, and Eldaah. All these were the children of Keturah. ⁵And Abraham gave all that he had unto Isaac. ⁶But unto the sons of the concubines, which Abraham had, Abraham gave gifts, and sent them away from Isaac his son, while he yet lived, eastward, unto the east country.

[7]And these are the days of the years of Abraham's life which he lived, an hundred threescore and fifteen years. [8]Then Abraham gave up the ghost, and died in a good old age, an old man, and full of years; and was gathered to his people. [9]And his sons Isaac and Ishmael buried him in the cave of Machpelah, in the field of Ephron the son of Zohar the Hittite, which is before Mamre; [10]The field which Abraham purchased of the sons of Heth: there was Abraham buried, and Sarah his wife.

[11]And it came to pass after the death of Abraham, that God blessed his son Isaac; and Isaac dwelt by the well Lahairoi. [12]Now these are the generations of Ishmael, Abraham's son, whom Hagar the Egyptian, Sarah's handmaid, bare unto Abraham: [13]And these are the names of the sons of Ishmael, by their names, according to their generations: the firstborn of Ishmael, Nebajoth; and Kedar, and Adbeel, and Mibsam, [14]And Mishma, and Dumah, and Massa, [15]Hadar, and Tema, Jetur, Naphish, and Kedemah: [16]These are the sons of Ishmael, and these are their names, by their towns, and by their castles; twelve princes according to their nations.

[17]And these are the years of the life of Ishmael, an hundred and thirty and seven years: and he gave up the ghost and died; and was gathered unto his people. [18]And they dwelt from Havilah unto Shur, that is before Egypt, as thou goest toward Assyria: and he died in the presence of all his brethren.

In Genesis 25:1 and 4b, the Hebrew prophet Moses went on record stating that subsequent to Sarah's death, Abraham took a wife named Keturah, who in turn bore Abraham, Zimran,

Jokshan, Medan, Midian, Ishbak, and Shua. After noting these additional children of Abraham, Moses stated emphatically in 25:5 that "Abraham gave all that he had unto Isaac," in conjunction with which he closed, noting that he likewise "gave gifts" to these other sons, whom he then "sent them away from Isaac his son, while he yet lived, eastward, unto the east country" (25:6). While granting—and reminding in no uncertain terms—that the seeded land promise was passed down to and through Isaac, as per Genesis 21:12 and 25:6, worth noting as well is that neither Ishmael nor his other brothers were utterly abandoned. Though the text reads, "In Isaac shall thy seed be called" (Gen. 21:12), God still went on to say in verse 13 that, "And also of the son of the bondwoman will I make a nation, because he is thy seed"—a reference to Ishmael, and to subsequent generations of Arab peoples by association. This promise was reaffirmed in 21:17–18, where Hagar was told: "Fear not…lift up the lad…for *I will make him a great nation*" (emphasis added). Moses then closed, noting that "God was with the lad" (21:20) and that "he dwelt [for a season] in the wilderness of Paran" (21:21).

As with Jacob later, Ishmael had twelve sons, who were born to him before he expired at the ripe and blessed age of one hundred thirty-seven. Moses identifies the sons as Nebajoth, Kedar, Abdeel, Mibsam, Mishma, Dumah, Massa, Hadar, Tema, Jetur, Naphish, and Kedmah in Genesis 25:13b–15, and then respectfully finishes, saying they were "twelve princes according to their nations" (25:16). Though they began with residence in the northern Sinai, as per 21:21 above, the blessed family apparently successfully spread out over time, evidenced by the parenthetical notation of their being "from Havilah unto Shur" (Gen. 25:18). Havilah was in north-central Arabia, with Shur being between Beersheba and Egypt.

It seems that Ishmael did well for himself—with God's help and because of God's blessing—does it not?

That Isaac was Abraham's principal beneficiary is amply noted in the literature thereinafter, in Genesis 25:19 and following, as is his subsequently bearing Jacob and Esau through his originally Syrian-based wife named Rebekah. Moses noted that, like Sarah, Rebekah was similarly "barren" (v. 21), but she "conceived" after Isaac's prayerful intercession. "Two nations" were predicted as being "in [her] womb" (v. 23), of which it was said "the elder shall serve the younger." Esau came first in verse 25, followed by Jacob, his brother. Let us now hear from Moses.

[19]This is the genealogy of Isaac, Abraham's son: Abraham begot Isaac. [20]And Isaac was forty years old when he took Rebekah as wife, the daughter of Bethuel the Syrian of Padan-aram, the sister of Laban the Syrian. [21]And Isaac entreated the LORD for his wife, because she was barren: and the LORD was entreated by him, and Rebekah, his wife, conceived. [22]And the children struggled together within her; and she said, "If it be so, why am I thus?" And she went to inquire of the LORD. [23]And the LORD said unto her: "Two nations are in thy womb, and two manner of people shall be born of thee; and the one people shall be stronger than the other people; and the elder shall serve the younger."

[24]And when her days to be delivered were fulfilled, behold, there were twins in her womb. [25]And the first came out red, all over like an hairy garment; and they called his name Esau. [26]And after that came his brother out, and his hand took hold on Esau's heel; and his name was called Jacob: and Isaac was [sixty years] old when she

bore them. [27]And the boys grew: and Esau was a skillful hunter, a man of the field; and Jacob was a quiet man, dwelling in tents. [28]And Isaac loved Esau, because he did eat of his venison: but Rebekah loved Jacob.

[29]And Jacob boiled pottage: and Esau came in from the field, and he was faint. [30]And Esau said to Jacob, "Feed me, I pray thee, with that same red pottage, for I am faint:" therefore was his name called Edom. [31]And Jacob said, "Sell me this day thy birthright." [32]And Esau said, "Behold, I am at the point to die: and what profit shall this birthright do to me?" [33]And Jacob said, "Swear to me this day;" And he swore unto him: and he sold his birthright unto Jacob. [34]Then Jacob gave Esau bread and pottage of lentils; and he did eat and drink, and rose up, and went his way: thus Esau despised his birthright. (Gen. 25:19–34)

As with tensions between Isaac and Ishmael, stories of legendary tensions between Esau and Jacob are unpacked immediately. In verses 29–34, Jacob's getting the better of his older and stronger brother is noted by his getting him to sell "his birthright to Jacob" (v. 33). In 27:1–29, Jacob stealthily secured Isaac's blessing, with an attachment that "people [shall] serve thee, and nations [shall] bow down to thee," and that even "thy mother's [other] sons [shall] bow down to thee" (v. 29). After learning of the mishap, Esau "cried with a great and exceedingly bitter cry" (v. 34), and begged his father to give him redress for his grievance and bless him, too. Not minded to retract the prophetic blessing, in response to his question of whether there was still a blessing for him (v. 36), Isaac said, "Behold, I have made him thy lord" (v. 37), but "thy dwelling shall be the fatness of the earth" and "by thy sword shalt thou live" (vv. 39–40). It seems that *success* was promised him, as was *strength*—characteristics evident in Arab peoples to this day.

Rebekah was less kindly disposed toward Esau (as was Sarah to Ishmael), and even Esau's wives were a source of grief to her. In Genesis 27:46, she lamented to her husband, "I am weary of my life because of the daughters of Heth" (cf. 26:34–35), in response to which Jacob was summoned by Isaac and sent off to Rebekah's family in Syria with the charge: "Thou shalt not take a wife from the daughters of Canaan…take thee a wife there of the daughters of Laban, thy mother's brother" (28:1–2). Jacob's blessing was reiterated in 28:3–4, where the "blessing of Abraham" was bestowed on Jacob and his descendants who, according to the text, will "inherit the land" (v. 4). When Esau discovered that his Syrian-based mother, Rebekah, did not like Canaanite-based women (v. 8), he then went to Ishmael in the East and married his daughter Mahalath. *While Abraham, Isaac, and Jacob are descendants of Shem, so too are Ishmael, Esau, Moab, Ammon, and others*—folk who frequent lands east of Judea and in the Arabian Peninsula. It is for this reason that one cannot say Arabs are anti-Semitic: They are Semitic—as are Jews. *We are all cut from the same cloth.*

Some of the ancient Arab peoples are now extinct; others have survived, however. The best known of the extinct Arabian peoples are the Amalekites—who drew God's angst on more than one occasion in the biblical narrative. A descendant of Shem (Gen. 36:12), they are further traced through Esau. His descendants are known to have occupied Bahrain, Oman, and Yemen, and are said to have been the first settlers of Yathrib—known today as Medina. They are believed to have settled around Mecca and Kheibar till displaced and finally destroyed. Both the Bible and the Koran note the Amalekites' inglorious end, with attendant disparaging tellings.

The southern Arabs claim to be descended from Qahtan, son of ʿAber, son of Shalikh, son of Arfakhshad, son of Shem, son of Noah. This Qahtan is undoubtedly the previously mentioned biblical personality named Joktan (Gen.10:26), as noted above in the consideration of the tables of nations in Genesis 10. Among Joktan's sons are Almodad, Hazarmaveth, Uzal, Sheba, Ophir, and Havilah (vv. 26–29). Of particular importance for our purposes is Joktan, who left an indelible mark upon the Arabian Peninsula.

To illustrate, a memorable descendant of Joktan is a queen known as Bilkis, whom Arabian historians identify with the Queen of Sheba who once visited Solomon (Koran, 38). Remnants of Bilkis' people, as others, fled northward when a dam built by Lokm at Marib in about the second century AD is said to have broken and forced the displacement of many Arabs. These migrating Arabs eventually formed the Ghassan kingdom, which had its capital in Damascus. There, monarchs carried the title name "Al-Harith." One known to New Testament readers as Artas, the King of Damascus in 2 Corinthians 11:32, is of this ilk. His kingdom, as with others, was allied with Greece and Rome; this kingdom, as with others, came to an end with the Islamic conquests of the seventh century AD by Mohammad's generals—more of which will be said later.[37]

THE ORIGIN OF THE PHILISTINES AND CANAANITES

Descending originally from Noah's son Japheth and then through Jovan, the Philistines were a seafaring people who, following a failed invasion of Egypt in 1190 BC, successfully secured a foot-hold on the eastern rim of the Mediterranean Sea, from where they went on to build five cities of note on the seaboard side of Canaan: Gaza, Ashdod, Askelon, Ekron, and Gath. Philistines are *not* native Arabian peoples, as alleged today by Islamic peoples claiming the name "Palestinians" for themselves—possibly to give credence to the mythology that they are from the original early settlers of the land. *They, in no uncertain terms, are not.*

Moses noted how sea invaders came from the island of Caphtor (known to us as Crete) and bested locals in Israel, saying the Caphtor "destroyed them, and dwelt in their stead" (Deut. 2:23). Jeremiah likewise noted the connection; while presaging the plunder of the Philistines, he referred to them as "the remnant of...Caphtor" (47:4). Amos, for his part, did much the same, attesting that "the Philistines [came] from Caphtor" (Amos 9:7).

The seafaring Philistines secured a temporary toehold in the eastern part of the Mediterranean world, not moving inland much beyond the shores. They successfully got the better of the Israelites (Judg. 13:1ff) till they were dislodged by various judges (15:1–20; cf. 3:31). Happily for the Hebrews, Philistine incursions were kept in check during Samuel's administration. In 1 Samuel 7:11, the Philistines were driven back; in verse 13, the writer says, "The Philistines were subdued, and they came no more into the border of Israel." The king's son Jonathan made a name for himself by getting the better of the Philistines (1 Sam. 14:1–46), as did David in 1 Samuel 17:1 and following. During Solomon's administration, the real seafaring Philistines were finally subdued (1 Kings 4:21).

As noted previously, common "Palestinian" rhetoric notwithstanding, the Philistines of the biblical era should not be confused with today's so-called Palestinians. For political reasons of their own, as noted, today's "Palestinians" are given to employing their variant of "Philistine" to confuse individuals who, as a result of their misappropriating the appellation, may more readily surmise that the present "Palestinians" should be associated with the "Philistines" who existed in Israel in a bygone era. *There is no connection between the seafaring Philistines of antiquity and the modern pretenders who came from the Arabian sands, marched under the banner of Islam, and pounced upon Israel two thousand years later.*

In any case, the Bible's Philistines were *not* Muslims. They worshipped Dagon, the infamous Ba'al, and his feminine counterpart, Ashtoreth. Commenting on particulars associated with the Philistines' capture of the Ark, 1 Samuel's chronicler notes how the Philistine idol Dagon fell "upon his face to the earth before the ark" of Jehovah (5:1–5, esp. vv. 3–4). That Ba'al was inquired of by the Philistines is noted in 2 Kings 1:2, where the king sent messengers to "inquire of Ba'al-zebub" (cf. Matt. 12:24). These, of course, were not Muslims, who would not accept idol worship and who, irrespective, came into their own many, many centuries later. While commenting on Saul's death, the writer of 1 Samuel noted how the real Philistines took the armor of the vanquished and deceased Saul, and "put his armor in the house of Ashtaroth" (31:10). For these and other reasons, not only are the present Islamic Palestinians not connected to the Philistines of the biblical era, but worth noting is that the real Philistines' amply attested proclivity toward idols and variant gods is patently offensive to Muslims.

"Canaanite" is a broad term denoting association with one of a number of the tribes resident in Canaan at the time of Joshua's conquest and Israel's consequential entrance. These include, and are not limited to, the Phoenicians, Philistines (not to be confused with those who maliciously and inaccurately employ the name today), Ammonites, Hittites, Jebusites, Amorites, and Hivites. To limited degrees, these have been noted previously in relation to their being descendants of Ham's fourth son, Canaan (as per Gen. 9:22–27; 10:6, 15–20).

Embedded in Canaan, these preexisting "-ites" founded cities that are well known to Bible readers. Foremost among them are Megiddo, Jericho, Sodom and Gomorrah, and, of course, Jerusalem. Megiddo is known through association with the climactic end-time battle, Armageddon (Rev. 16:12–16)—and more will be said of this later; Jericho, for its part, commemorates the famous first-time battle when the walls came down at the start of Canaan's conquest under Joshua (Josh. 6:1–21); Sodom and Gomorrah are known for their association with illicit sexuality (Gen. 19:1–29); and Jerusalem, of course, is known as being the place "whither the tribes go up, the tribes of the LORD…to give thanks unto the name of the LORD" (Ps. 122:4).

Instructions for the methodical displacement of the Canaanites are noted in the text, much as various battles are amply attested in Numbers 31:1–24; Deuteronomy 2:26–3:22, 20:1–20, and 21:10–14; and Joshua 1:1–11:23. Though granting that the systemic eradication of a population—as per Deuteronomy 7:1–5 and 20:10–15 and Joshua 9:24—may well seem incongruous with a more kindly disposed orientation and application of biblical faith and virtue, the perspective may be ameliorated if one considers the actual nature of Canaanite religion and practice—construed by ancients beyond the pale of biblical influence to be so very heinous.

In Genesis 13:13, residents of Sodom are noted as being "exceedingly" sinful. The "iniquity of the Amorites" reaching full measure is noted in 15:16, much as an outcry against Sodom is noted in 18:20, as is mention of their sin being so very "grievous." Moses' noting that local Moabite men used thousands upon thousands of their daughters to sexually lure Israelite men away from

Jehovah, in Numbers 25:1–18, represents a seemingly unprecedented low point in uncivilized behavior—another testimony to Canaanite debauchery. In Judges 19:22, grossly perverted men, "base fellows" with unrestrained lust, gave vent to their misguided passions and killed an innocent girl as they sexually abused her (vv. 26–30). Biblical literature offers these and other examples as symbols of a wild world gone bad, and not as isolated examples of blemishes in an otherwise noble and stable society.

That Canaanite religion bears blame for these lusty improprieties is evident in its royal family. The Canaanites' head deity was El, who had a wife named Asherah. Not content with her alone, El likewise married his three sisters, one of whom was Astarte. One of El's most famous—better, infamous—sons was one known as Ba'al. According to the mythology, this El went on to kill his brother and some of his own sons, but he also is said to have cut off his daughter's head, castrated his father and himself, and compelled his associates to do likewise. As if this all were not strange enough, Ba'al's sister, Anat, was a violent goddess of passion and war. Bizarre, is it not? *That this was the religious narrative in Canaan before the Israelite entrance makes it easier to appreciate why the religion was rejected outright.*

Genesis readers learn that a reasonably well-to-do Lot fell upon hard times after a fiery conflagration leveled Sodom and Gomorrah. After suffering the untimely destruction of his married daughters, sons-in-law, and grandchildren (Gen. 19:12–23), and after experiencing the death of his wife, who impulsively "looked back" (v. 26), Lot pressed on. After the fire fell upon the cities (vv. 12–29) and claimed the better part of his family in the process, Lot made his way to Zoar. There he dwelt in the mountains with his two remaining daughters, living as an impoverished hermit. With no means to secure spouses at their disposal,

Lot's daughters concocted a scheme to inebriate their father and then seduce him to secure children through him (vv. 32–35). The plot proved successful, with the result that "both the daughters of Lot [were] with child by their father" (v. 36). Moses informed that the firstborn incestuous son was subsequently named Moab, from whom came the Moabites, and that the second was called Ammon, from whom came the Ammonites (vv. 37–38)—an inglorious beginning to be sure.

The author of 1 Kings 11:5 and 7 informed that the Ammonites lent religious credence to an "abomination" named "Milcom." Particularly abominable was the fact that this thirsty god claimed blood—human blood. He was known to be particularly appeased by the sacrificial burning of children.

In 2 Kings 16:3, the Judean king Ahaz was critiqued for his embrace of the regional religion, as a consequence of which he "made his son to pass through the fire, according to the abominations of the nations, whom the LORD cast out." While noting the reign of Judean King Manasseh, the chronicler noted in 2 Kings 21:6 that "he," also, "made his son pass through the fire," adding that he "observed times, and used enchantments, and dealt with mediums and wizards; he wrought much wickedness in the sight of the LORD, to provoke Him to anger." Ezekiel castigated individuals for doing likewise, saying in 16:20–21, "Thou hast taken thy sons and thy daughters...and these hast thou sacrificed...[and] caused them to pass through the fire" (cf. 23:37). Archeological evidence in Canaanite areas corroborates the above—as travelers to Israel with me see firsthand. The remains of hundreds of children, approximately four through twelve years in age, have been unearthed, with evidence that they were burned in sacrifice to Canaanite gods.

The aforementioned references do not exhaust the evidence

attesting to various forms of Canaanite debauchery. It is hoped, though, that the adumbrated treatment will suffice as an explanation of why the Canaanites incurred God's forceful judgment during the early Israelite conquests of a land once known as Canaan.

THE ORIGIN OF THE EGYPTIANS

Egypt was fortified by a variety of natural barriers. The great sea to the north provided a bulwark against would-be land invaders, as did the deserts to the west, south, and east. Though indeed significant, benefits from the natural protections pale in comparison to the benefits of the country's natural provider: its life-source, the Nile River itself. The Nile runs for more than four thousand miles, beginning in Lake Victoria, Central Africa, and running all the way to the Mediterranean Sea. A gentle breeze assists boatmen who employ the natural waterway when making out a living, as does the gentle current. The ancients derived a variety of benefits from the Nile: It provided irrigation for otherwise dry fields and attracted wildlife to the region in the process; it proved a rich and reasonably easy source of fishing; and it provided an invaluable source of transportation. For these and other reasons, the Nile was Egypt's prize possession and the envy of others round about.

Civilizations grew up in Egypt and great rulers along with them. The first pyramid was built by Pharaoh Zoser, as evidence thereof what was likely an Egyptian improvisation of the ziggurats (stepped towers) built in ancient Mesopotamia (as per Gen. 11:1–8). The Great Pyramid was built by a hundred thousand men over a twenty-year period at the behest of Pharaoh Khufu (also Cheops). The Egyptian marvel was considered by the Greeks to be one of the wonders of the ancient world. Perhaps not wanting to be outdone by his father Khufu, his successor, Khafre, joined a lion's body that extended for two hundred forty feet with a pharaoh's head that was sixty-six feet high. Besides these, Pepi II is well known as a powerful monarch, but shortly after his ninety-year reign, his kingdom came to an end. Sometimes called the "Feudal Age," the subsequent two-hundred-year era was rife with political intrigue and social instability; commerce and industry waned considerably against the backdrop of which civil war ripped the country apart. Abraham is said to have visited Egypt during this era, around 2085 BC (Gen. 12:10–20).

Amenhotep I, of the eleventh dynasty, reunited Egypt, built up trade, and prompted Egypt to once again emerge as a world force. It was during his dynasty that Joseph was sold into slavery (Gen. 37:12–36), with his family following sometime thereafter (Gen. 46:28–34), around 1875 BC.

Soon, the political turmoil that marked the preceding dynasties brought forces to bear upon the present one. It came in the form of the Hyksos invaders (shepherd kings). Armed with two-edged daggers, double-curved bows, and short, bronze-tipped arrows, and sporting fast-moving chariots, the Hyksos swarmed the delta from Syria and Asia and conquered northern Egypt with relative ease. Finally, an Egyptian national named Ahmose I drove out the hated Hyksos in 1580 BC. In his wake came a resurgent nationalistic spirit; it may have been during this time when foreigners were looked at with suspicion that the Hebrews—who were related to the just-expelled Hyksos—may have been pressed into the servitude that is the object of Moses' attention in early Exodus.

If this perspective prevails, the "new king over Egypt who knew not Joseph" in Exodus 1:8 was Thutmose I. The "daughter of Pharaoh" noted in 2:5 who was kindly disposed to Moses was

Hatshepsut. The pharaoh who then sought to kill Moses in 2:15 would have been Thutmose III; he was a stepson of Hatshepsut who hated her and eventually deposed her. As a consequence, it would come as no surprise that, given his friendship with her, Moses would incur Thutmose III's angst as well. The pharaoh for the ten plagues was then arguably Amenhotep II. While much could—and perhaps should—be said, for purposes of biblical history, Pharaoh Necho II is the next important monarch. He killed Josiah—one of Judah's greatest kings—in 2 Kings 23:29 and came to an inglorious end himself later, when defeated by the Babylonians at the Battle of Carchemish in 605 BC.

Hebrews and Egyptians have been involved in intrigue since near the dawn of their respective recorded histories. That Egypt factors into the present Middle East quagmire should thus come as no surprise.

THE ORIGIN OF THE AKKADIANS, SUMERIANS, AND BABYLONIANS

Genesis 11 records the story of the Tower of Babel, during which time people were "scattered...upon the face of...the earth" (v. 9). By 3000 BC, a people known as the Akkadians had settled into the upper portion of a tract of land called Mesopotamia—a posh, fertile land situated between the Tigris and Euphrates rivers. The lower valleys were occupied by a group known as the Sumerians—from whence came the Bible's beloved Abraham.

Ur (of Chaldea) was a famous southern city, as were Eridu, Kish, Lagash, Larsa, Nippur, Umma, and Urak. Between 2500 and 2300 BC, Ur gained prominence over Sumeria, which in turn invaded and bested those in the north—in Akkadia. In time, however, Akkadia rebounded and invaded Sumeria at the behest of a powerful Akkadian general named Sargon. Having gotten the better of the contest militarily, Sargon employed his administrative savvy and forged a united Mesopotamian kingdom headquartered in a city called Babylon. As is often the case, those who survived him were unable to thrive in his absence: Barbarian mountain men called Gutians conquered Sumer and held sway for a hundred years. Eventually, however, Sumerians threw off their yoke and established themselves afresh from their capital in Ur. They dominated until they were pressed upon and dislodged by the Elamites.

In the second millennium BC, the Mesopotamian lands between the Tigris and Euphrates rivers were controlled by the aforementioned warring Elamites. We learn of them in Genesis 10:22 (as per the above) and in Genesis 14:1, where Elamite King Chedorlaomer, with other bellicose Mesopotamian warlords, made an incursion into Canaan and carried off Lot and his family for a season. Abraham is said to have overtaken and gotten the better of the war party and brought back his family, friends, and possessions (vv. 13–20). His minor victory did nothing to offset the balance of power in the region. After attending to that business, God affirmed His promise to Abraham (Genesis 15), noting that his descendants would be akin to the number of the stars (15:1ff).

In 1760 BC, the Elamites were successfully bested and dislodged by an Amorite general named Hammurabi, who conquered the Tigris-Euphrates Valley and subsequently founded the old Babylonian kingdom. In conjunction with founding the empire, Hammurabi is remembered for establishing a systematized code to govern it—of which the Mosaic constitution bears some minor similarities, though distinguished from it still.

The empire is said to have fared well under Hammurabi's administration. Shortly after his death, however, the Hittites invaded old Babylonia and controlled it for almost two hundred years. The founder of the Hittites was Heth, who was previously noted in Genesis 10:15. In Genesis 23:1 and following, Abraham purchased a lot from one of his descendants (v. 20). That Abraham got along with them better than Isaac is noted in 27:46, where his bride Rebekah is on record as being beside herself because of the "daughters of Heth," and not wanting her mothered baby boy Jacob to marry any of them. Though concerned about arrangements for love, others were more interested in arrangements for war. After Heth's Hittite descendants were in power in Babylonia for one hundred seventy years, they were subdued by the Kassites, who controlled the region until bested finally by the Assyrians and Elamites.

In about 620 BC, the Chaldeans came and rebuilt Babylon, which had laid in waste since leveled by the Assyrians in 721 BC. Nabopolassar became governor of the city of Babylon, after which he arranged for his son to marry the daughter of the king of Media. Later, in 612 BC, Nabopolassar's son, Nebuchadnezzar, led a successful attack against the Assyrian capital of Nineveh, in the process establishing the new Babylonian empire. After getting the better of the Egyptians in 606 BC at the famous battle of Carchemish, the new dominion was secured.

In the course of taking on Egypt, at his western flank, Nebuchadnezzar brought Israel under his sway. In 605 BC, he placed Jerusalem under his puppet king, Jehoiakim. In 597 BC he returned, and then again in 586 BC, when he punished Zedekiah for his rebellion, destroyed the Judean Temple, and brought the period of the first commonwealth to an end. Nebuchadnezzar's end came in 562 BC, when death claimed him after an illustrious career. Nebuchadnezzar was succeeded by his son, Nabonidus, who abdicated power to his son Belshazzar and moved east. On October 13, 539 BC, a weakened Babylon fell to a Persian confederacy, an event that brought to an end the new Babylonian kingdom.

THE ORIGIN OF THE ASSYRIANS AND PERSIANS

Known as the cruelest people in ancient history, the Assyrians conquered and ruled by brute force. They mastered "siege warfare," using battering rams and other highly developed military machinery. After savagely vanquishing their foes, they made haste to displace the defeated and deflated locals by sending them off as slaves and then, in turn, replacing the dispirited and deported indigenous population with transplants from other parts of their domain.

The capital of Assyria was in Nineveh, on the eastern shore of the Tigris. Nineveh was guarded by sixty miles of walls that were one hundred feet high and about eighteen feet thick. The walls were guarded by twelve hundred towers, each said to have been two hundred feet high, giving ample protection to the six hundred thousand who called Nineveh home. Its gates were guarded by massive bulls and lions sculpted into the stone. Roofs were supported by cedar resting on Cyprus columns, themselves strengthened by iron and sculpted silver. Its palace is said to have adorned the fabulous city, with courts and walls taking up in the vicinity of one hundred acres. Hanging gardens were a wonder to behold. Both here and elsewhere, Assyrian kings built massive dwellings, replete with enormous gateways, arches, and towers.

All are said to have been adorned in ways that defied imagination. Sargon II, for example, is said to have had a palace with two hundred large rooms, with room for eighty thousand guests. Even if that is overstated, I am sure it was quite a spread—all of which was built by slave labor.

The Assyrian King Tiglath-pileser I (1114–1076 BC) called himself the "ruler of the earth." Though his claiming to have personally killed four buffalo, ten elephants, and one hundred twenty lions is arguably overstated, his political power was not. Not content to receive the world as given, when Ashur-nasir-pal (883–859 BC) later came to power, he began a policy of expansionism. His son Shalmaneser III (858–824 BC) unwittingly assisted Bible readers. His records corroborate the Bible, noting the existence of a Hebrew King Ahab who was involved in a war with him. The empire began to degenerate after this powerful king's death.

Tiglath-pileser III (746–728 BC) usurped the throne, fired up the engines of the weakened empire, and forged the Assyrians into a world-class warrior class. Bible writers pick him up and note his conquests in various places. In 2 Kings 15:29, for example, the historian notes that "Tiglath-pileser, king of Assyria, [came] and took Ijon, and Abel-beth-maachah, and Janoah, and Kedesh, and Hazor, and Gilead, and Galilee, all the land of Naphtali, and carried them captive to Assyria." Shalmaneser V (727–722 BC) followed him and, in like manner, is noted in the Sacred Text. In his case, it was for capturing and killing the last northern king of Israel—Hoshea (2 Kings 17:1–4). His general, Sargon II (721–705 BC), mentioned in Isaiah 20:1, finished the demise of the northern kingdom of Israel and was later assassinated.

Sennacherib (705–681 BC) was the governor of Babylon at the time of his father Sargon's death, and took up the mantle of pillaging and plundering. He invaded Judea, minded as he was to secure more leverage over its subjects. Lengthy swatches of biblical literature tell and retell tales of his ill-fated invasion and siege of Jerusalem, one held during the political administration of Hezekiah and the prophetic administration of Isaiah. Biblical writers inform that one hundred eighty-five thousand Assyrian soldiers mysteriously died (2 Kings 18–19; 2 Chron. 32; Isa. 36–37) and that the monarch was later murdered by one of his own sons in a temple. Esarhaddon (681–669 BC) followed. He proved to be a capable king. During his administration, he rebuilt Babylon. Lastly, Ashurbanipal (668–626 BC) ruled. Under his administration, the Samaritans came into their own: "The king of Assyria brought men from Babylon, and from Cuthah, and from Ava, and from Hamath, and from Sepharvaim, and placed them in the cities of Samaria instead of the children of Israel; and they possessed Samaria, and dwelt in its cities" (2 Kings 17:24).

The Assyrian empire survived Ashurbanipal by only fifteen years. Nabopolassar, king of Babylon, tried to sack Nineveh three times, but was repelled each time. Finally, however, he got the better of them and brought the proud city down. The destruction of Nineveh was so thorough that Alexander the Great walked over the city years later without even knowing he was walking atop the ruins.

In 550 BC, a Persian general called Cyrus the Great subdued the Medes and assimilated them into a world-class fighting force with the Persians. In 547 BC, he conquered the wealthy Croesus, who ruled the land between the Mediterranean and Black seas and extended to the borders of India. In 539 BC, he took the city of Babylon and executed Belshazzar. Secure and administratively savvy as they were, from 550–330 BC, the strong and efficient Persians ruled one of the most extensive empires in history and intersected with biblical history in the process.

In Daniel 1:21, Cyrus is noted. Much as in 6:28, Daniel is said to have prospered in the reign of Cyrus. Bible writers note Cyrus often, and depict him in a good light—usually as God's instrument to accomplish His purposes on the earth. In Isaiah 44:28, for example, Cyrus is referred to as God's "shepherd" and one who "perform[s] all My pleasure"—i.e., God's pleasure. In 45:1, Isaiah says that Cyrus is God's "anointed," designated and empowered by God to "subdue nations" and "loose the [armor] of kings" (45:1).

Because death claims all—the powerful and the powerless alike—it eventually claimed great Cyrus. He was succeeded by his son Cambyses II, who, upon discovering a revolt against him, took his own life. Happily for the weakening Persians, Darius the Great succeeded Cambyses II and restored order. His zero tolerance for dissent is attested by the cruel measures he employed against it. Noting rumblings against him in Babylon, for example, he crucified three thousand of the city's leaders. In 490 BC, he led sixty thousand Persian foot soldiers and cavalry on an ill-fated advance upon Greece. His inglorious defeat at the hands of a much smaller number of Greek soldiers at the Battle of Marathon took the luster out of his persona and forced him into a retreat mode. He was followed by his son Xerxes—known as Ahasuerus in the book of Esther—who, in like manner, would be humbled by human experience.

In 480 BC, Xerxes crossed the Dardanelles with hundreds of ships and more than one hundred thousand men. His advance on Greece was briefly stopped by a famed three hundred Spartans at a pass called Thermopylae. Though he eventually got the better of the Greeks there, the stand purchased for the Greeks some much-needed time to regroup, plus the story of the brave stand gave the Greeks heroic visions that inflamed the imaginations of their countrymen. Though the Persians marched on Athens and got the better of the city, most of the Greeks fled—but for the time being only. Xerxes then went in hot pursuit of the Greeks, who had escaped to an island called Salamis. Outnumbered though they were, the Greeks put up such a fight that the Persians crumbled beneath their weight. A deflated Xerxes left Greece a defeated man and the decay of his empire soon followed. Artaxerxes followed him, and was the king during the time of Ezra and Nehemiah (Ezra 7:1; Neh. 2:1). Darius III followed, and was eventually overrun by Alexander the Great, a defeat that brought Persian domination to an end.

THE ORIGIN OF THE GREEKS AND ROMANS

The defeat and retreat of the Persians inaugurated a new and golden age for the Greeks, led by Pericles (461–429 BC). This period turned up some of the better-known Greek contributors to Western civilization's arts and sciences. Herodotus (490–431 BC), the father of history, emerged then, as did Hippocrates (460–370 BC), the father of modern medicine. Fathers of modern philosophy—Socrates (469–399 BC), Plato (427–347 BC), and Aristotle (385–322 BC)—left an indelible mark on Western thought and likely need no introduction here. The philosophers apparently fared better than the administrators and generals. Preferring the force of arms over and against civil discourse, Sparta and Athens took to arms in conflicts that extended from 459–404 BC, with Sparta eventually getting the better of Athens in the aforementioned Peloponnesian Wars.

In 338 BC, Phillip of Macedon conquered Greece. He ruled for two years, after which he was assassinated in 336 BC. He was followed to the throne by his son—the famous Alexander the Great. Immediately after coming to power, Alexander set his sights on Persia—to settle an old score.

He crossed the Hellespont in 334 BC and defeated the Persians at Granicus in 334 BC. In 333 BC, he took them on again at Issus with the same result. He decisively defeated the Persians at Arabela in 331 BC and became the master of their empire. In a reasonably short period, Alexander secured power in Greece and held sway over all of Persia. The Egyptians welcomed and surrendered to him, and Jerusalem made peace with him as well. Still not content, against the objections of some of his own, Alexander pressed on and made haste to take on India in 327 BC. There it is said he died of disease in 323 BC. His vast empire was subsequently carved up by his generals. Cassander was granted sovereignty over Greece and Macedonia; Lysimachus was given Asia Minor—modern Turkey; Ptolemy ruled Egypt; and Seleucus ruled Syria. Around this time, Rome had control over little more than central Italy. But things were about to change.

Rome flexed its muscles through its engagement in three wars with the better-respected masters of the Mediterranean's sea and lands: the Carthaginians. The first war extended from 264–241 BC, the second went from 218–202 BC, and the third from 149–146 BC, culminating in the final Roman triumph and the consequential burning of Carthage. Secure as they were as masters of the sea, Romans set their sights on mastering more and more land. The empire expanded eastward, eventually reaching Israel, where Pompei annexed Judea as a Roman holding in 64 BC.

Rome attended to outward business better than its inward affairs. The Roman ability to acquire territory outperformed her ability to manage it. Once she became powerful, questions of the means by which power would be employed and shared occupied many of its nobles. A period of civil wars ensued. Julius Caesar rose to prominence, but was cut down by his thought-to-be loyal friends, Brutus and Cassius, in Rome on the Ides of March in 44 BC. Octavius—who later took the name Augustus Caesar—defeated Brutus and Cassius at Philippi in 42 BC, as he did Mark Anthony and Cleopatra at the Battle of Actium, and thus secured imperial Roman power for himself thereinafter.

Jesus was born during the administration of Octavius (Luke 2:1). Octavius was succeeded by Tiberius Caesar (AD 14–37), and it was during his administration that the ministry of John the Baptist was launched, as with Jesus' own. Tiberius was followed by the ruthless Caligula (AD 37–41), during whose time the fledgling Messianic movement advanced in and from Judea—popularly though mistakenly called "early Christianity." Paul conducted his various missionary journeys during the reign of Claudius (AD 41–54). Nero followed him to power and is said to have started off reasonably well only to be later bested by his maniacal dementia. Peter and Paul are said to have died at his cruel hand. Nero ruled till he committed suicide in AD 68. A general named Vespasian followed and ruled from AD 68–79. His son Titus, who had destroyed the Temple in Judea in AD 70, came to the throne in AD 79 and ruled till AD 81. In that year, Domitian ascended to power and banished John the Apostle to the island of Patmos (Rev. 1:9).

SUMMARY

The Bible offers a brief telling of the origin, rise, and happenings of various people groups. Because Abraham's Promised Land was the natural landbridge connecting three continents—Africa,

Asia, and Europe—its forever being hotly contested and incessantly acted upon by various people groups is only to be expected. It indeed lived up to that expectation over and again—then, as now. Various nations that grew up around Israel are noted in Israel's literature time and time again, making coming to terms with the Bible's story impossible without developing an appreciation for the other regional and national actors in its mysterious and unfolding dramas. This, of course, calls for paying minimum attention to the political entities noted above, which set in motion various desert storms in bygone biblical eras. *When one thinks of storms to come, it is amply attested that a tempest builds in the East and makes its way to Judea,* and it is to that coming cataclysmic war with the people of the sands that we will now attend.

III

ARABIAN PEOPLE AND LANDS
AT THE END OF SACRED TIME

Eschatology: Arabian Geopolitical
Intrigue at the Ragged Edge of Time

The *Oxford American Dictionary* describes the word "Armageddon" as a noun denoting "the last battle between good and evil before the Day of Judgment" and as a "dramatic and catastrophic conflict, typically seen as likely to destroy the world or the human race." While it could be said that the world does not know much about the real Jesus, it could also be said that it at least knows something about the real Armageddon. Armageddon has made its way into secular consciousness and imagination, and is known and dreaded by individuals who know little if anything else of the Bible's story.

Programming on the History Channel can speak to things past; anchors on ABC, NBC, CBS, FOX, and others can speak of things present. While various sorts of news sources can content themselves by going to the different parts of the *world*, and reporting from various places in it, ministerial ordination requires religious commentators like myself to give pride of place to going to different parts of the *Word* and reporting from it—and about

the world. In the interest of shedding biblical light on the aforementioned anticipated geopolitical explosion, we will here enter a
time machine and journey back a few millennia. We will go back
thousands of years to places that are thousands of miles removed
from us; from these places that are far away in time and space, I
will speak about things to come and wars with the people of the
sand—after I first hear from the biblical text.

WHAT THE BOOK OF REVELATION REVEALS

Though called "the Revelation," it has been said that what is
really revealed in Revelation is a matter of speculation. While
opinions vary on its interpretation, the earth's descent into dire
straits is agreed upon, as is a culminating and climactic struggle
between wicked and righteous forces—referred to as the Battle of
Armageddon. These elements are non-negotiable and are fixed in
eschatology as the North Star is fixed in the evening sky.

Though known from the Greek, the word "Armageddon"
really comes from the Hebrew har měgiddōn, meaning the "hill
of Megiddo." The Apostle John popularized it for Christians'
consumption when making reference to it in his New Testament
Revelation. It is from there that the term made its way into the
minds of Western culture's rank and file. Though principally concerned with Armageddon alone, believing that it behooves us to
appreciate the context within which the Armageddon story and
attendant Islamic-related invasion story are played out, I will now
go on to offer a very brief overview of Revelation itself.[38]

Revelation presents twenty-two chapters containing a total
of four hundred and three verses combined. Of these, only sixty-
three verses contain explicit statements and instructions said to

be from the lips of Jesus.[39] The three hundred and forty remaining Revelation verses contain fantastic, heavenly throne-room images (4:1–5:14), apocalyptic decrees noting merciless ravages to be unleashed upon weary earth dwellers (6:1–17), and a faithful, struggling Israelite witness (7:1–8) amidst a Great Tribulation unleashed upon the righteous, given their resolve to remain loyal to the testimony of Jesus during this time (7:9–17). Through seven angels (8:1–6) comes notice of impending cataclysmic upheavals on the earth that follow in 8:7–9:21; an inserted exhortation that deliverance from on high is soon coming (10:1–7); and that John—and all believers by association—must endure and serve faithfully until the deliverance arrives (10:8–11) is noted. The slaughter of two witnesses follows immediately thereafter in 11:1–10, with an appendage informing of their consequential resurrection (vv. 11–14), after which the seventh angel proceeds to proclaim the Kingdom's eventual inauguration (11:15–19). Though its coming is hastening, the Kingdom's arrival is not yet. Believers are exhorted to bear up and maintain their testimonies amidst the turbulence of trying times. Apocalyptic images of a woman with child fleeing from a dragon hell-bent on her demise capture readers' attention in 12:1–17, as do those of horrific beasts coming from the sea (13:1–10) and earth (13:1–18), given to unleashing their pent-up fury upon those who will not accept their wicked domain and receive the "mark of the beast" noted in 13:17. That a select few do, in fact, bear up under the imposed pressure is noted in 14:1–13. Notice of more "woes" upon bewitched fellows follows in verses 14–20, as does a telling of God's eventual triumph thereinafter in 15:1–8. The Revelation then offers a countdown to the climactic battle, which, as we shall see, in no uncertain terms is launched from what would be modern-day Iran.

Reminiscent of the ten plagues and the consequential Exodus under Moses' administration, loathsome sores are predicted to one day plague humankind in 16:2. Stories of water turning to blood follow in verses 4 through 7. Men are scorched in verses 8 and 9, much as they are disoriented by darkness in verses 10 and 11. Though they hark back to the Exodus narrative, these predictions could just as well be symptoms of nuclear explosion and fallout.

The drying up of the Euphrates River then follows in the narrative. Though akin in ways to the parting of the Red Sea in Exodus, this one is differentiated from it, given that this crossing opens up the way for invading hordes staging in and/or passing through lands just east of the Euphrates (i.e. modern Iran) to come to Israel for war. This culminates in the long-anticipated Battle of Armageddon (Rev. 16:12–16) and the subsequent shaking of the seduced and defiled earth (vv. 17–21). Noting that the vile world will be embroiled in a tempestuous conflagration, in 17:1–6 the Revelation turns to announcing the evil empire's final death blow, with the empire referred to as "the whore"—"BABYLON THE GREAT: THE MOTHER OF HARLOTS AND ABOMINATIONS OF THE EARTH" (v. 5).

Did we hear "Babylon"? Yes we did: right there in Revelation.

It arguably was a cryptic designation for Rome. Today, the land once known as Babylon is known by another name: "Iraq." A telling of unfolding events follows in 17:7–18, after which the narrative returns to unpacking Babylon's sins and the defiled earth's by association (18:1ff). Word of the famous Marriage Supper of the Lamb follows upon the heels of the wicked "whore's" demise in 19:1–10. Judgment falls upon Babylon (a revived Rome?) and the world then, subsequent to which restoration is happily envisioned, followed by a telling of the climactic battle that will sweep the earth clean of its wicked agents—for the moment.

John went on: "Heaven opened" in 19:11, and, "behold, a white horse; and He that sat upon him was called Faithful and True, and in righteousness He doth judge and make war." The royal personality on the white horse goes by the name "KING OF KINGS, AND LORD OF LORDS" (v. 16). With His gaze set on re-conquest, He sets His sights on defeating the Iranian-launched armies, which drew others into its vortex, assembled at Armageddon (vv. 17–21). The victorious Savior gets the better of the beast soon thereafter, and utterly destroys its army (vv. 19–21). Having done so, "the dragon, that old serpent, who is the Devil and Satan," is "bound" for "a thousand years, And cast...into the bottomless pit" (20:2–3). Notice of the Kingdom's establishment follows in verses 4 through 6 which, in turn, is followed by a note of a brief, unsuccessful rebellion that will be crushed (vv. 7–10).

All things then completed, a "new heaven and a new earth" follow (21:1–8), along with "that great city, the holy Jerusalem, descending out of heaven from God, Having the glory of God" (vv. 9–27, esp. 10–11a). The Revelation ends with a picture of paradise restored (22:1–5), which, in turn, is followed by exhortations to keep in the ready (vv. 6–21). Chapter 22 ends with: "Behold, I come quickly!"—noted in three times in verses 7, 12, and 20. There is another "Alpha and Omega" reference placed between, in verse 13 (cf. 1:8, 11). In between the introduction and conclusion and in conjunction with the mention of the coming Armageddon conflict in chapter 16 (vv. 12–16), Jesus reminds that He is coming "as a thief" and that believers ought to be ready (v. 15). He picks up this theme at the close, stressing the importance of keeping "the words of the prophecy" (22:7), reminding that individuals will be judged "according [to] his work" (v. 12) and that He has "sent mine angel to testify unto you these things in the churches. I am the root and the offspring of David, and the bright and morning Star" (v. 16).

What it means to "keep the words of the prophecy" is interesting for a variety of reasons.[40] Hoping the above will suffice as a reasonable overview of the eschatological-oriented book of Revelation,[41] I will now turn my focus more directly to the object of my attention in this particular chapter, beginning with a look at how the Iranian-launched Armageddon battle is developed in Revelation and then at how the coming invasion beckons readers back to Genesis—thus a climactic battle with the warriors of the sand.

THE BATTLE OF ARMAGEDDON

In Revelation 9:14, the "disciple whom Jesus loved" prophesied: "Loose the four angels who are bound at the great river, Euphrates" after which, in verse 15, he said those unleashed forces will kill a third of humankind. Dramatic, forceful, and horrible, is it not? He followed in verse 16, saying that a fighting force of 200 million—if you can imagine that—will one day be mobilized, and then a plague from them will decimate humanity "by the fire, and by the smoke, and by the brimstone" (v. 18). Unpleasant reading, to be sure.

The references to incessant burning have led some expositors to conclude that John envisioned a nuclear component to the great conflagration. Irrespective, given the improbability that a singular nation-state can muster forces of 200 million fighters,[42] one wonders if envisioning some sort of transnational religion would be better. Could it be that religion will inspire adherents to throw caution to the wind and call forth pent-up energies that will culminate in warfare of epic proportions? If one wonders which world religion might conceivably do that, only one stands out as seeming to be both interested and capable—but more on that later.

Later in Revelation, John picked up on the invasion force and gave more particulars. He said they would one day amass by the Euphrates River, and from there will launch an ill-fated strike aimed at Israel. In 16:12, John informed, "The great river, Euphrates, and its water was dried up, that the way of the kings of the east might be prepared." He then explained in verse 14 that "demons" will "go forth unto the kings of the earth and of the whole world, to gather them to the battle of that great day of God Almighty," after which John closed with: "And He gathered them together into a place called in the Hebrew tongue Armageddon" (v. 16).

Massive army? Driven by demons? Marshaled just east of the Euphrates River? Does this sound at all familiar? Interestingly, it is—and all too familiar, I might add.

For some time, I have been daunted by the realization that the aforementioned Armageddon conflict is spirited along by forces marshaled just east of the Euphrates River that, when unleashed, are slated to bring their fury to bear upon Israel. That the country just east of the Euphrates is Iran, a nuclear-capable nation hell-bent on Israel's demise, has me concerned. Is there a correlation between what was predicted in the ancient Word and what is happening in the modern world—in and through Iran? This is the million-dollar question.

It all may be just one big, cosmic coincidence that Revelation's endgame *seems* to correlate with Iran's anticipated war-game. It may be, though, that we are living in a world where prophecy is unfolding. On that score, I am inclined to think the latter, not the former. In any case, I am sure you will agree that the nature of the situation, as with its seeming to correlate with Revelation, warrants serious consideration and further Bible study, if nothing else.

What can generate the kind of momentum that will result in the unleashing of such energies and miseries? Why the Euphrates area? To answer these questions, Bible readers need to leave Revelation's endgame and go to the Bible's start-up story—in Genesis.

BACK TO THE FUTURE

The doorway to Revelation opens in Genesis—as with Ezekiel, Daniel, and others. That *Genesis motifs abound at Revelation's close* is evident from but a casual reading of the story.

John's noting the wiping of tears from eyes with "no more death, neither sorrow" (21:4) reminds of the "pre-fall" condition in the Garden of Eden. All was well in Eden, once upon a time, till sin made its entrance onto the stage of the human drama and the race became defiled. Sin-infected humanity, as you may recall, was expunged from the garden—cast out of paradise. In the wake of their so being, the conditions of sin, death, decay, and curse became normative and ubiquitous, as with a host of consequential associated miseries. Humankind is represented in the literature as having lost its once-happy estate; happily, however, the paradise lost in Genesis is envisioned as being recovered in Revelation— which brings us to the point here.

That in Revelation 22:1–2 there is a "pure river of water of life" and a "tree of life" on its banks harks back to the lost para- dise described in Genesis 2:8, where Moses described Eden and where, in verses 9 and 10, "the tree of life [was] also in the midst of the garden…and a river went out of Eden to water the garden." John's noting in Revelation 22:3 that there is "no more curse" in the paradise he is referring to likewise reminds readers of early Genesis. In Revelation, the writer is drawing upon Genesis motifs and in the process is taking his readers back to the future. That he is doing so is obvious; the reason he is doing so is not.

In Genesis 2:10, a river went forth from Eden that split into four rivers, two of which were known as the Tigris (or Hiddekel) and the other as the Euphrates (2:14). That the Garden of Eden was located by the fountainhead is indeed significant, in part because when one consults a map today to find where the Tigris and Euphrates rivers meet, inquirers are beckoned to the land known as Iraq—what was Babylon yesterday and where Eden was situated in days gone by. Coincidence? I think not!

The ancient Garden of Eden was located in what moderns call Iraq—in the center of the sand people's world! It was from Iraq/Babylon where sin originally manifested onto the stage of the human drama, where the human race was initially defiled and from where humans were banished from paradise and from God's presence. The human problem is said to have begun there—*much as it will end and close from there.*

After describing the Armageddon conflagration in some detail and after noting that God's Messianic forces will get the better of the evil ones laying siege to the planet, the victory is described with Eden-reminding language: John said that the Messiah "laid hold on the dragon, that old serpent, who is the Devil and Satan…. And cast him into the bottomless pit" (Rev. 20:2–3a). Does this ring a bell?

Serpent? Devil? Satan? Have we heard this story before? I think we have—and I trust that you are following the trail to where it obviously leads.

In Genesis, the evil one is depicted as a cunning serpent (3:1a), one who got the better of Eve (3:1b–8). Moses said the serpent talked the woman into laying hold of the fruit in a garden—fruit that was hanging about the "tree of life" (vv. 2–3). Subtly, the woman was seduced into reaching for it and then, in turn, she talked her husband into violating the divine command as well. After being found out, both were expunged from Eden—and the rest is history. Played out at the dawn of biblical time, the serpent got the upper hand over both humans in the aforementioned contest. In the book of Revelation, during the end-time contest predicted to be played out at the very dusk of biblical history, John says the vanquished "serpent of old" will be taken by the hand and then banished for an extended period.

Is it not interesting that John turns his readers' attention back to that part of the biblical world and Word when speaking prophetically about things to come, and while noting the redemption to come at the climax of human history? *It is more than just a coincidence that the Euphrates area hosts the Bible's start-up scenario as with its endgame.*

The global upheaval described in John's revelation and in Revelation actually dovetails with the spirit and word of various Old Testament prophets. As with John, the Hebrew Bible's prophets envisioned a world ablaze at day's end, with Israel caught in the middle of a host of trying contests.

Like John in the Revelation, Zechariah envisioned that "all the nations of the earth be gathered against" Jerusalem (12:3 and 9), but that Israel would ultimately prevail in a contest (v. 10). He predicted that God will "gather all nations against Jerusalem to battle; and the city shall be taken, and the houses rifled, and the women ravished" (14:2). Thus noted, in verse 3, he said God "will go forth, and fight against those nations, as when He fought in the day of battle." The upshot of the victory is that "the LORD shall be King over all the earth" (v. 9a), and no longer will there be "utter destruction; but Jerusalem shall be safely inhabited" (v. 11).

Similarly, Ezekiel noted that a confederacy of nations will participate in a climactic war against Israel. "Gog, of the land of Magog," is the object of Ezekiel's rebuke in 38:2, as are the princes of Rosh, Meshech, and Tubal. Persia, Ethiopia, and Libya are noted in the anti-Israel federation in v. 5—noted previously in this volume, as you may recall. Happily for Israel, however, their advance will be stopped by a fire flash: "I will rain upon him, and upon his hordes, and upon the many peoples that are with him, an overflowing rain, and great hailstones, fire, and brimstone" (v. 22). I could be wrong, but this sounds nuclear to me.[43]

When offering a telling of the world at the ragged edge of history, as with the aforementioned authors, Daniel weighed in with visions of wars with Persia and Greece (8:1–27) and speaks of Antichrist-inspired troop movements all over the Middle East in 8:11–12.[44]

SUMMARY

The Apostle John—along with the prophets Ezekiel, Daniel, Zechariah, and others (as we shall see later)—opined that regional forces around Israel will one day bring their weight to bear against a reconstituted Israel at the ragged edge of human history. I am not raising this issue here to explain it further just now as much as I am doing so to draw attention to the fact that *coming to term with history's endgame is impossible without developing a working knowledge of the first game,* and with the people and terms employed in describing it.

According to Revelation, the Armageddon conflict is played out against the backdrop of demon-inspired forces making their way into Israel via Iran—the land east of the Euphrates. From there, John said they will "go forth unto the kings of the earth and of the whole world, to gather them to the battle of that great day of God Almighty" (16:14), after which John closed by saying, "And He gathered them together into a place called in the Hebrew tongue Armageddon" (v. 16).

What force in human experience can call forth such energies and propel peoples to war? Can disputes over territories alone muster such enthusiasm? I think not! While the Israeli-Palestinian issue—so called—is used as a lightning rod, the issue does not inflame Arab angst on the basis of perceived wrongs being perpetrated against Arab cousins in the region as much as it does because *it arouses their religious passions.*

Though tense moments are observed between Israelis and Arabs in the biblical narratives, when the sun set over the Old and New Testament's stories many years ago, Arabs and Jews seem to have developed an aptitude to live reasonably well together. *There simply was not enough pent-up energy in the system to bring about a cataclysmic war.*

That was then. This is now!

ARABIAN RELIGION IN
THE MIDDLE OF TIME

Heterology: Arabian Religious Intrigue
in the Middle of Time

Prior to Mohammed and the advent of Islam, Jewish tribes dwelt alongside Arabs in Arab lands beyond Israel, where they seemed to have fit in reasonably well. Jews spoke like their Arab cousins, dressed like their Arab friends and associates, and interacted with Arabs in a reasonably comfortable manner. Jews, in fact, made up a sizeable amount of the aggregate population of Medina. Ten years after Mohammed's arrival there, however, all the Jews were killed or displaced and all of their land and former holdings were in Arab hands. Being of Jewish extract myself, I—Jeffrey Seif—have a rather keen interest in the relationship between Jewish and Muslim people.[45]

Islam was introduced into the Arabic bloodstream six hundred years after the New Testament's principal story and approximately twelve hundred years after the close of the Old Testament's. Though the religion claims that the Hebrew Bible has been corrupted from its original and pure Islamic version, the outlandish and disparaging claim has no basis in time and circumstance.

Many hundreds of years after the biblical canon's close, Islam happened; its forceful emergence redefined the nature of the relationship between Semitic peoples in the region. Believing that we do well to consider what Islam is and how its nature affected the Middle East's equilibrium, a heterological examination is in order.

In scientific nomenclature, "heterology" denotes the lack of correspondence between organic parts; it thus focuses on abnormalities. Similarly, in the sometimes abstract-sounding world of theological inquiry, "heterology" is a doctrinal category under which various spiritual maladies are considered—*sin,* particularly.

I subscribe to Judeo-Christian literature and religion, and do so without apology. I believe that Jesus is "the [right] way" (John 14:6) and that folks would fare better in this life and the next by coming to terms with Him. While believing this to be so, at the risk of being misunderstood, let me say that I tend to think that even a wrong religion can still have a better effect on most people than no religion at all. As a result, I have made room to be both tolerant and appreciative of world religions, given that they do provide moral guidance to individuals who perhaps would not otherwise be there to assist them. Thus minded and guided, I think religious people in ill-informed systems can and often do perform better than non-religious persons. Though I believe that individuals need to be "saved" through Jesus, I still believe folks can be helped along in life by moral virtues espoused in other belief systems. While I hold this to be true generally, I have trouble finding much redeeming character in the history of the religion called Islam today.

Even though I am not minded to take issue with Arab peoples (or any peoples), *I do take issue with the radical telling of the philosophical system that defines and drives many.* Given that the religion has extended way beyond the Arabian Peninsula and is growing in Indonesia, Africa, and elsewhere, construing Islam as an Arabian religion is overly simplistic, on the basis of its being much more than that. *Today, only 17 percent of Muslims are Arabs.* The religion does have its origins in Arabia, true; so to Arabia we now turn, in the interest of coming to terms with its origin and development, and the bearing the religion has had on history and seemingly will have on prophecy.

WHAT IS ARABIAN ISLAM?

We do well to *not* make generalizations about Islam. On the one hand, Islam certainly is a religion—true; on the other, however, it is not a religion in the sense that most Christians and Jews think about religion and religious systems. *Islam is a political entity as much as it is a religious one,* with no distinction between the two, as is the case in Judeo-Christian cultures.

To a fault, the doctrine of the separation of church and state is sacred in American democracy. It is upheld on the basis of a founding promise that we shall make no laws with respect to religion, nor shall we require it of our citizens who, by virtue of their being citizens, are entitled to the pursuit of "life, liberty, and happiness" according to the dictates of their own consciences. *America cherishes pluralism and freedom, freedom that includes one's being able to opt for any religion—or no religion, if preferred.* With our founders, I believe this right should be held inviolate.

The result is that religious leaders in America are not vested with social or juridical authorization. Religious ministers, of course, can suggest a course of action, which individuals may or may not opt to accept. Pastors can encourage right living, good marital relationships, prudent business relationships, and the like. But we ministers cannot enforce our exhortations by imposing various punishments for noncompliance. The levying of fines, imprisonments, and/or capital punishment is state business in our nation and does not fall under the purview of the church or synagogue. This is our world; it is not the Islamic world, however.

By way of contradistinction, *Mohammed founded an Arabian-based system in which he controlled both the religion and the empire.* The dichotomy between *regnum* (state) and *sacerdotium* (church)—central and sacred in present-day Judeo-Christian political science dogma—meant nothing to Mohammed (then, or many of his followers now). He was bent on forging *both* a religious and a political entity through his religion—and in one stroke.[46]

There is a responsible argument that Mohammed was one of the greatest leaders who ever lived, and certainly the greatest Arabian leader who ever lived. If a leader is one who enhances the overall prestige of his constituents, fills his and their coffers with accumulated wealth, and expands the borders of his lands as with the holdings of their followers, then surely Mohammed was one of the greatest in the world, and certainly the best in the Arabian world. Alexander the Great of Greece, Napoleon of France, Ramses of Egypt, and Octavian of Rome are noted for their exploits, as are many, many others. These men were "great" not because they were paragons of moral virtue, but because they enhanced and expanded their respective realms and left an indelible mark on history in the process. Mohammed was just such a great man.

Though I see Mohammed as one of the greatest leaders in human history, I do not see him as a great moral and spiritual leader in history. As with the aforementioned military men, his hands were stained with way too much blood, his coffers were filled with way too much "dirty money," and his bedroom was filled with way too many illicitly gained women. Though I personally think him to be lacking as a moral and religious guide, I am still prepared to respectfully grant him his place in world history as a leader who stood head and shoulders above his contemporaries in so many ways—and ahead of many others who came both before and afterward. Because he mercilessly removed the heads from the shoulders of many unarmed Jews in Arabia and took their homes—as well as their lands and families—for his own purposes, I simply cannot bring myself to accept him as a righteous prophet, much as his religion will never be construed by me as the "religion of peace"—as per today's politically correct mantra. *My nonacceptance of him and his religion is not based on race, however; it is based on principle.*

Since inception, based on a belief that its immutable standards came directly from God, Islam was understood to have provided the only acceptable social mechanism to order one's personal and social life. What is true for individuals was true for collections of individuals in states. The late Ayatollah Khomeini is revealing in this regard. He said, "Islam is politics or it is nothing." Accepting his authoritative understanding of the nature of Islam, I say that Mohammed's religion was not a religion in the classical sense that most Judeo-Christian sorts construe religion. We do well to keep this in mind.

Though many so-called Christian countries in the West are, in truth, no longer decidedly religiously "Christian" by any serious standard—including America, in a variety of respects—the same does not hold true for societies in the Middle East, where governments are profoundly religious. In the Middle East, Islam is not simply a matter of private faith—as religion is here. *Mohammed's religion provides the overarching philosophical system that enables otherwise disenfranchised males who subscribe to it to forge a strong corporate identity and participate in an empowering world that comes replete with domestic power, political power, and military power.* The religion gives meaning, social cohesion, and strength to otherwise disempowered masses of frustrated individuals. In addition to delivering on a sense of "belonging," Islam gives deep meaning to drab and impoverished lives. Through it, individuals transcend the hopeless and mundane and, like the knights of a bygone era in "Christian" Europe, are afforded through jihad the opportunity to opt for a religious quest that will stimulate otherwise dormant heroic impulses—ones that seem to have no other foreseeable outlet.

Members of the Islamic community are deemed to be part of *Dar al-Islam* (i.e., the "House of Islam"). Those of us outside the family are construed as being *Dar al-Harb* (i.e., of the "House of War"). Mohammed "unleashed the dogs of war" upon the non-compliant outsiders and had absolutely no tolerance for those of his own who turned away from armed struggle on his religion's behalf. Those who set their sights on war—as the "prophet" did himself, time and time again—were promised plunder and paradise as their rewards. What a deal! Through jihad, any lonely and disrespected Arabian beggar could be thrust into paradise, where he would be surrounded by dozens upon dozens of young virgins, there for him and ready to serve his every appetite and fantasy. It is little wonder that the religion infuses the imaginations of adherents between the ages of seventeen and twenty-five, and mobilizes their energies in the quest for the ultimate prize.

"Hadiths" are elaborations of Islam's holy book. Therein, the aforementioned proclivities are expressed with statements like, "A day and a night fighting on the frontier is better than a month of fasting and prayer," and, "He who dies without taking part in a campaign dies in a kind of disbelief." The following Islamic dictum sums it up perfectly: "Paradise is in the shadow of the swords." Again, for understandable reasons, young men can see great opportunity in and through jihad—which historically has been waged militarily, and not morally, as per today's propaganda.

As the sun set over Mohammed's earthly existence in the last nine years of his life, the religion's founder personally attended twenty-seven raids, battles, and military expeditions and ordered thirty-eight others that he did not attend. *These, coupled with the assassinations and executions he was directly involved in, underscore the militant and warring nature of the man and his movement—* mistakenly called the "religion of peace" today by revisionist sorts not minded to come to terms with the religion's history and reality. That said, though war was indeed part of the prophet Mohammed's doctrine and practice—as we shall see below—the random slaughter of innocent civilians through brazen acts of terror is considered by many Muslims to be something of a modern innovation born out of the frustration of the times—American meddling and Israel's emergence particularly. Though granting some merit to this exceedingly gracious assessment, I find this kindly disposed analysis to be overly simplistic and an exercise in self-deceit.

MOHAMMED AND THE JEWISH PEOPLE

Leaving that thorny and broader question of Islam's relationships with outsiders aside for the moment, in the interest of coming to terms with the troubling tensions between Muslims and Jews in particular, a brief telling of Mohammed's interactions with Jewish people is deemed necessary, as is the offering of a historical treatment of how the two groups fared together after the prophet's departure.

As for the history, we know that the prophet Mohammed began his preaching in the famous Arabian city of Mecca. A few years labor there yielded less than two hundred followers at first, and left him frustrated—as you might well imagine. He left Mecca as a marginalized and unrecognized religious fanatic and, with his small band of devotees in tow, set his sights on Medina. His presence and message took root there as he labored to discover what fortunes would befall him.

At that time, about half the population of Medina was Jewish. Culturally assimilated as they were, none of the Jews had Hebrew names. Jews in Medina spoke the native Arabic language and embraced the native Arabian culture. *Jews and Arabs were kindred sorts, cousins, and we got along reasonably well*—at least till Mohammed's arrival and his political religion's advent.

Mohammed arrived in Medina and claimed to be the last of the Jewish prophets—in the line of noteworthy biblical heroes. When, like the Arab leaders in Mecca, the Jewish community's leaders in Medina did not accept Mohammed's bold claim, they invoked the prophet's ire—*as did everyone who did not accept what many thought to be his delusional authority*. As a result, the Jewish community was annihilated in Medina—as elsewhere. Less than two years after rejecting his prophetic claim, there were no Jews left in Medina. Many were slaughtered, with the lucky simply dispossessed.

When all was said and done, the Muslims had the Jews' possessions. Jewish men were mercilessly slaughtered—some simply for sport. Jewish women became slaves and concubines. Children were taken and raised as Muslims. This was a portent of things to come, an evidence of what becomes of those who do not come to terms with what today is called "the religion of peace"—Islam.

As if the annihilation of the Jews in Medina were not enough to satisfy the bloodlust, when Mohammed was on his deathbed, one of his last decrees banished Jews from the entire Arabian Peninsula—and not only from Medina. The founder of the "Religion of Peace" construed Jews and Christians as "cursed by Allah," and the aforementioned punishments were construed as our just deserve. "Liars" by nature, we Jews were assumed to be untrustworthy by nature. Supposed Jewish deceit, for example, was epitomized in the way Jews were alleged to have corrupted the Scripture.

Islam teaches that Abraham was originally a Muslim and that Ishmael was Allah's "chosen," as the firstborn son. According to Islamic doctrine, Jews changed the Bible from its original Islamic meaning by twisting and perverting the words of Moses as with others. The facts that Mohammed lived two thousand years *after* Moses and that the Old Testament had been in circulation for centuries in its known and present form meant nothing. *Never mind the facts!* Mohammed proffered the belief that Jews—and Christians too!—rearranged the Bible to hide the fact that it was an Islamic story at the outset. After being repeated over and again, it is simply accepted, incredible though the claim most certainly is.

For Mohammed, Jews were and are vitiated, deceitful sub-humans. Jews were construed by him as pathetic "apes," and Christians were referred to as "pigs." Searching for more colorful ways to defame Jews still, Mohammed once said, "A tribe of Benai Y'Irael ["sons of Israel"] disappeared. I do not know what became of them, but I think they mutated and became rats." This was construed by Mohammed as divine judgment. Jews were said to have incurred God's wrath because they changed their Scriptures to hide the truth of Islam. According to this line of reasoning, much as God punished Jews for disregarding their own Scriptures, it should come as no surprise that they would also disregard he who came to teach them more properly—Mohammed. As much as one does not want rats in one's home or wild apes in one's vicinity, so too, Mohammed opined that Arabia would be better were it not infested by these Jewish creatures. Anxious to please him, his lieutenant Umar complied efficiently after his death and eradicated the Jews.

Though Mohammed ordered the removal of Jews from Arabia, Islam deemed that there were times when it was prudent to keep Jews around. When it was judged necessary to keep folks to do the servile work, Islam found ways to accommodate Jews— as with Christians. In certain cases, Jews and Christians could exist as *dhimmis,* as members of a second class, a servant class, in Islamic societies. This we could do in order to do the servile work that was beneath the dignity of Islamic overlords. This was typically the best we could hope for.

The following scene, pulled from Wilkie Young's memoirs of his time in Turkey in 1908, is descriptive of the norm that prevailed:

> The attitude of the Muslims towards the Christians and Jews…is that of a master towards slaves whom he treats with a certain lordly tolerance so long as they keep their place. Any sign of pretension to equality is promptly repressed. It is often noticed in the street that almost any Christian submissively makes way even for a Muslim child. Only a few days ago the writer saw two respectable-looking, middle-aged Jews walking in a garden. A small Muslim boy, who could not have been more than eight

years old, passed by and, as he did so, picked up a large stone and threw it at them—and then another—with the utmost nonchalance, just as a small boy elsewhere might aim at a dog or bird. The Jews stopped and avoided the aim, which was a good one, but made no further protest.[47]

Jews who would not convert to Islam were humbled incessantly and in various ways. Unrepentant, non-Islamic Hebrews could not wear nice clothing, could not build nice buildings, and had to be distinguished from Muslims in their dress and headgear. Yellow patches were affixed to clothing to designate membership in the inferior Jewish race—an idea popularized by Hitler more recently. Jews were forced into servile work, laboring as hangmen, gutter cleaners, and the like. Inordinately high taxes were forever a problem for Jews, as was the realization that the lands they worked and the homes they lived in could be confiscated at the pleasure of their Muslim overlords.

ISLAM AND THE JEWISH STATE IN ANTIQUITY

Against this backdrop, one can perhaps best perceive the present-day problem between Jews and Muslims: *Jews are construed as runaway slaves,* as subordinated humans who have escaped the grasp of their former masters in the Middle East—Arab Muslims.

That Jews are outperforming Muslims in commerce, industry, statecraft, brain trust, and more is another source of grief for them. It not only calls into question the Islamic notion that Muslims are superior to other people, but it also serves notice of the reality of what Islam is coming to terms with, namely that *Islamic civilization has been in decline for many years.* In fact, Islamic civilization has grown sterile and has shown itself unable to contribute to humanity's present or future. As long as Arab Muslims are constrained by the totalitarian framework of a rigid reading of their Islamic faith's requirements, change doesn't seem likely. This is the real reason many Muslim males are so frustrated, and it has nothing to do with Christian or Jewish intrusions or malice. *The past glory of Islam has been fading for centuries and it offends the sensibilities of its men.*

Though the image of a "golden age" lives on in Islamic memory, in many ways it lives *only* in memory, save in the lives and experiences of the fortunate super-rich, who fortunately derive their means from fossil fuels. Good fortune in the southern sands aside, the declining Islamic empire is nothing compared to what it used to be. Against the backdrop of Islam's slow and painful demise, Judaism has arisen—and with it, a forceful state on top. Not only have the Jewish people fared better than Muslims individually—barring revenues from fossil fuels—but the State of Israel has emerged over and against the military and political protestations of Muslim Arabs, many of whom are unable to come to terms with the divestment of their former slave-class and their greedily acquired land holdings. This is why the current Arab-Jewish struggle, fought under the banner of Islam, must restore the memory of the once-friendly coexistence between the presently estranged cousins without deliberately overlooking the traumatic events at the inception of Islam that stained this relationship with much violence and blood, and harbored hatred and resentment ever since.

Muslims protested Israel's emergence with both their words and their swords. Islamic nations put poorly equipped and undis-

ciplined armies in the field, only to have them summarily humili-
ated by Jewish troops in successive conflicts. *It may well be that the
fielding and romanticizing of today's so-called suicide bombers*—better, "homicide bombers," in my estimation—*is little more than a
dying culture's way of demonstrating against a modern world that it
has failed to enter, and protesting against a Jewish world that it simply could not keep under its thumb.* In that sense, then, the battle
for Israel and its capital, Jerusalem, is more psychological and
spiritual than material.

In his *Clash of Civilizations*, the late Professor Samuel P.
Huntington, who taught the Science of Government at Harvard
University, answered why there will be a clash of civilizations.
Huntington opined that civilizations are differentiated from each
other by many components, with religion being the most impor-
tant. In defining the influence of religion alone, he said:

> The people of different civilizations have different views
> on the relations between God and man, the individual
> and the group, the citizen and the state, parents and chil-
> dren, husband and wife, as well as differing views of the
> relative importance of rights and responsibilities, liberty
> and authority, equality and hierarchy. These differences
> are the product of centuries. They will not soon disappear.
> They are far more fundamental than differences among
> political ideologies and political regimes. Differences
> do not necessarily mean conflict, and conflict does not
> necessarily mean violence. Over the centuries, however,
> differences among civilizations have generated the most
> prolonged and the most violent conflicts. Conflict along
> the fault line between Western and Islamic civilizations
> has been going on for thirteen hundred years.[48]

Even before Huntington's piece, Professor Bernard Lewis of Princeton University predicted such confrontation, saying the following in his article entitled, "The Roots of Muslim Rage" in *The Atlantic Monthly*:[49]

> We are facing a need and a movement far transcending the level of issues and policies and the governments that pursue them. This is no less than a clash of civilizations—the perhaps irrational but surely historic reaction of an ancient rival against our Judeo-Christian heritage, our secular present, and the worldwide expansion of both.

The rivalry surfaces in the battle for Jerusalem.

Israel's capital, Jerusalem, *has no real history or mention in Islamic lore.* The battle over Israel and for Jerusalem is thus not intrinsically related to some sort of reclaiming of the Muslims' hearts as if, let us say, Mecca or Medina had fallen into Christian and/or Jewish hands. Given the way those cities and their surrounding lands factor into Islamic religion, suffering Medina's or Mecca's loss would understandably be considered intolerable to them. Israel is another story, however.

Israel came into the Islamic fold well after Mohammed and was not even part of his domain. In the interest of better understanding the battle for Jerusalem—culminating finally in the Battle of Armageddon—we do well to step back and consider its history, beginning in Scripture and extending then into the modern era.[50]

Mount Moriah was noted early in the Genesis narrative (22:1ff), but came to prominence as an Israelite holding much later. David's acquisition of the threshing floor on Moriah from Araunah the Jebusite (2 Sam. 24:21–25) is noted as the time when it came into Jewish hands. Solomon's development of the site for the Temple (1 Kings 3:1) fixed it in space and time, making it the center point of Jewish civic and religious life.[51]

In 586 BC, the Babylonians conquered Jerusalem and, as noted in 2 Kings 25:8–10, wrought havoc upon the city. Babylonian sway over the Israelites came to an end when they did, however. The Persians, fortuitously, got the better of them and in 538 BC Cyrus decreed that the displaced Judeans could return and rebuild the Temple in their ancestral homeland (Ezra 1:2–3). Zerubbabel was a major figure who led the first wave back from Babylon/Persia. Ezra—called the "Second Moses"—was significant during this time as well. The reconstruction of the destroyed Temple consumed a good twenty years and was eventually completed in 516 BC. Later, in 444 BC, Nehemiah was appointed governor, in the wake of which he exerted considerable influence upon the city's wall-building (cf. Neh. 2–3; 12:27–43).

In 332 BC, Alexander the Great conquered Judea, which was subsequently drawn into the Hellenistic domain. In the wake of Alexander's death, Judea was annexed as part of the large province of Syro-Phoenicia, then under Ptolemaic rule. In 200 BC, Antiochus III Megas conquered Jerusalem with the result that the city came under Seleucid—not Ptolemaic—administration.

During the reign of Megas' son, Antiochus IV Epiphanes, Greek-Syrian soldiers were stationed in Jerusalem. Temple ritual was impeded, as were personal, familial, and social Jewish practices.

A revolt broke out, led by Hasmoneans. In 164 BC, the Jewish Temple in Jerusalem was reclaimed and rededicated. Soon thereafter, Josephus noted that Simeon the Hasmonean razed the Syrian's Akra fortress to the ground (142–134 BC).[52] Weakened by strife over the years, the Hasmonean rule ended in 37 BC, when the Roman senate confirmed Herod the Great as king of Judea. Herod subsequently built the Antonia Fortress adjacent to the Temple's northwestern corner, in addition to which he built a theater and hippodrome. His most well-attested project, however, was the Temple itself.

The renovation project began in 20 BC and was completed during the procuratorship of Albinus (AD 62–64). Josephus said that this project alone employed eleven thousand workers. It was indeed a marvel to behold—evidenced today by remains of the Herodian ashlar stones, ruins from the Royal Stoa, remains of Robinson's Arch, excavations from the street running along the western and southern walls, Warren's shaft, the Huldah Gates, and more.

Architectural marvels did not assuage the Jews' disdain for the interloper Herod. Jews wanted neither Roman rulers nor their client kings, so war broke out. The Roman V, X, XII, and XV legions were brought in to quell the rebellion, with the X legion staying on in the wake of the revolt's quelling. In fact, that legion was garrisoned in Jerusalem thereinafter, for hundreds of years.

In AD 130, the Emperor Hadrian (AD 117–138) founded a Roman pagan city atop Jerusalem's ruins, which he named Aelia Capitolina. Aelia was named after the emperor himself (with his name being Publius Aelius Hadrianus); Capitolina harks back to the Capitoline gods (i.e., Jupiter, Juno, and Minerva)—an appellation likewise possessing faint reverberations of another grouping— i.e., the "Palestinians." Jerusalem was divided into two sectors: to the south was the longstanding headquarters of the tenth legion camp and the northern section was the urban-civilian area.

When Constantine the Great took control of the Eastern Roman Empire in AD 324, he ushered in a new era in the church's history—not to mention Jerusalem's. By AD 335, a church edifice was constructed atop the site believed to be the burial place of Jesus—the Church of the Holy Sepulchre—with other ones springing up throughout the land.

A two-year break in Jerusalem's "Christianization" was secured when Julian (called "the Apostate") came to power. In AD 362, he allowed the Jews to rebuild the previously destroyed Temple—an ambition that came to naught when Julian fell in battle in AD 363. Throughout the century's remainder, the church construction went unabated and Jerusalem became a major Christian pilgrim center.

Shortly thereafter, Emperor Theodosius II's (AD 408–450) wife Eudocia invested inordinate energies in Jerusalem's resurrection as a Christian city. She herself took residency in the city from AD 444–460 and was proactive in the development of churches, hospitals, and hospices. She also used her influence to build up the city's fortifications.

In the sixth century, under the reign of Emperor Justinian (AD 527–565), Jerusalem reached its post-Israelite zenith. The oldest extant depiction of Jerusalem's city-plan, from Madaba, is from this era. The Western and Valley "cardos" were extended during this time. Evidenced as well was the abandonment of the Temple Mount—given Jesus saying that the stones would "fall one upon another," churchmen were not given to various reconstructions atop the sacred precincts. It was left in ruins as a reminder.

In AD 614, Jerusalem was breached by the Persians and a number of its monasteries and churches were torched. The Persians ruled for only fifteen years, though, after which time the city briefly reverted back to Byzantine rule—until the Muslim conquest in AD 638.

After Mohammed's death, his commanders gathered neighboring Arab tribesmen from Hijaz, Najd, and Yemen, which were commissioned for jihad—the "holy war." In AD 634, followers of "the prophet" commenced to attack Gaza in the interest of securing some profit—in the name of the prophet.

The marauding bands of Islamic brigands bent on easy conquest overran the weak countryside. In response, Jewish and Christian town dwellers in Jerusalem, Jaffa, Nabulus, Beth Shean, and elsewhere simply closed the doors of their cities and retreated into lockdown mode behind their walls. All was lost, and it was only a question of time till famine claimed them before the Islamic sword most certainly would.[53]

Prior to the Islamic invasion, the Byzantines doled out bribes and negotiated treaties with Muslims at their borders in the interest of keeping the Islamic hordes at bay. One Christian governor named Farwa is said to have converted to Islam, perhaps in the interest of placating the Muslims. Attempts at appeasement notwithstanding, seeing an opportunity to fulfill Mohammed's interest in domination (not to mention their own), the Muslims were eventually able to exploit the Christians' "lack of a coherent strategy for defense," which precipitated some of the most savage early clashes between Byzantines and Muslims.[54]

In AD 634, Sophronius—the Christian patriarch of Jerusalem—lamented that folks in the towns were "chained and nailed for fear." The previously developed contract between the Byzantine Jews and Christians purchased nothing save some false security. Ultimately, many, many thousands of Jews and Christians were mercilessly slaughtered.

No doubt, many of the living counted the dead to be more fortunate. Jewish and Christian survivors were sold into slavery. Captured women were passed around as pleasure-objects for the Muslim hordes—who used and abused them with no known

ARABIAN RELIGION IN THE MIDDLE OF TIME

pangs of religious conscience. Women were even raped in the presence of their own husbands to humiliate them both and to dramatically and graphically attest to the Islamic triumph!

The slaughter of the resident population and the molestation of unfortunate Christian and Jewish women were construed as Allah-given rites and rights. As stated, no objections were raised on the basis of these acts contradicting Islamic, religious virtue. To the contrary, they were construed as a sign of the dawning of a new era—and seen as a testimony that the glorious age of Islamic conquest had come.

How did the land and people fare under their Islamic lords?

City life diminished considerably in the Holy Land as the total number of cities declined from fifty-eight to seventeen. Farmland mismanagement precipitated soil erosion that contributed to the abandonment of farming enterprises. Incessant intertribal warfare between the various Arab-Muslim "brothers" was a problem as well. Bested by their own ineptness, social forces of their own making pressed the members of the Arabic population backward to their wandering, nomadic existence. They conquered Israel by the sword only to, in effect, relinquish much of their gains, given their inability to manage both themselves and others.

The desert sands overtook many cities, and the world retreated into barbarism.

Sir Winston Churchill, the former British prime minister and world-class leader, concurred and eloquently expressed the death of city life—and of civilization in general—at the hand of Muslims in his 1899 account of the Sudanese campaign, saying:

How dreadful are the curses which Mohammedanism lays on its votaries! Besides the fanatical frenzy, which is as dangerous in a man as hydrophobia in a dog, there is this fearful fatalistic apathy. Improvident [irresponsible] habits, slovenly [sloppy] systems of agriculture, sluggish methods of commerce, and insecurity of property exist wherever the followers of the Prophet rule or live. A degraded sensualism deprives this life of its grace and refinement; the next of its dignity and sanctity. The fact that in Mohammedan law every woman must belong to some man as his absolute property—either as a child, a wife, or a concubine—must delay the final extinction of slavery until the faith of Islam has ceased to be a great power among men.

Individual Moslems may show splendid qualities. Thousands become the brave and loyal soldiers of the Queen: All know how to die. But the influence of the religion paralyzes the social development of those who follow it. No stronger retrograde [backward] force exists in the world. Far from being moribund [declining], Mohammedanism is a militant and proselytizing faith. It has already spread throughout Central Africa, raising fearless warriors at every step; and were it not that Christianity is sheltered in the strong arms of science—the science against which it had vainly struggled—the civilization of modern Europe might fall, as fell the civilization of ancient Rome.[55]

Churchill's forceful assessment—one that would be deemed very politically incorrect today—is corroborated by history.

As briefly noted previously, during the Abbasid caliphates of Harun al-Rashid and al-Mutawwakil, Jews and Christians were forced to wear yellow patches on their clothing as an indication of their differentiation, subjugation, and inherent inferiority. This and other degradations of the holy people continued and culminated in further insults to the holy people and places time and time and time again.

Author Yahya b. Sa'id gave a description of the desecration and destruction of the Church of the Holy Sepulchure. Referring to the Muslim destruction of holy places, Andrew Bostom quotes Moshe Gil as saying:

> They dismantled the Church of the Resurrection to its very foundation…they destroyed Golgotha…as well as all the sacred grave stones. They even tried to dig up all the graves and wipe out all traces of their existence…the authorities took all the other property belonging to the Church of the Holy Sepulchre and its pious foundations.[56]

Then, leaning upon the Muslim writers ibn Khallikan and ibn al-Athir, Gil goes on to speak of "thousands of churches which were destroyed."

An extract from the following poem, written by a disconcerted Jew named Solomon ha-Kohen who lived and wrote during the days of the Muslim-Arab slaughter, reflects the sentiment of those times. Of the Muslims, ha-Kohen says:

> They were a strange and cruel people, girt with garments of many colors. Armed and officered-chiefs among the "Terrible Ones," and capped with helmets black and red, with bow and spear and full of quivers…. They laid waste the cities, and they were made desolate…and they

rejoiced in their hearts.... They do not resemble men.
They are like beasts.... They had no mercy on the widow
and pitied not the orphan.

Tragic, is it not?

The Byzantines' opting for a treaty with the Muslims seems
to have proved completely ineffectual. The border arrangements
whereby Arabs would live in the outer lands, with Jews and
Christians in theirs, seemed to be only a convenient mechanism
by means of which the Muslims were able to purchase time to
effect their own grand scheme—the complete conquest of Israel.
In AD 638, the caliph Umar ibn el-Khattab conquered Jerusalem,
beginning an Islamic rule that lasted for four hundred sixty years,
till retaken by Crusaders in AD 1099. Umar visited the Temple
Mount and ordered the rubble accumulated during the Byzantine
era cleared. He then built a mosque on the hill's southern portion, identified by Muslims as the site from which Mohammad
made his nocturnal journey from Mecca. His mosque held three
thousand worshippers. During this Islamic administration, the
ban on Jewish residency in Jerusalem—imposed by Gentiles since
the days of the Bar Kokhba revolt—was lifted. A Jewish neigh-
borhood was established adjacent the Temple Mount. A Cairo
Geniza document confirms the meeting between the Jews and
caliph Umar ibn el-Khattab that precipitated the aforementioned
development. That there existed a more tolerant administration extends some measured promise for a brighter tomorrow—
unlikely though I think it to be as of this writing.

Later, caliph Mu'awiya established the Umayyad dynasty from
Syria. The Damascus-controlled dynasty was able to garner noto-
riety, given its proximity to the Temple Mount. Perhaps in order

to increase its influence, the Umayyad caliph ʿAbd al-Malik (AD 685–705) built a mosque over a foundation rock on the mount (alleged to be the place from which the "prophet" ascended into heaven). This was followed by caliph al-Walid's construction of the al-Aqsa Mosque (the site to which the prophet was said to have transported from Arabia by night). An extremely well-planned caliphs' complex was, likewise, developed along the mount's southern portion—signs of the city's rising prominence, later in the game. Later, in AD 750, the Syria-based Umayyad dynasty came to an end when the Baghdad-centered House of ʿAbbas came to power and exerted its influence over the city. Given Jerusalem's distance from the new power center, the city's newly cultivated influence waned considerably during this time.

In AD 969, Jerusalem was conquered by caliph al-Muʿizz li Din Allah, founder of the Egyptian-based Fatimid dynasty. In AD 1033, a severe earthquake destroyed Jerusalem's city walls. The Fatimid caliph Tahir ʿAli (AD 1021–1036) rebuilt the walls. They could not keep out the coming Crusaders, however, and the city fell into their hands in AD 1099, after which it became the capital of a new and independent kingdom—the essentially Christian "Kingdom of Jerusalem."

The so-called Christians commenced with a great slaughter in Jerusalem; with the native population(s) decimated, a Christian majority reigned—at least for a season. The Temple Mount was subsequently settled by the Order of the Knights Templar, founded in AD 1118. Al-Aqsa Mosque was renovated and became their headquarters, and was referred to by them as the Templum Solomonis. The Dome of the Rock, so called, was likewise reconstituted—this time as a church called Templum Domini.

In AD 1187, an Islamic army under Saladin won a decisive

battle (the Battle of the Horns of Hattin) in the wake of which the Christian occupation of the Kingdom of Jerusalem came to an end. Jerusalem was subsequently refortified by the Muslims, owing to concerns over the impending crusade under Richard the Lion-Heart (AD 1189–1192). Later, concerned that he was unable to hold the city against an advancing Crusader threat, the Ayyubid caliph al-Mu'zzam (AD 1218–1227) adopted a "scorched-earth" policy and had the city's walls razed—so as not to provide protection for the Christians.

The city remained without walls throughout the Mameluke period, which followed on the heels of the Ayyubids' demise. At the end of AD 1516, the Ottoman sultan Selim I (AD 1512–1520) took Jerusalem without a battle.

The Ottomans rebuilt the city, reestablished it as a significant Islamic pilgrim site, and experienced increased pilgrim traffic as a result. Selim I's famous son, Suleiman the Magnificent (AD 1520–1566), led the Ottomans to their "golden age." The city's water system was developed, as were its present-day walls, admired by modern pilgrims at the present. Jerusalem's rise as an Islamic holy city escalated during his term—many centuries removed from Islam's founding.

The Turkish Ottoman Empire's sway ended when its Jerusalem holding was passed on to the British, who then passed it on the United Nations. A partition agreement—dividing Israel into Jewish and Arab holdings—was drawn up, but was met unfavorably by local Arabs. When modern Israelis declared their independence in accordance with the world-authorized UN mandate, Arabs mobilized energies to defeat the fledgling Jewish State. Their efforts were to no avail; however, modern Israel expanded the more so with much of Jerusalem finally coming back into Jewish hands—where it fortuitously remains till this very day.

Some in the region claim that Jews had no presence till this day. Given the popularity this theory enjoys, a brief word to the contrary is in order here.

JEWISH PARTICIPATION IN AND CONTRIBUTION TO MIDDLE EASTERN LIFE AND LITERATURE

Let's pause and gaze at the medieval era. If someone in the here and now looks at the Jewish fabric in Israel as "alien" to the Middle Eastern embroidery, let us then examine how embedded Jews were, and still are, in the tapestry of the Middle East as an original fabric that harmoniously blends in.

Manufacturing, industry, and technology were still many centuries ahead of the Middle Ages, where literature was the principal progressive "industry" of the time and thus the arena where individuals demonstrated creativity. Living in the same part of the world for millennia with the Jews speaking Hebrew and the Arabs speaking Arabic, a Judeo-Arabic inter-pollination had to occur. Temporally speaking, *this Judeo-Arabic inter-pollination has the longest recorded history that extends from the pre-Islamic time to the present.* Topographically speaking, this interaction spanned the widest geographical area, from Spain to Yemen to Iraq.[57] In fact, this segment of the Jewish history was "one of the foremost periods of Jewish cultural and intellectual creativity."[58]

Language and linguistic disciplines are essential parts in the development of literature and literary works. What is interesting to know, and what functions as evidence of the authenticity of belongingness of the Jewish community to the Middle East, is the way Hebrew and Arabic languages interacted and influenced each other.

Apparently, mutual linguistic influence in the absence of the satellite age could not have happened without regional coexistence and geographical proximity. Although the biblical record stops at the fact of the Jewish settlement in the land formerly called Canaan—after the Exodus from Egypt—with Arab and Arab-related kinfolk to the east, later secular history notes the Jewish penetration into the south and of Jewish settlement in the Arab Peninsula. There is plenty of evidence "to show how the powerful Jewish communities in the north and [later] in the south of the peninsula came to be established there."[59] Despite the scarcity of any scrap of evidence regarding the reason and/or the time of the southward Jewish migration, it is obvious that by the time of Mohammad, the Jewish were already settled, became part of the local culture, spoke Arabic, and embraced Arabic names. They were also clustered in the form of large family groups, clans, or tribes ("tribes" here should be understood in a regional-cultural sense, not biblical). In this regard, Griess says:

> Generally speaking, the precise period of the first settlement of Jews in Arabia during the pre-Islamic era is unknown, and it is therefore impossible to say when the Arabic language was first employed by them. Historical data concerning the Jews of Arabia do not reach further back than the first century AD. However, the purely Arabic names which they bore suggested that they must have already been settled in the country for several centuries.[60]

The pieces of evidence of the Jewish involvement in, interaction with, and eventual contribution to the Middle Eastern culture and literature are countless. Let us come closer to examine how each group influenced the other positively in literature, and more particularly on the linguistics track.

As early as the beginning of the eighth century, scarcely fifty years after the Islamic conquest of the Levant, the Fertile Crescent, as with other parts of the Middle East, a Babylonian Jew by the name of Jawaih de Bassora translated a major medical work from Syriac to Arabic.[61]

Reciprocally, the adoption of the Arabic language by the Jews residing in Muslim countries—particularly in Iraq and Egypt—had a salutary effect on the Hebrew tongue. The Jews, in effect, were led to turn their attention to the deplorable state of their own language. They set about polishing it, as it were, and created a grammar for it modeled after that of Arabic.[62] Thus, the influence Arabic exerted on the Hebrew language is indisputable, according to the testimonies of language historians on both sides. In this regard, Dr. W. Bacher states:

> The stimulus for the study of Hebrew philology was, it is true, strengthened by external influence, namely, the example furnished by Arabic philology, which continued to influence materially the character of the Hebrew science; and it was the Arabic model which, being that of a kindred language, directed the development of Hebrew philology into the right path, and led it to permanent results.[63]

Dr. Hartwig Hirschfeld, on the other hand, furthers the point though on another axis. He asserts that the earliest works by Jews on the Hebrew language are not only written in Arabic, but are also arranged on the plan of their Arabic models and adopt their terminology. In fact, he makes an additional important note that while for Arab grammarians these elaborations were an end of themselves, Jews brought these elaborations into the service of the holy writings.[64] Dr. Philip Alexander states that the scientific study of Hebrew grammar began under the impact of Jewish scholars who applied the sophisticated contemporary theories of Arabic grammar to Hebrew.[65]

Not only was Arabic a matter of interest for Jewish scholarship, but even the average Jewish populace all over the Middle East spoke Arabic from the seventh century AD onwards. Nevertheless, their mastering of Classical Arabic and their devotion to their own language gave rise to the Judeo-Arabic literature teeming with Middle Arabic elements.[66]

Examples of this are numerous.

Abu al-Faraj Harun, one of the most prominent Jewish scholars of the eleventh century AD (AD 1000–1050), wrote several Arabic works on the Hebrew language. The most famous of all was the Egyptian Jew, Rabbi Sa'adya al-Fayyumi Gaon (AD 882–942), who wrote his masterpieces in Arabic and under the influence of Arabic philology. The Moroccan Jew, Judah ben Hayyuj of the tenth century AD, was the first to solve the mystery of the Hebrew root and its triliteral aspect because of his better grasp of Arabic and its grammar. This is besides many others—like Abdul Walid ibn Marwan ibn Janah (AD 990–1050), ibn Qoreish (the tenth-century North African Jewish scholar), ibn Barun (the Spanish Jew of the eleventh century), Moses ben Samuel ben Chiqatilla of Cordoba of the twelfth century (the most prominent Jewish biblical commentator that used Arabic in his writings), etc. All of these and many others significantly contributed to the literary and intellectual lives of Arabs and Jews equally.[67] The composition of works in Arabic by Jews continued to be much more prevalent in the East, where Arabic continued to be used as the spoken language of the entire region.

In sum, a wide variety of scholarly works were the prod-
ucts of the collaboration of the cousins of that era—the sons
of Isaac and the sons of Ishmael, along with their confederates.
This included works translated into Arabic, originated in Arabic
by Jewish scholars, and others written in transliterated Arabic
(which means Arabic text written in Hebrew script). The Jews, in
addition, enriched the Arabic library by literary works from their
own library, which included liturgical works, exegetical works,
and translations of Hebrew pietistic works. Meanwhile, *they used
Arabic to revive their Hebrew language and save it from extinction,
which had a great impact on the Hebrew Bible and later spawned
the magnificent and meticulous Masoretic Text* used worldwide to
date. Furthermore, a new breed of literature was born, namely,
Judeo-Arabic literature.

Returning to our downward-spiraling historical narrative
now, let it be said that this enriching productivity and mutual
interaction and collaboration was eclipsed by the fact that the
interrelationship of Judaism and Islam has gone hostile.

ISLAM AND THE JEWISH STATE
IN MODERNITY

Immediately after Israel declared her independence on May 14,
1948, the fledgling Jewish country was invaded by forces from
Egypt, Jordan, Iraq, Syria, and Lebanon, pitting a civilization
constituted by about 45 million Islamic-inspired Arabs against
forty-five thousand Jews. The Jews won. On October 29, 1956,
the Sinai War began in response to Egyptian instigations. Israel
won. Relative peace was secured between 1957 and 1966 till once
again the engines of Arabic discontent erupted and the Six-Day

War began on June 5, 1967, and extended till June 10. Israel won. The Yom Kippur War followed, beginning on October 6, 1973, and going till October 25 of the same year. Israel won. Unable to get the better of the Jews through "conventional" military action, an "unconventional" war is presently being played out, spirited along by disenfranchised youth, ad hoc ragtag militia, homicide bombers, and various sorts of "terrorists." These frenzied sorts work from and among civilian Arabs, and, from among them, then go on to strike at civilian targets both in their own world and around the world—a world that, since 9/11, apparently includes the United States of America. Is Israel winning this quasi-war? Is America? Hard to tell. How do you win it?

Not only are Zionist Israel and "secular" America the objects of Islamic angst, but so are the gentler, nonpolitical sectors of their very own world. That this is so is attested by the recent takeover of Bethlehem.

In days past, visitors anxious to get a glimpse of Jesus' possible birthplace would offload their buses and make haste to get to the famous Church of the Nativity. En route, pilgrims would be swarmed by a plethora of street vendors peddling wares, much as they would be greeted by established merchants calling out from their storefronts. Tourists were forever beckoned to the shops, where they were urged to take the proprietors up on their great "deals" and "discounts" on an assortment of Christian nativity-related paraphernalia. That was Bethlehem back *then*—during the "boom." What is of the city of Jesus' birth, *now*?

Though the situation is improving some, it could be said that Bethlehem has tragically pretty much gone "bust"—at least when compared to days past.

Though "wise men still seek Him," fewer are seeking Him in the city of His birth. In days past, for example, 91,276 pilgrims typically visited Bethlehem each and every month—before the Muslim occupation; now, by contrast, according to the city's mayor Victor Bataresh, tourism is down more than 90 percent.

Upon arrival these days, uplifted pilgrims are greeted by the spirits of the downcast locals. Gone are the enthusiasm and optimism that once resonated from Manger Square and permeated the bustling city of the Messiah's birth. Now, a travailing misery index is cascading upwards as the economic index is plummeting downwards. With a 65 percent unemployment rate and with no forecasted turnaround in sight, the city that once brought light into the world now sits in darkness, gloom, and despair—ever since the days of the Islamic occupation.

Unlike Mary, who was once turned away to the tune of there being "no room at the inn," those wanting to stay the night in Bethlehem now have no problem finding a room. The once-bustling tourist city averages two thousand empty hotel rooms per night. It will be much easier to find a room in the city of Jesus' birth than it will be to find a Christian, I might add: An exodus is on there, as Christians are fleeing Bethlehem en masse.

In 1948, the Christian population in Bethlehem was 85 percent. It is now but 12 percent—and declining fast. Reporting in the Ummah News Links under "Christian Population on Decline in the Holy Land," Sami Awad, executive director of a Bethlehem-based peace group, said, "Most of the Christians here [in Bethlehem] are either in the process of leaving, planning to leave, or thinking of leaving." In conjunction with that particular trend, Ummah noted that the "native Arab-Christian population has dipped below 2 percent of the West Bank, Gaza Strip, and Arab East Jerusalem." With the overshadowing Muslim Palestinian birthrate among the highest in the world, there are concerns that the Christian minority will become an "extinct" breed in the city of Jesus' birth and in the region within the next sixty years. Tragic! Demonic-inspired Jew-bashing aside, unreported—or under-reported anyway—are the abuses Christian Arabs suffer under the administrations of their Muslim Arab overlords, pressing them to seek better lives for themselves outside of Islamic jurisdictions. This is the real problem. The Palestinian Authority seems either unwilling or unable to assist Arab citizens of Christian persuasion.

As is to be expected, many blame the Jews for the above—even the victims. As with just about every other problem on planet earth, Jews are seen as the principal culprits.

In this regard, the Tunisian Reformist Abdelwahab Meddeb, in his *La Maladie de l'Islam and Contre-Prêches*, eloquently expresses the problem as an insider, saying: "The current anti-Semitism in Arab countries is directed against imaginary Jews." According to Meddeb, one of the chief symptoms of the malady of Islam is resentment. This resentment is particularly strong, as he indicates, against the West, and more particularly against the Jews. It affects even secular Arab Muslims.

> Preachers and even "secular" editorialists view the disasters that have befallen their community through [the prism of] acute xenophobia. They invent an imaginary conspiracy and attribute it to the other who fulfils the role of the enemy. [Both] the faults of the collective and the shortcomings of individuals are attributed to the evil and malignant foreigner.... What better way to rid oneself of responsibility after ridding oneself of guilt? [According to this view,] the Muslims' misery is caused by the West... and by Israel, whose success is a source of vexation [for the Muslims] in light of their own failure, which they are unable to acknowledge.[68]

CONCLUSION

Though today's Middle East conflict is played out against the backdrop of Arab-Israeli intrigue, *I believe this is indeed overly simplistic.* Discontented non-Arab Egyptians reside to the west of Israel and express their displeasure over its existence; non-Arab Turks reside to the north and do likewise, as do the non-Arab Persian-Iranians who abide in the east of Israel. *The angst is inspired by Islam!*

The bloody history of Islam from its inception to date is indescribable. In fact, its teaching legalizes violence, labels it as "religious" obligation, ignites it as being *for* the sake of Allah, and seals it with the approval of his messenger. The alleged tolerance of Islam toward the indigenous conquered populations is no more than a smoke screen to camouflage centuries of atrocities that never occurred in history, not even under barbarians. Even a prominent Islamic figure as Saladin, usually portrayed as a noble warrior, was ruthless in his dealings with indigenous Jews and Christians.

Islam traditionally dominates by the "fear factor." Fatima Mernissi, a Moroccan Muslim scholar, outlined her *Islam and Democracy: Fear of the Modern World*[69] in ten chapters, and seven of them start with the word "fear." Islam inculcates in the personhood and society matchless fear of almost everything. This fear includes: (1) *Fear of Allah*—since his overall image is that of a capricious god that would ultimately do whatever he wants in deciding the person's fate regardless of what the person did or did not do; (2) *Fear of hell*—with no solid guarantee of escaping it; (3) *Fear of apostasy*—which is met by merciless death, i.e., execution; (4) *Fear of freedom of thought*—because it blunts the edge of their only and favorite tool, the "sword." This is why you find that it is only in the Muslim world that free thinkers are accused (falsely, of course) of being anti-Islam and are murdered to quiescence them permanently; (5) *Fear of the West*—because the West is associated in their minds with Christianity. They divided the world into two camps, as noted previously—*Dar al-Islam* ("House of Islam") and *Dar al-Harb* ("Camp of War"); they have no place in mind for the "Camp of War" except the western part of the world.

In such an overwhelming sphere of fear of almost anything and everything, love surely must disappear—and it does, doesn't it? Not only does the Koran not attribute to Allah any sort of love, but the very word "love" itself is totally absent from the Koranic text, despite the attempts of some translators to "push" it into the translated text illegitimately. (In contrast, we remember what the Bible says in 1 John 4:18: "There is no fear in love, but perfect love casteth out fear, because fear hath punishment. He that feareth is not made perfect in love." This is but one of many references.)

When Muslims started their expansive campaigns, they were preoccupied with only one concern in the newly conquered territories—*exacting money and extorting properties.* In fact, the head-quarters—whether in Mecca, Damascus, or Baghdad—adopted a policy, coined in a proverbial statement implemented throughout the conquered territories, that was employed down through the centuries. The statement that came out in poetic form said: "Milk the udder until it dries; then suck the blood until it dies." Think about that. Nations, to them, were no more than "cows to milk" until the cows were dead. Decadence to the point of collapse was the guaranteed result. For example, Egypt had already had 6 million acres of cultivated land when the Muslims first invaded the country. It took only seventy years for this cultivated land to shrink to only 3 million acres.

Save Islam, every expansive civilization left something behind upon retreating from formerly conquered territories. If we take Egypt as a case in point, the French who occupied Egypt for only three years tabulated all the Ancient Egyptian monuments. In addition, they deciphered the Rosetta Stone, which opened the world's eyes to the mysteries of one of the greatest ancient civilizations. The Brits who followed built the railway road and revived the idea of digging Suez Canal throughout their seventy years of occupation. By way of comparison, it is worth noting that Islamic civilization *left absolutely nothing after fifteen centuries of occupation.*

Without delving into too many details, legalizing polygamy (which asserts the right of loving *and* marrying several others), which Islam offers as a reward to its followers, is out of keeping with the modern era, not to mention its being profoundly hazardous. Anthropologists have documented that as people modernize, they tend to opt for monogamy, and the contrary is proved equally true. The inevitable sexual imbalance between several wives eventually leads to grim consequences (like immorality), even in the most conservative societies. With so many unattended children, the crime rate proves to be higher in polygamous societies; with Islamization on top, crime develops into terrorism—where it is legitimized through social and religious sanction.

Non-Muslims are persecuted in Muslim-controlled lands. Persecution is here construed as unwarranted violence against people or properties that includes individual and mass murder. This also includes physical expulsion and other forms of discrimination (for example, bias, restrictions on displaying one's religion, restricting religious practices, negative attitude, false statements, etc.). All of this is carried out by unlawful compulsion in order to bring about forced conversion. Systematized persecution by

Islamic states is a very potent strategy, one carried out on many levels and on different fronts to bring about either elimination of non-Muslims or their forced conversion.

The spectrum of Islamic persecution includes non-Muslims in general, but Jews and Christians in particular. Atheists have the least of their attention. Jews and Christians are *infidels* par excellence. In fact, since Israel was reinstituted as an independent nation, one often hears this statement in the Middle East usually mentioned by Muslims, "First comes Saturday, then Sunday." What is meant by this statement is that after Muslims are "finished" with the Jews (referred to by their Sabbath), it is the turn of the Christians (referred to by the day of our Lord) to be dealt with, which means "exterminated."

Wherever Islam spreads, it creates an atmosphere of fear and utter despair due to the following factors: collapse of the state, social injustice, persecution of the minorities, familial instability, high divorce rate, high reproduction rate, poverty, cultural repression, hopelessness at improving the current historical situation, overwhelming fear of God, eternal insecurity, etc. All of these miserable factors collectively form a fertile ground for the spawning of terrorism. It is an atmosphere of utter misery expressed in the irrational outbreak of masses' rage, with an external object being the construed source of the angst: Jews, Israel, and/or the West. This has clearly been seen on TV during the crisis of the Danish cartoons when riots went out of proportion, accompanied by the burning of flags, the vandalizing of properties, and the calling for boycotts and diplomatic cuts and the like.

Since its emergence on the stage of history, Islam fashioned the world in a new order: *Dar al-Islam* ("House/Camp of Islam") and *Dar al-Harb* ("House/Camp of War"). *It declared war on anyone and everyone who did not follow its way.* September 11, 2001, was another day when Islam placed the entire world into a new (dis)order, with the then-circulating statement, "You are either with us, or against us," polarizing the world into two camps—terroristic and anti-terroristic. In other words, from its beginning and up to date, Islam has challenged the world and the world system out of neutrality, (quasi) stability, and peace into the quagmire of war and terrorism.

Mindful of the above, we do well to not delude ourselves with the popular, politically correct fantasy that by ceding more and more real estate to Muslim terrorists, we are purchasing peace for the peoples of the Middle East. *It may sound good in theory, but it is not born out in practice*; it is, in truth, just another ploy to attack Jews in their ancestral homeland.

If peace is not to be secured by conceding to terrorists, what then? Believing that it is better to light candles than it is to curse the darkness, we would do well to turn our attention to what the Bible says about an eventual peace in the region.

ARABIAN RELIGION AND HOSTILITY AT THE END OF TIME

Soteriology: Cessation of Arabian Hostilities at the End of Time

"Soteriology" in theological nomenclature speaks of healing, wholeness, salvation, and the like. The Bible begins by
noting sin's entrance and finishes with the inauguration of the
Kingdom of God and its consequential and eventual just, righteous, and orderly society. The means by which this will be actu-
alized is worth noting here, with attention given to implications
for Jewish-Arab intrigue played out in and around Judea.

The story of sin's entrance onto the stage of the human drama
(Gen. 3:1–24) is often told and retold. That one brother killed
another brother immediately thereafter (Gen. 4) was a telltale
sign of bad things to come and attested to the emergence of frac-
ture and war within human society. Abraham's eventual emergence and quest for the "promised land" (11:27–12:3)—in the
ancient world's only landbridge connecting Africa, Arabia, Asia,
and Europe—guaranteed that wars would come to the region…
and they did. Situated precariously at the crossroads of ancient
civilizations, biblical Israel was established, with Abraham's being

beckoned to go there and with his eking out an existence in that tempestuous part of the world.

Scripture's singling out Abraham and making him and his progeny the object of divine attention is well attested in the narrative, as is the fact that thorny problems with his sons Ishmael and Jacob facilitated feudal tensions that have endured with the passage of time. Down to the modern time, the perennial Arab-Jewish conflicts form the basis for unresolved problems that continue to vex the planet's greatest minds here in the present modern era.

In the interest of coming to terms with our making peace with the people of the sand, we will now direct our gaze that direction and consider the prophetic Word. Political personalities wrestle with problems and proffer solutions to the Middle East quagmire. Believing that we do better to look to God than man—though appreciative of well-intended human efforts—I believe we would do well to consider what the Scriptures say.

Believing Middle East problems to be more spiritual than material, I do not believe that perennial Middle-Eastern tensions stem from fossil fuels, from petty territorial disputes with Israel, or from simple grudges between rival Islamic clansmen. If the problems are not rooted in human interests, needs, and squabbles, then they are not going to be solved by human peace-keeping endeavors alone—well-intended though they indeed may be. If there is a spiritual, religious component that needs addressed, then a consideration of the Bible's doctrine of health, healing, and saving should be expanded to include what God will do on His earth to bring about its restoration and equilibrium for humankind. In the interest of coming to terms with world-impacting judgment and salvation motifs, a brief assessment will be offered here—beginning with an appraisal of the prophet Ezekiel.

EZEKIEL

Draconian, anti-Judaic judgment motifs abound in Ezekiel. Chapters 2:1–21:27 are rife with horrific images and tension-producing messages, all pointing to an impending destruction said to be coming upon the Hebrew people and the world. In what follows, we'll swiftly move both to and through samplings of Ezekiel's diatribe to give a sense of their essence and to briefly explore their substance.

For example, in 2:3, the Lord is on record commissioning Ezekiel: "I send thee to…a rebellious nation that hath rebelled against Me." Ezekiel, in turn, is encouraged with, "Be thou not rebellious like that rebellious house; open thy mouth" (v. 8). In 6:3, God says, "I will bring a sword upon you [Judah]," and verse 6 states that "cities shall be laid waste." In 7:2–3, God notes "the end is come," stating in verse 5 that it is a disaster, and that He will "not spare" or "have pity" upon Judeans (v. 9). While a number of things invoke God's ire, in 12:24, He says, "There shall be no more any vain vision nor flattering divination within the house of Israel," and in 13:8, God states, "Because ye have spoken vanity, and seen lies, therefore, behold, I am against you." For this and other reasons, judgment upon Judah is said to be forthcoming in Ezekiel. This is further attested in 21:24 and 27, where God says: "Because ye have made your iniquity to be remembered, in that your transgressions are uncovered…I will overturn, overturn, overturn it, and it shall be no more, until He comes whose right it is, And I will give it to Him."

The Lord is displeased, is He not?

Similarly, border nations are said to have likewise incurred God's wrath. In Ezekiel 21:28–32, the Ammonites (located in modern-day Jordan) are the object of His fury, too. In 21:28, we hear: "Concerning the Ammonites.... The sword, the sword is drawn; for the slaughter is it polished." Ezekiel 22:1–24:27 picks up with more judgment themes directed against the Jewish people, after which the narrative describes judgment against various border states. Moab and Edom (likewise associated with modern Jordan) are noted in 25:8–14. In verse 9, the Lord says, "I will open the side of Moab from the cities," and then in verse 10, He states, "Unto the men of the east with the Ammonites, and will give them in possession." He goes on in verse 13 commenting on Edom's demise: "I will also stretch out Mine hand against Edom," and in verse 14 He says, "I will lay My vengeance upon Edom."

Philistia—which is comparable to the Gaza area occupied by individuals who interestingly and incorrectly refer to themselves as "Palestinians"—is then the object of divine rebuke in 25:15–17. Scripture says, "Because the Philistines have dealt by revenge…with a despiteful heart," and because of "the old hatred" (v. 15). Therefore, God says, "I will stretch out Mine hand upon the Philistines" (v. 16) and "I will execute My vengeance upon them" (v. 17).

Next, Tyre and Sidon—located in southern modern Lebanon—come under the knife in 26:1–28:24. The Lord says, "Behold I am against thee, O Tyre, and will cause many nations to come against thee" (26:3). This is but one of the many prophetic invectives aimed at what would be Lebanon today. "How art thou destroyed" is another in 26:17a, as is, "I will bring strangers upon thee, the terrible of the nations, and they shall draw their swords against the beauty of thy wisdom, and they shall defile thy brightness" (28:7). As for Sidon, God's Word says, "Behold I am against thee, O Sidon.... For I will send into her pestilence…blood into her streets, and the wounded shall be judged in the midst of her by the sword upon her on every side" (vv. 22–23).

Prophetic denunciation against Egypt and her allies follows in Ezekiel 29:1–32:32. "Set thy face against Pharaoh, king of Egypt, and prophesy against him" is God's command in 29:2. Immediately after, Egypt's Pharaoh is likened to a crocodile, whom He calls a "great monster that lieth in the midst of his rivers." He says, "I will put hooks in thy jaws, and…I will bring thee up out of the midst of the rivers," where Pharaoh will then "fall on the open fields" (29:3–5). The image is clear: God will judge the beast that dwells by the Nile—Pharaoh of Egypt.

"Alas for the day!" is the word in 30:2, "for the day is near… the sword shall come upon Egypt" (vv. 3–4). The Lord says, "I will also make the multitude of Egypt to cease," (v. 10) and "I will break Pharaoh's arms, and he shall groan…with the groanings of a deadly wounded man" (v. 24). "Pharaoh and all his army," says the Lord is "slain by the sword…. For *I have caused My terror in the land of the living*" (32:31–32).

The objective is clear.

After prophetically touring modern Israel and uttering prophetic invectives against those to the east (the Ammonites, Moabites, and Edomites), to the immediate west (noting Philistia), and then to the north (Tyre and Sidon), Ezekiel went farther west (and took on Egypt). Then he finished with a final word against Mount Seir—a kindred name for Edom: "O Mount Seir, I am against thee; and I will stretch out Mine hand against thee, and I will make thee most desolate. I will lay thy cities waste, and thou shalt be desolate, and thou shalt know that I am the LORD" (35:3–4).

Having begun his prophetic rebuke in what would be modern Jordan and then ending there, Ezekiel goes on to unfold a variety of restoration motifs and prophecies. Once the previously noted horrific judgments run their course, the prophet notes that Israel will be wonderfully restored, according to 36:1–38. In 37:1–14, a fantastic prophetic image of Israel coming to life is employed, with bones coming together to form skeletons that, in turn, take on organs, skin, breath, and life. Thus revived, Ezekiel notes, the people's reemergence in the land of the living invokes the ire of those around and about (38:1–17).

The upshot is that regional forces will be mobilized against the Jews in the reconstituted Jewish State—arguably modern-day Israel. Ezekiel employs names that had otherwise fallen off the pages of the biblical narrative, names like Gog, Magog, Rosh, Meshech, Tubal, Gomer, and Togarmah (38:1–3 and 6). The more commonly known nations of Persia, Ethiopia, and Libya are prophetically noted in verse 5. Therein, readers are told that in the "latter years," forces from them will "come into the land that is brought back from the sword, and is gathered out of many peoples, against the mountains of Israel" (v. 8), and that they will "come up against My people Israel…in the latter days" (v. 16).

Today's events show striking parallels. Scripture informs that those who rally their energies and forces against Israel will incur "the fire of [God's] wrath" (v. 19). In verse 21, God is on record saying He will "call for a sword against" those and bring them to "judgment with pestilence and with blood" (v. 22). He follows up with, "I will rain…overflowing rain, and great hailstones, fire, and brimstone." The regional powers' destruction is noted in chapter 39:1–20, with an appendage that, by means of so doing, God will "set My glory among the nations, and all the nations shall see My judgment that I have executed, and My hand that I have laid upon them" (v. 21). The prophet then states that God will bring back the captives of Jacob and "have mercy on the whole house of Israel, and [He] will be jealous for [His] holy Name" (v. 25).

God is on record saying that He will make Himself known through world events centered on Israel and involving various regional forces.

In the wake of the glorious and well-attested triumph, the establishment of a Temple on the Temple Mount in Jerusalem is described in great detail in 40:1–46:24. Once the Temple is established, blessings flow from Jerusalem and extend not just to Jewish people, but to the Arab peoples to the immediate east as well—and to those beyond by association. *I personally am fascinated by this, and think it is a gracious restoration story needing to be heralded.*

In 47:1–5, waters are said to gush mysteriously from a rebuilt Jerusalem Temple complex and, in turn, flow due east. "Hast thou seen this?" asks the Lord rhetorically in verse 6. He goes on to say: "These waters issue out toward the east country, and go down into the Arabah, and go into the sea, and being brought forth into the sea, the waters shall be healed" (v. 8).

The Judean wilderness to the immediate east of Jerusalem is exceedingly dry. The lifeless patch of deserted mountain pitches eastward, descending to the lowest point on earth and to what's appropriately called the Dead Sea or Salt Sea. The real estate is stark and basically uninhabitable, save for the likes of the Bedouin, who know how to eke out a meager, temporary existence there—helped along by their tapping into Israel's water pipes. Though chemical extract plants translate to profit, the saline content of the sea's water makes sustaining life through the sea impossible, much as the land yields no bounty to speak of. God says He will change all of this, however, and that Arabs will benefit—as will others.

With this image, Ezekiel notes that water will flow from the House of the God of Israel and bring life to this barren region, healing both the land and the sea in the process. As for the once-Dead Sea, 47:9 notes the resultant "great multitude of fish, because [God's healing] waters shall come there; for they shall be healed; and everything shall live." Ezekiel goes on to state in verse 10 that fishermen and others will one day reap bounty from the waters, precisely because "water flows from the Sanctuary." The prophet closes by saying that the "fruit shall be for food, and its leaf for medicine" (v. 12).

Worthy of note for our purposes is the fact that *prosperity, healing, and health are envisioned as coming to Arab peoples*—those dwelling east of the Promised Land. That this is accentuated is further attested in verse 22, where Israelites are reminded to be kindly disposed toward Arabs resident in the newly reconstituted State of Israel.

Speaking of land allotments, Ezekiel says, "Divide this land unto you" (v. 21), following with, "The aliens that sojourn among you, who shall beget children among you; and they shall be unto you as born in the country among the children of Israel; they shall have an inheritance with you among the tribes of Israel. And it shall come to pass that, in what tribe the stranger sojourneth, there shall ye give him his inheritance, saith the LORD God." I find the implications to be striking!

God's kind disposition toward Arab peoples is amply attested. Though the descendants of Esau and Ishmael incurred God's judgment along with the Jewish people, they likewise will receive rejuvenation along with the Jewish people—proof of God's abiding love for them, the same.

JEREMIAH

Like Ezekiel's, the words of "Jeremiah, the son of Hilkiah" (Jer. 1:1) are both prophetic and poignant. Jeremiah, like Ezekiel, is called into a thankless ministry, though at a younger age himself (around 20; 1:6). Commanded not to marry or have children, Jeremiah is commissioned to marry his miserable work—that of preaching an unpopular message to his people, a recalcitrant and sin-hardened people. Not an easy assignment, to be sure.

Commentators call this unfortunate and lonely man the "weeping prophet" because of his sorrowful manner. In 9:1, he says, "Oh, that my head were waters, and mine eyes a fountain of tears, that I might weep day and night for the slain of the daughter of my people!" Similarly, in 13:17, he says: "If ye will not hear it, my soul shall weep in secret places for your pride; and mine eye shall weep bitterly, and run down with tears, because the LORD's flock has been taken captive."

Jeremiah knows the present and sees the future, and this sensitive and sad man is made the worse off through what he envisions. In 11:18–23, Jeremiah says that God gave him "knowledge" and showed him Judah's evil "doings" (v. 18). He, by his own reckoning, "was like a lamb…brought to the slaughter" (v. 19), not knowing that his own Jewish people "devised plots" against him, saying, "Let us destroy the tree with its fruit, and let us cut him off from the land of the living, that his name be no more remembered" (v. 19). Advocating for him in response to his complaint, Jeremiah gives a corresponding "thus says the LORD" in verses 21–23: "Behold," says God, "I will punish them; the young men shall die by the sword; their sons and their daughters shall die by famine…. I will bring evil upon the men…even the year of their judgment" (vv. 22–23). Tense, is it not?

Disconcerted by their sinfulness, Jeremiah gives voice to his complaint in 12:1 and following. "Pull them out like sheep for the slaughter, and prepare them for the day of slaughter" is his imprecatory prayer in verse 3. Figuratively speaking, Jeremiah sees that the land of Israel "mourn[s]," that the "herbs of every field wither," and that even the animals are chagrined because of the wickedness of Israel (v. 4). Even Jeremiah's brothers in the "house of thy father" speak "fair words" against Jeremiah, and deal "treacherously" with him (v. 6). He is essentially friendless in an increasingly unfriendly world.

Jeremiah is commissioned to deliver an unpopular message to Judea's leaders, who are minded to "walk after [their] own plans" and "do the imagination of [their own] evil [and irreligious] heart[s]" (18:12). They have "forgotten" God (v. 15) and "stumble in their ways," prompting God to deliver through Jeremiah the words, "I will show them [My] back, and not [My] face, in the day of their calamity" (v. 17). Displeased by Jeremiah's messages as they understandably are, "They say, 'Come, and let us devise plots against Jeremiah,'" in verse 18. By way of response, as before, Jeremiah turns around and says: "Pour out their blood by the force of the sword…forgive not their iniquity, neither blot out their sin, but let them be overthrown before thee" (vv. 21–23).

His prayers are answered.

These are but small samplings from a book rife with judgment motifs aimed at recalcitrant Judah. Judgment motifs are ubiquitous in chapters 2 through 45, with imprecatory verbiage aimed at Gentiles noted in chapters 46 through 51.

After a general introduction in 46:1 about prophecies to come "against the nations," as God's mouthpiece, Jeremiah zeroes in on Egypt in verses 2–26. "Draw near to battle," says the Lord in verses 3–4. He follows with: "Harness the horses…polish the spears, and put on the coats of mail" (v. 4). "Come up, ye horses; and rage, ye chariots" are His words to Egypt, as noted in verse 9. "Declare ye in Egypt," He says in verse 14; "Prepare [yourselves]; for the sword shall devour round about thee." The "valiant men" of Egypt are "swept away" (v. 15) by a God who says, "I will deliver them into the hand of those who seek their lives" (v. 26a).

When God's providential judgment runs its course against Egypt, however, Jeremiah notes—as did Ezekiel previously with those in Jordan—that God's graces will come to Egypt: "'*Afterward it shall be inhabited*, as in the days of old,' saith the LORD," (v. 26b, emphasis added). *The restoration motif is but more striking testimony to the fact that God is not just about the business of restoring the "apple of His eye," Israel, but that He also has His eye on the people round about, and has plans for their good successes much the same.*

With Egypt thus forcefully and graciously attended to—with negative and positive predictions on record—Jeremiah turns to Philistia, which, as noted previously, is the area occupied by individuals in Gaza today who falsely pride themselves as being "Palestinians."

"The word of the LORD...came to Jeremiah...against the Philistines" (47:1), and speaks of a coming day when the "LORD will spoil the Philistines" (v. 4). The Scripture says that "baldness is come to Gaza" in verse 5. Jeremiah continues by noting that "Ashkelon is cut off" (v. 5), pointing out that the Lord has given "a charge against...[the people who dwell by the] seashore"—the Philistines (v. 7). The prophet is graphic here, as with the above.

Similarly, Moab, Ammon, and Edom—modern Jordan today—are the objects of divine discontent in the following prophecies. "No more praise of Moab" is exclaimed in Jeremiah 48:2, given that it is "destroyed," with "her little ones" having "caused a cry" (v. 4). "The spoiler shall come upon every city" and "no city shall escape" (v. 8). "Give wings unto Moab, that it may flee and get away" is the word in verse 9—though she will not be spared. There is no escaping judgment: "Moab shall be ashamed"

(v. 13), for "the calamity of Moab is near to come" (v. 16). "Woe be unto thee, O Moab!" are some of Jeremiah's finishing words in verse 46, for "thy sons are taken captives, and thy daughters, captives."

Interestingly, however, as with Egypt above (in 47:26), God isn't minded to leave Moab/Jordan writhing in agony forever and overrun with concomitant despair. After the judgment runs its course, He closes, saying: "'Yet will I bring again the captivity of Moab in the latter days,' saith the LORD," after which he finishes with: "Thus far is the judgment of Moab" (48:47, emphasis added).

A trend is observed in the denunciation literature: *God judges Jews and Arab-related peoples alike.* As much as Judah is found wanting over and again, and God is minded to bring His weight to bear against her, so too is He minded to restore. Similarly, *the same prophets who give voice to God's displeasure over His treasured people, Israel, likewise remember the beloved descendants of Isaac and Ishmael's other sons and associates, and note that they will arise and stand in God's economy in, to use the language of Jeremiah, "the latter days"* (48:17).

Let's continue.

"Concerning the Ammonites" is the opening phrase in 49:1. Scripture says the villages "shall be burned with fire" (v. 2) as evidence of their having incurred God's displeasure. "'I will bring a fear upon thee,' saith the LORD GOD of hosts, 'from all those who are about thee; and ye shall be driven out every man right forth, and none shall gather up him that wandereth'" (v. 5)—sort of.

The hyphenated notation above is not accidental. In saying "none shall gather up him that wandereth," Jeremiah is no doubt referencing those who are warring against them. That this is clear is evidenced by the fact that the final word to these Arab peoples is not their utter demise but, as noted previously, the text closes in verse 6 with: "'And afterward *I will bring again the captivity of the children of Ammon,*' saith the LORD" (emphasis added).

There is a restoration. Those in what's called Jordan today are beloved too, and they live!

Scripture is speaking emphatically about an abiding love for the peoples round about Israel. This should serve notice to Bible readers that we do well to take note and consider the positive implications.

God says He will demonstrate judgment against Edom (v. 7), however, whom He will make "bare" (v. 10). "His seed is spoiled" and "he is not" (v. 10). "Thou shalt not go unpunished" is the word in verse 12, as is the prediction that the once high and lofty Edom would be made "small among the nations" (v. 15), and a "desolation" (v. 17), and that "the heart of the mighty men of Edom" shall "be like the heart of a woman in her pangs" (v. 22). Judgment is forceful here as elsewhere. *But grace comes even so.*

Having taken on those in the ancient countries occupying modern Jordan, Jeremiah then visits Damascus—in what would be modern Syria. Beginning with "concerning Damascus" in verse 23, Jeremiah describes people who are "confounded" and "fainthearted." Damascus is referred to as "feeble" and "fear[ful]" in verse 24, where she "turneth herself to flee" when "fear hath seized on her," and when—as with Edom above—"anguish and sorrows have taken her, as of a woman in travail." The "young men shall fall in her streets," and "the men of war shall be cut off in that day" by a "fire" that God will "kindle" (vv. 26–27).

"Concerning Kedar" is the opening of the next prophetic invective. In 49:28–33, Jeremiah addresses these nomadic Ishmaelite tribes, said to be of Kedar and Hazor. The people of Kedar are known in Genesis 25:12–13 as frequenting the Arabian Desert. A clan of nomadic warriors, they are famous for their archery skills. Isaiah 21:16–17 refers to the "glory of Kedar" along with the "number of archers, [and] the mighty men of the children of Kedar." The "sharp arrows of the mighty" are similarly noted in Psalm 120:4, as is a reference to the "tents of Kedar" (v. 5), with a reference to their hatred for peace (v. 6). Combined, these cross references lend credence to the notion that these sons of Ishmael were a very strong and warlike Arabian people.

"Spoil the men of the east" is the word in Jeremiah 49:28. "Their tents and their flocks shall [be taken] away," as will their "vessels, and their camels" (v. 29). "Their camels shall be a booty, and the multitude of their cattle a spoil," says Jeremiah in verse 32. After noting the demise of the nomadic, Arabian nation— described as secure (v. 31), though it has "neither gates nor bars"— Jeremiah turns his attention to the Elamites—ancient Elam being inhabited by those in and around Iran today.

"Behold I will break the bow of Elam, the chief of their might" is the prophet's opening salvo (49:35). "And upon Elam will I bring the four winds," he continues in verse 36, "and will scatter them toward all those winds." After adding, "I will cause Elam to be dismayed before their enemies, and before those who seek their life; and I will bring evil upon them" (v. 37), Jeremiah follows with, "I will send the sword after them, till I have consumed them." While this is the story, it is not the final story.

Before getting to it, let us focus afresh on where Elam was and is on the map.

Recorded history actually began with a record of the Elamites settling on the tract of land that is now Iran, in approximately 3000 BC. They were followed by Indo-Europeans, who successfully forged kingdoms in the region around 2000 BC. The Medes came and flourished, holding sway over their territory— what is presently the Iranian landmass—from 728–550 BC, till they were overthrown by the Persians under Cyrus II. The land is known today as *Jomhuri-ye Eslami-ye Iran* (the "Islamic Republic of Iran"), referring to the political entity presently inextricably entrenched on the 634,734-square-mile parcel east of the Euphrates and Tigris rivers in southwestern Asia. The land, as we have seen, was known to the ancients much earlier as Elam—as it was known to Jeremiah, who goes on to castigate them.

Though Jeremiah speaks of God's "fierce anger" against them and of forthcoming disasters (49:37), this is not the prophet's final word. As noted a few times already, he closes in verse 39 with: "'It shall come to pass in the latter days, that *I will bring again the captivity of Elam,' saith the LORD.*'" Here again, *God's abiding affection for this non-Israelite people is noted through a coming restoration,* one slated for the "latter days."

Beyond these expressions, which could understandably be construed as superfluous by now, worth noting is something unique. Just prior to underscoring His plan to redeem Elam, God is on record saying: "I will set My throne in Elam" (v. 38). Beyond just a notice of a coming restoration is mention of God's making the land a special place of habitation. This is interesting for a variety of reasons.

Previously in this volume, taking our lead from Revelation 16:12 and following, we noted that the dreaded Battle of Armageddon is to be played out by demon-inspired forces marshaled in this very land. *That this very place is the Islamic nexus for anti-Zionist rhetoric and is calling for destruction today should give Bible observers cause to pause and wonder.*[70] Fascinating, on top, is the fact that God will eventually be particularly known in Elam—a land that, as with Israel itself, He is said to have His eye upon and one that, as with Israel, He is minded to make a special place in His Name and power—later. Iran. Interesting!

In sum, readers of Jeremiah's prophecies note that the prophet minces no words about Judah's sins and consequential judgment. Similarly, Jeremiah decries the sinfulness of those around about, and sees an unpleasant visitation upon Israel's neighbors that will leave them greatly humbled, as with Judah. Like Ezekiel, however, Jeremiah knows that a new and better day will dawn upon humankind—including a better day for Israel's neighbors.

ISAIAH

Isaiah is the prophet most oft employed in the New Testament. New Testament writers were given to underscoring how Isaiah's writings predicted the coming of the Messiah; for our purposes, we are principally interested in whatever light they may shine upon judgment and restoration motifs, and how these might find application for Arab peoples who inhabit the world in proximity to the Messiah's second coming.

As noted previously in this volume, in Isaiah 60:1 and following, Isaiah says, "arise, shine" in anticipation of a rising light. In verse 3, he sees that "the nations shall come to thy light," and that folks will "see…and be enlarged" (v. 5). Of these Gentiles, *Arabs are noted as being foremost amongst them.* Leaving this prophetic word that has profound implications for just a moment, at the risk of sounding like I am just restating points made previously in this volume, let me note that, as with the other Hebrew prophets, Isaiah speaks about the good news of coming deliverance. He, as we know, likewise shares the bad news of coming destructions— in advance of their arrival. In the book that bears his name, he calls Judeans to account for invoking the ire of the "Holy One of Israel,"[71] and everyone is pleased with him.

Isaiah makes his entrance onto the stage of the human drama at a time when Judean culture is in serious decline and the community's "misery index" is seriously on the rise. Unabashedly, the emboldened prophet decries Jewish leadership's social and spiritual indifferences as with its abuses and speaks of God's impending judgment on Judah as a result of perennial disobedience to the Torah's moral and spiritual demands.

From a biblical perspective, Isaiah was arguably the greatest man of his time.[72] Isaiah's early prestige may well have made him the envy of some Old Testament prophets, some of whom even quoted him. As noted, he was indeed popular with New Testament writers as well, evidenced by his being quoted by them 411 times—slightly more than the Psalms and more than Moses. It could be said with ease that Isaiah was "set apart" from the rest. And speaking of being "set apart," worth noting is that King Hezekiah's son Manasseh was not the least bit kindly disposed toward Isaiah, and is said to have "set him apart" as well—but in another way. Manasseh is remembered in history as being the king who put Isaiah to death by sawing him in two,[73] chagrined as he was by the prophet's forceful message and manner.

When one hears him out, that he would incur such wrath is easy to understand. After noting that the Jewish people are akin to "dumb asses" in Isaiah 1:3, the prophet predicts a near total annihilation in verse 7. As if that were not engaging enough, in verse 10, he tells Judean men that they are a nation of homosexuals, and then likens the capital Jerusalem to a slut, a "harlot" (v. 21). Commenting on his "calling" to the ministry in 6:8a and his subsequent surrender to the call in 8b, Isaiah notes the Lord is informing that his tenure as a prophet will extend "until the cities be wasted without inhabitant, and the houses without man, and the land be utterly desolate" (v. 11). Not a pleasant picture.

Isaiah boldly addresses the social and spiritual decay in his day and calls for prophet, priest, and king alike to repent while informing them of the consequences of failing to do so. Isaiah's "gloom-and-doom" messages eventually invoke the ire of King Manasseh. Isaiah loses his life as a result, given the king's inability to stomach the insults and the images. Lastly though, worth noting is how Isaiah is a hopeful prophet—and not just a prophet of doom. While chapters 1–35 are largely preoccupied with predictions of judgment, chapters 40–66 are largely filled with messages of future restoration—with an ultimate fulfillment in the Messiah.[74] What comes between them will be the object of our attention here.

A court prophet, Isaiah acts like a district attorney and represents the sovereign's case against his law-breaking subjects. Trial language appears in Isaiah's introduction (cf., e.g., 3:9, 13–14). To make an arrest, one must produce specific facts that would lead a reasonable person to believe that a particular crime has been committed and that a particular person is responsible for that particular crime. The "elements of an offense" must then be "proved up"—something Isaiah clearly does.

Injustice leaps out immediately in 1:16–17, where the condition is to be remedied by "refus[ing] the evil, and choos[ing] the good," correcting oppression, and bringing justice to the fatherless and widows—i.e., those whose life circumstances have left them weak and ill-protected. Isaiah adds to the aforementioned social defilements, noting an infusion of spiritual ones in 2:6–8. Returning then to social concerns, in 3:13–26, Judah is said to have "eaten up the vineyard," leaving "the spoil of the poor...in your houses" (v. 14). That this follows with the question—"What mean ye that ye beat My people to pieces, and grind the faces of the poor?"—lends credence to the proposition that class abuses

are rife, further denoting that the affluent and powerful are running roughshod over the disempowered, weaker underclasses.
God mocks the haughty and wealthy sorts and pronounces judgment upon them in verses 16–26. Disregard, injustice, and indifference are then characterized in 5:7b and 8, where a warning is
added to those who devour others. Drunkenness and affluence are
addressed in verses 11–12 and 22, followed by a stinging rebuke
of the corrupt in verse 23. Isaiah's "sin list" reads *unlike* many of
our own, given the prophet's interest in social sins more than in
private ones—as is often the focus today.

In Isaiah 1:2–9, the prophet stings his hearers with words
from God like: "I [the LORD] have…brought up children, and
they have rebelled against Me," (v. 2) and the "ox…and the ass"
know their masters, "but Israel doth not know" and is thus, in
effect, dumber than even the dumb asses. Judah is a "sinful nation,
a people laden with iniquity…children that are corrupters" (v. 4),
who "have provoked the Holy One of Israel to anger."

The upshot is that Judah's "country is [seen as] desolate," "cities are burned with fire," and "foreigners devour" the land (v. 7).
Isaiah not only sees this and gives voice to it prophetically, but
he forcefully takes on those responsible for it, likening them to
"rulers of Sodom" and the "people of Gomorrah" in verse 10.
Likening men to homosexuals isn't a way to endear oneself to
men. This is not Isaiah's objective, however. In 1:21, Jerusalem is
likened to a prostitute with: "How is the faithful city become an
harlot!" Leaders are further reviled as being "rebellious" princes
(v. 23) and are compared to "thieves" who love "bribes." Their
wives are likened to proverbial "dizzy blonds" in 3:16–23. They
are "haughty," with "stretched forth necks and wanton eyes"
(v. 16), prancing about as they go. In verses 18–23, these arrogant
snots will have their "tinkling anklets," "headbands, "crescents,"

"pendants," "bracelets," "veils," fancy "headdresses," "armlets," "sashes," "perfume boxes," "amulets," "rings," "nose rings," "festival robes," "mantles," "cloaks," "handbags," "hand mirrors," "linen wrappers," "turbans," and "veils" taken from them.

According to Isaiah, Judah's ladies can expect that "instead of sweet fragrance there shall be rottenness; and instead of a girdle, a rope; and instead of well-set hair, baldness; and instead of a rich robe, a girding of sackcloth" (v. 24). Decimated as Jerusalem will be, and devastated as the women and men will be, the prophet closes in verse 26 with: "Her gates shall lament and mourn; and she, being desolate, shall sit upon the ground." This, says Isaiah, is a fitting judgment for a people who "have cast away the law of the LORD of Hosts and despised the word of the Holy One of Israel" (5:24).

In addition to calling attention to Israel's sin and judgment, Isaiah addresses other nations as well. That he is a "court preacher" is amply attested on the basis of the interest he has both in other people and in world events, evident in the way he speaks to and about Babylon, Assyria, Philistia, Moab, Syria, Ethiopia, Egypt (then Egypt and Ethiopia together), Edom, Arabia, Shebna, and lastly, Tyre.

Babylon is considered in 13:1–14:23 and then again in 21:1–10. In 13:9, a day comes, "cruel both with wrath and fierce anger." In verse 11, God is minded to "punish the world for its evil" and lay Babylon waste, something seen as coming to pass in 21:1 and following.

Assyria draws Isaiah's attention in 14:24–27. "I will break the Assyrian in My land, and upon My mountains tread him under foot," is the word in verse 25, something said to be "purposed" by the Lord" (vv. 26–27).

Philistia is similarly the object of divine rebuke in 14:28–32.

"I will kill thy root with famine" is the message in verse 30. In verse 31, Isaiah exclaims: "Howl, O gate; cry, O city; thou, O Philistia, art dissolved." He finishes with the following point in verse 32: "The LORD hath founded Zion, and the poor of His people shall trust in it."

Moab draws fire in 15:1–16:13. "He is very proud," says Isaiah in 16:6. The people of a once-proud Moab will be humbled and will learn that their religion will not be able to save them from the judgment due them. "He," says God in verse 12, "shall come to his sanctuary to pray; but he shall not prevail."

The Syrian capital of Damascus, says Isaiah in 17:1, will cease from being a city. Other Syrian cities are destined to fall, according to 17:1–14, as well—judgment for what they did to Judah. "This," says the Sacred Text in verse 14, "is the portion of those who spoil us, and the lot of those who rob us."

According to Isaiah, the people of Ethiopia are tall and smooth of skin (18:2), much as they are "terrible" and powerful. When God "bloweth a trumpet" for war, however, as per verse 3, people will be humbled and a "present [will] be brought unto the Lord of hosts by a people scattered and stripped, and from…a nation measured out and trampled under" (v. 7).

Ethiopia's proud neighbor in the region, Egypt, is noted separately in 19:1–17 (and together with Ethiopia in 20:1–6). In 19:1, "The LORD…shall come into Egypt," where there will be great upheaval (v. 2). Verses 3 through 10 state that Egypt will fall when its foundations are "broken" (v. 10). The Lord makes sport of Pharaoh's "wise" counselors (vv. 12–13) who fail to steady Egypt, construed later by Him as "a drunken man [staggering] in his vomit" (v. 14).

Edom is briefly considered in 21:11–12 with a warning of imminent destruction. Arabia is addressed in 21:13–17. "The burden upon Arabia" is the all-too-familiar opening in verse 13. It will surely "fail" is the word of reckoning in verse 16, as is the promise of its "diminish[ment]" in verse 17. Sheba's fall is noted in 22:15–25, as is Tyre's finally in 23:1–18.

In sum, while it is indeed true that Isaiah has an eye for Judah's sins and circumstance, he, likewise, has his eyes on others'. Not only that, but as we shall see, he looks beyond his day and toward a distant point in time. *He looks over the gloomy horizon and sees a day when Judah will be regenerated and, with her, the world.*

"Comfort ye, comfort ye My people" is his opening in 40:1, followed by, "Speak comfort to Jerusalem, and cry unto her, that her warfare is accomplished, that her iniquity is pardoned; for she hath received from the LORD's hand double for all her sins" (v. 2). "Fear not; for I have redeemed thee," is the word in 43:1, with the reminder that at days' end, "thou art Mine." In 44:1, Jacob is "My servant" and is referred to as "chosen"; reference to God's future "blessing upon thine offspring" follows fast in verse 3. After all, He says in verses 21–22: "O Israel, thou shalt not be forgotten by Me. I have blotted out, like a thick cloud, thy transgressions." Furthermore, verse 28 states: "Jerusalem, 'Thou shalt be built; and to the temple, Thy foundation shall be laid.'"

He who—if our memory serves correctly—boldly stripped proud women of their finery says in 52:1 that it is time to now "put on thy beautiful garments." He actually expands, saying: "Put on thy beautiful, O Jerusalem, the holy city." Unholy Jerusalem, previously represented as a faithless prostitute in Isaiah's earlier diatribe, is now referred to as "holy" and amply adorned.

Something has changed, has it not?

Judah's coming rejuvenation is noted, as is the fact that it is not just for Judah's benefit. In 56:3, Isaiah is explicit in saying, "Neither let the son of the foreigner…[say] 'The LORD hath utterly separated me from His people.'" Even "unto them" says He, *"within My walls [I will give them] a place and a name"* that shall not be cut off (v. 5, emphasis added). To the "sons of the foreigner[s]" (v. 6), God promises that "even them *will I bring to My holy mountain"* (v. 7, emphasis added); for God's "house shall be called an *house of prayer for all peoples,"* and "the LORD GOD who gathereth the outcasts of Israel" will likewise be "gathered unto him" (vv. 7–8, emphasis added). Interesting.

The new day that is prophetically realized in the aforementioned passages is likewise presaged in the earlier part of Isaiah. In 2:2, Isaiah opens his initially disturbing book with: "It shall come to pass in the last days, that the mountain of the LORD's house shall be established…and all *nations shall flow unto it"* (emphasis added)—a word that includes the Arab nations and peoples round about. "Many people shall come"—not just Jewish people—and these will then say, "'Come ye, and let us go up to the mountain of the LORD, to the house of the God of Jacob; and He will teach us His ways, and we will walk in His paths;' for out of Zion shall go forth the law, and the word of the LORD from Jerusalem" (v. 3). That Judah's warfare is over—and the world's too, for that matter—is noted in what follows, in verse 4: "They shall beat their swords into plowshares, and their spears into pruning hooks; nation shall not lift up sword against nation, neither shall they learn war anymore."

Oh what a day! May the Lord hasten its coming—as with the attendant global regeneration and salvation! Until that day dawns, we would do well to work the question: *How might Judeo-Christian sorts make peace with our estranged Arab friends?* This question will be the object of our attention in that which follows.

OUTREACH AND EVANGELISM

We have already considered the interrelationship between Israelites and their Arab neighbors—who surround Israel like a crescent. It seems to us that the essence of the Jewish-Arab quandary is intrinsically spiritual and is not in any way simply a squabble over a little piece of land, claims to the contrary notwithstanding. If the problem is spiritual, then the answer is, too. How, then, can we deal with the problem spiritually, if not materially? Moreover, if we assume that the problem is inherently spirited along by Islamic dogma, then how can we deal with Islam as a belief system and spiritual force? Simply put: How will the Prince of Peace bring peace and healing? To understand this, we need to explore "salvation" in an Islamic-related context.

WHY WE SHOULD REACH
OUT TO MUSLIM PEOPLES

Islam casts its dark shadow not only over Jewish-Arab relationships but over the entire world. What we now call 9/11 was and still is vivid evidence of this. Israel is surrounded by approximately 325 million Arabs and Arab confederates, of which at least 315 million are Muslims. Muslims comprise almost 20 percent of the global population, while Catholics, in comparison, are only 17.4 percent. So, if the current world population is about 7 billion, Muslims alone are about 1.4 billion. By virtue of their outstanding population, they have control over many Middle East nations, the Far East, and a few European countries like Bosnia, Albania, and Turkey. The sheer size of the population beckons us to come to better terms with the religion and its adherents.

Issues with bulk aside, given that since 9/11 most global problems are centered upon Islamic terrorism, detecting terrorists, and curtailing their activities, the need to come to terms with Islam is the more pressing. Beyond this, and more importantly for our immediate purposes, Jesus dying for these billions of helpless and hopeless souls born into Islam imposes upon those sensitive to His interests a mandate to wrestle with the question of how we might reach them. The mandate—"Go ye, therefore, and teach all nations, baptizing them in the name of the Father, and of the Son, and of the Holy Spirit, Teaching them to observe all things whatsoever I have commanded you; and lo, I am with you always, even unto the end of the age" (Matt. 28:20)—beckons believers their way, doesn't it? And, if we may add, it is also our mandate to "show forth the praises of Him who hath called you [and them] out of darkness into His marvelous light" (1 Pet. 2:9). This a given, the principal question is simple: How?

What may take you by surprise is that the "praises of Him" (Jesus) are not only attested by the Judeo-Christian Bible, but also by the Muslims' holy scripture, the Koran. Believing we'd do well to become acquainted with the Muslims' view of Jesus, a cursory glance at some of their relevant passages is in order here.

THE KORAN'S TESTIMONY OF JESUS

Before attempting to build spiritual bridges to Muslims, it is important to know the Koran's testimony about Jesus. For example, the Koran testifies to the following (with emphasis added):

His Virgin Birth: "And Marium [Mary]...kept her chastity, and we *breathed into her of Our Spirit*, and she believed in the word of her Lord and was obedient" (Sura of "The Prohibition" [#66] v. 12). Notice here that the Koranic text acknowledges that Jesus was birthed by the Spirit of God.

He is God's Word: "But Christ Jesus, the son of Marium, is God's apostle, *His Word… and a Spirit of Him*" (Sura of "The Women" [#4] v. 171). With no need for any further comments, this, in essence, is a testimony of Jesus' divinity.

He would be a sign: "Says your Lord, 'It is easy for me; *and we will make him a sign unto people* and mercy from us; and the matter is decreed'" (Sura of "Marium" [#19] v. 21).

He is the peacemaker par excellence: "And peace be on me the day I was born, the day I die, and the day I will be raised alive" (Sura of "Marium" [#19] v. 33).

He Himself is a statement of truth: "This is Jesus the son of Marium, the oracle of truth, about whom they argue" (Sura of "Marium" [#19] v. 34).

He is a Creator: "And [Jesus is] an apostle to the sons of Israel, [saying] 'I have come to you with *a sign from your Lord.… I create* for you, out of dust, the form of a bird, and I will breathe in it, and it will be a [living] bird according to Allah's will. And I will heal the blind and the leper, and will raise the dead by Allah's will, and I will tell you what you eat and what you treasure in your homes, and this is indeed for you a sign if you believe'" (Sura of "Family of Imran" [#3] v. 49). "O Jesus, Son of Mary, remember My favor on you when I supported you with the Holy Spirit so that you spoke to the people in the cradle and in maturity;

and when I taught you writing wisdom, the Torah and the gospel" (Sura of "Table" [#5] v. 110). It is noteworthy here that the Koranic testimony indicates that Jesus was birthed by the breath of God and that that His ministry was facilitated by the Spirit. *He has miraculous ability:* "And you healed those born blind, and the lepers by My permission, and when you brought forth the dead by my permission" (Sura of "Table" [#5] v. 110).

He possesses the testimony of Mohammad: Narrated by Abu Huraira, the prophet Mohammad says: "When every human being is born, Satan touched him at both sides of his body with his two fingers, except Jesus the son of Mary whom Satan tried to touch but failed" (Hadith 6:324; 54.10.506). This, in essence, is a testimony of Jesus' inherent sinlessness.

In sum, Islam teaches that Jesus is sinless, flawless, born miraculously from a virgin by God's breath, a Spirit of God and a Word from Him, a sign, taught in wisdom, given the Book, verifying the sacred past history, endorsed by the Holy Spirit, and is able to create, heal, raise the dead, and prophesy. *This list of features is not found in any other person, including Mohammad.*

HOW DO MUSLIMS REALLY PERCEIVE JESUS?

Mindful of the above, we do well to ask the following: How do Muslims really perceive Jesus? Believing it is imperative that we understand our Muslim friends' perception of Jesus before attempting to talk to them about Jesus, a brief treatment of this is in order. At the outset, please realize that Muslims are *not* altogether clueless about Jesus. Still, despite the Koranic testimony of

Jesus, His image in their minds is not a wholesome one. At first, the Koranic name of Jesus is altered into "Isa," which, linguistically speaking, does not relate to Jesus in any given way. Second, the aforementioned references aside, there are marked differences between the Bible's Jesus and the Koran's.

By analyzing the rest of the Koranic view of Jesus, one can easily detect that His redemptive work is deliberately obscured. Though a prophet, Jesus does not die for sins in Islam. Redemption by blood unto salvation is *the* very characteristic feature of Mosaic religion and the Christian faith, without which biblical faith is reduced to the level of other worldly religions. If Christianity lacks the blood of Jesus, there really is no real difference between Christianity and Islam. Jesus' blood is not salvific in Islam.

Muslim clerics fear that adherents might find real answers somewhere else and abandon Islam as a consequence. By losing its expansive population, Islam would become no more than a house of cards. In order to counteract any possibility of folks moving from Islam to Christianity by way of conversion, Islam openly (in counter-evangelism) invites Jews and Christians to believe in Mohammad as Allah's last messenger and in the Koran as Allah's final revelation (cf. Suras al-Ma'idah 5:15; al-Hadid 57:28; and an-Nisa' 4:47). Furthermore, *Muslim clerics take pains to hem their population in, with adherents having little to no contact with the broader culture, the world beyond the clerics' control.*

HOW DO MUSLIMS REALLY LOOK AT CHRISTIANS?

The Koranic text bluntly and unabashedly commands Muslims not to establish relationships with either Jews or Christians. Sura of the "Table" (#5) v.51 says, "O ye who believe! Take not the Jews and the Christians for your friends and protectors: They are but friends and protectors to each other. And he amongst you that turns to them (for friendship) is of them." It would have been a passive form of hostility if the Koran stopped at this point, but the Koran, again unabashedly, commands an aggressive form of hostility toward Jews and Christians. Sura al-Tuba (#9) verse 29 says:

> Fight those who believe not in Allah [god of Islam] nor the Last Day, nor hold that forbidden which has been forbidden by Allah [god of Islam] and His Messenger [Mohammad], nor embrace the religion of Truth [Islam], (even if they are) of the People of the Book [i.e., Jews and Christians], until they pay the Jizya [poll-tax] with willing submission, and feel themselves subdued [rather, humiliated].

In other words, *the Koran commands Muslims to look down at Jews and Christians should they refuse to embrace Islam, exact all the possible money from them, and humiliate them.* The list of Koranic verses and parts of the Hadith collections that follow this ominous stream are numerous.

HOW MUSLIMS ONCE VIEWED
THE BIBLE RESPECTFULLY

In its present form, the Scripture is not construed as an authoritative religious source in modern-day Islam, given Islam's alleging that Jews and Christians changed its original form—a form that is said was really Islamic at the start.

The New Testament's claim notwithstanding, the Islamic prophet Jesus did not die on the cross for people's salvation. The Koran denies Jesus' crucifixion, saying: "They declared: 'We have put to death the Messiah, Jesus son of Mary, the apostle of Allah.' They did not kill him, nor did they crucify him, but they thought they did" (Sura of "Women" [# 4] v.157).

As noted, Muslims are indoctrinated into thinking the Bible in its Jewish and Christian forms is corrupt. In accordance, whatever we claim using our Bible is already deprived of its credibility in their minds' eyes. Interestingly, however, and to the surprise of most, the Koranic stand actually affirms the authenticity of the Bible—a point worth underscoring. While many Muslims today say the Bible is corrupt, nothing in the Koran actually supports this allegation. Not one word in the Koran teaches that the Scriptures of the Jews and Christians have been perverted by men. In fact, the opposite is true: The Koran actually supports the Bible. For example:

> *And He [God] will instruct him [Jesus] in the Scriptures* and in wisdom, the Torah and the gospel. And [make Him] an apostle to the sons of Israel. He will say: "I bring you a sign from your Lord." And *verifying of what was before,* the Torah, and to make lawful to you some of the forbidden things [in reference to the ceremonial law]. I bring to you a sign from your Lord, therefore fear God and obey me. (Sura of "The Family of Imran" [#3] vv. 48–50, emphasis added)
>
> And we [God] revealed the Torah, in which there is guidance and light, and with which the prophets make judgment...[judgment that belongs to] the rabbis and priests because *they preserved (kept) the divine Scripture*

and bore witness to it ...And after them we sent Jesus, the
son of Mary, *verifying what he has already had, the torah,
and we gave to him the gospel, in which there is guidance
and light.* (Sura of "The Food" [#5]) vv. 44–47, emphasis
added)

By analyzing the aforementioned Koranic testimonies, we
find the following: (1) A testimony that the Jews preserved what
we now call the Old Testament (the Hebrew Bible); (2) The content of that Hebrew Bible was verified by God by the time Jesus
arrived on the stage of human history; (3) Both of these statements seal the Hebrew Bible with authenticity and truthfulness
without any charge or even hint of alleged corruption; (4) These
two suras bear testimony that the Gospel (which is used in reference to the New Testament) is divinely inspired; and (5) The
Koranic testimony establishes continuity between the Torah (Old
Testament) and the Gospel (New Testament) in terms of being
guidance and light. In other words, not only the content, but also
the functionality of the entire Bible has been preserved.

"And do not argue with the People of the Book [Jews and
Christians] except by what is best [which means, "be courteous"]
...and say [urging Muslims], '*We believe in what was inspired to us
and to you, and that Our God and your God is One*'" (Sura of "The
Spider" [#29] v. 46, emphasis added).

By looking at this particular quotation, one will find that up
to the time of Mohammad, Muslims were urged to believe in the
entire Bible with both its testaments. Obviously, no one invites
one's followers to believe in something under the suspicion of
corruption or doubted integrity. "If you were in doubt as to what
We [God] have revealed unto you," said Mohammad, "then ask
those who have been reading the Book [Bible] from before you"

(Sura of "Yunus [= John]" [# 10] v. 94). By looking at this Koranic verse, one cannot help but notice that the Bible formed the frame of reference regarding theological inquiries Muslims might have made. Again, one cannot recommend a given book to be a reference without having absolute certainty about the integrity of its content.

In sum, it is to be observed that: (1) The Koran declares the totality of Scripture (Old and New Testaments) to be the Word of God and "guide to the believers"; (2) Muslims are under obligation to confess their faith in *all* the books of former Scriptures; (3) These books already existed before and during the time of Mohammad; and (4) Nowhere does the Koran say that these Scriptures were corrupt.

Is it not interesting that the Muslims' Koran has nothing substantial to say about the corruption of the Scriptures—the source-book of the largest religion on earth? During Mohammad's time, Christian influence was known in Mecca. There were Jewish and Christian settlements in Hijaz, and Christianity ringed the Saudi peninsula. Yet not one negative word was uttered by "Allah" concerning those Scriptures. It is also obvious from the totality of these verses that Mohammad truly believed the Bible to be God's Word. Repeatedly, he confirmed the Bible. There is no mention of a "partial" confirmation. There was no statement that said, "Confirm only that which I agree with." Instead, *Mohammad addressed the Scripture of the people of the Book, confirming its integrity, truthfulness, and accuracy.*

In what follows, we'll sample medieval and modern Islamic scholarship and ascertain how the anti-Scriptural bias entered the mainstream of Islamic thought, despite its having no origin in the religion's founding prophet.

Medieval Islamic scholarship: Muslim scholars, polemicists, and traditionalists—like al-Tabari, al-Bukhari, al-Ghazali (died in AD 1111), and Fakhruddin Razi (died in AD 1209)—never charged the Bible with corruption. For example, al-Tabari, in his *The Book of Religion and Empire*,[75] says, "As to the Gospel which is in the hands of the Christians, the greater part of it is the history of the Christ, His birth, and His life." It is certainly noteworthy that he did not make any allegation of corruption or twisting—as is the norm in Islamic circles today. Quite the opposite, he expressed his appreciation for the historical part of the Bible, which indirectly affirms its authenticity. This testimony by itself is enough to cover the time span from the seventh to the twelfth centuries AD as void of any alleged corruption of the Bible.

Modern Islamic scholarship: Let's consider Imam Muhammad ʿAbdu, the nineteenth-century-AD Egyptian grand jurist. The position of a grand jury in and by itself secures the highest possible Islamic legal office—not only in Egypt, but extending to the four corners of the Islamic world (as Egypt was and still contains the "Harvard" of Islamic scholarship and Islamic religious studies). In other words, this grand jurist's voice is an authoritative one. His well-attested scholarship reached far and beyond the contours of his time and space. In his *Jesus, the Life of the Messiah*,[76] Imam Muhammad ʿAbdu said: "The charge of corruption of the Biblical texts *makes no sense at all.* It would not have been possible for Jews and Christians everywhere to agree on changing the text. Even if those in Arabia had done it, the difference would have been obvious between their book and those in other parts." A statement like this coming from a matchless scholar and grand jurist like him should utterly refute any charge of biblical corruption raised by any Muslim anytime, anywhere.

We believe it is of utmost importance that whenever a Christian outreaches to a Muslim, he or she should be able to respond to any accusation regarding the integrity of our Scripture as our only reliable source of the salvation story. Therefore, knowing the aforementioned refutations is important. However, if the Muslim keeps on reiterating the charges of corruption he or she has heard somewhere, then the Christian can ask: When did the biblical text get corrupted? Was it before or after Mohammad's affirmation? If before, then Mohammad's testimony is a false one; if after, then when? Where? Why? How? By whom? In what way? Where is the original, then?

WHERE DID THE ISLAMIC CHARGE OF TEXTUAL CORRUPTION COME?

As Muslims learned more and more about the true teachings of the Bible, they realized that the Koran and the New Testament were not truly compatible. One had to be wrong. Differences were too concrete to be glossed over as mere "misunderstandings" or "misinterpretations." Muslims believed that Jesus spoke the Gospel. Their dilemma was how both the Koran and the New Testament could be true if they completely contradict each other on many fundamental doctrines. They were in a quandary, and understandably so. Consequently, they chose to attack the integrity of the Bible in order to protect their scripture. They, of course, had no real alternative. It was the easy way out for the so-called Muslim scholars to fool their fellow Muslims. When it comes to the Bible, most Muslims are clueless—as are many Jews and Christians, sadly. Muslims just reiterate what they hear from their sheikhs (leaders). As a rule, they do not critically reflect on what their teachers tell them, nor do they analyze what their Koran teaches on the subject. Instead of scrutinizing what the Bible teaches, they follow the easy way and borrow from the work of others who have already attacked the Bible's credibility, given their concern that it attacks their own.

Writing in his *Dear Abdullah*, Gerhard Nehls says:

> The [notion of the] Bible being corrupt was first promoted by ibn Khazem (died in 1064 AD) as a means of avoiding the obvious contradictions between the Bible and the Koran. Believing that the Koran could not possibly have been corrupted, he then assumed that it was the Bible that underwent textual modifications. This, he felt, must have been the case.[77]

Knowing what Muslims believe is not, and should not, be dissociated from what they feel. This raises the next question: *How do Muslims feel?*

Insecure!

Insecurity is a term that explains much of the inner feelings of Muslims. Could there possibly be something wrong with their belief system and their prophet, Mohammad? This dread thought prompts anxiety.

A Moroccan woman in her twenties—who had already converted from Islam to Christianity—shared that she always thought that neither Islam nor Mohammad was true…Mohammad's life was amply indicative of inferiority. Fearing cultural alienation and possible punitive acts, however, she kept her thoughts to herself, so long as she remained in her country of provenance, Morocco. When she moved to France to pursue a college degree, she found the audacity to share her feelings and thoughts with her close high school girlfriend who followed the same academic pursuit. Surprisingly enough, her girlfriend had the same thoughts and feelings. From that point, another pursuit started—a pursuit after truth.

Is this simply an individual case that does not express the majority? We think not! A standard expression of Muslims' subconscious anxiety is their unsettled question: *Is Islam a true religion or not?* Sometimes this question comes out in an atmosphere enshrouded with confidentiality, and other times in an atmosphere charged with defiance. Irrespective, it is still a haunting expression of their lack of assurance in what they believe.

Many of us can recall with certainty when Jesus was in His most vulnerable moment on the cross. There, He was naked, exposed, beaten, and whipped—with nails driven through His flesh. He, however, had all the security, authority, and ability to give the repentant thief an *explicit promise* to be with Him in paradise. The promise had a temporal element to it that made it all the more *definite:* "*Today* shalt thou be with Me in the paradise" (Luke 23:43). The Koran, by contrast, has never given Muslims any explicit promise that they would have eternal bliss. In fact, Mohammad himself—as their prophet and guide—was uncertain whether Allah would eventually save him or not. Look at this excerpt from the Koran:

> Or do they say, "He has forged it?" Say: "If I have forged it, *you have no power to help me against Allah.* He knows very well what you are pressing upon; He suffices as a witness between me and you; He is the All-forgiving, the All-compassionate." Say: "I am not an innovation among the Messengers, *and I know not what shall be done with*

me or with you. I only follow what is revealed to me; I am only a clear warner." (Sura of "al-Ahqaf" [# 46] vv. 8–9, emphasis added)

"I know not what shall be done with me or you." This reference and many like it should trouble many Muslims. If Mohammad himself, the very founder and prophet of the religion of Islam, was uncertain where he would spend eternity, how then can any Muslim know where he will spend it? If the leader is consciously blind when it comes to his eternal fate, how would it be for the followers? Beyond extending a promise that suicide bombers will inherit paradise, little is held out to assure others.

WHAT TYPES OF MUSLIMS WILL AN OUTREACHING CHRISTIAN ENCOUNTER?

This is a significantly important question because not all Muslims are alike. Let's consider some of the basic types of Muslims that one may encounter today.

Sincere fundamentalists: These can also be called "true seekers of Allah." They are preoccupied with their religious duties and memorize the entire Koran and the teachings of Mohammad in the Hadith. Their ultimate goal is to replicate the life of Mohammad on earth, expressed in the way they dress, bathe, groom, pray, eat, etc. Pietistic to the core, they tend to be backward and reactionary in their worldview. The picture of *Ayatollah Khomeini, the deceased spiritual leader of Iran, comes to mind when referring to this group, him being a probable representative of this type.*

Political fundamentalists: These are craftier than many others. In fact, they are very much like a chameleon by nature. They have some of the external features of the former group, but also with some differences. Not nearly as otherworldly as the pietistic sorts, they are more prone to garner political power, and can fairly be called "power-seekers." They can be very manipulative, possessing as they do a hidden agenda in their hearts. They look pious on the outside, but the inside is something else. The image of the Iranian president, Mahmoud Ahmadinejad, comes to mind when referring to this group, him being an ample representative of political fundamentalists.

Ignorant fundamentalists: These are the masses you see on TV demonstrating, burning flags, vandalizing properties, and shouting, "Death to Israel and death to America!" etc. They barely know anything about the religion of Islam, with the exception of a few verses that call them to jihad. Their pent-up anger is given a religious voice and expression in the religion of Islam. They are extremely violent and can be triggered at any time. The religious virtues of integrity, piety, and character building are not matters of concern to the members of this group. They seem to be principally driven by someone else and/or by external stimuli, and not by a well-formed spiritual worldview.

Well-informed moderates: Diplomats, university professors, and high-profile figures who are often highly educated are the representatives for this particular group. They usually distance themselves from fundamentalist Islam, reckoning association with it as an undesirable stigma. Nevertheless, they maintain loyalty to Islam in a moderate and perfunctory way. Their lifestyle is a blend of conservatism and secularism. They understand that this lifestyle is contradictory to the fundamental teachings of Islam, yet they have already made up their minds and made their decisions. If they are found in the position of power or authority, they will be in a continuous struggle to keep the political fundamentalists at bay—in a respectful manner, if possible, knowing that they themselves are in danger should they incur their displeasure.

Secular moderates: These folk care less about religion than their more spiritual contemporaries, and prefer to live out their lives as they like. They are often highly approachable and peaceful. They are not usually given to religious duties or theological thoughts, and will be embarrassed by how their religiously minded associates carry themselves.

Sunni or Shi'ite: This distinction takes us to another level. It is not a categorization like the aforementioned types, and the differences are way too complicated to be discussed in this volume. What may concern you, as you seek to build bridges and spread the Gospel, is that the Shi'ites (who comprise only 10 percent of the total Muslims' population) believe in the idea of the *Mahdi* (an Arabic adjective meaning "the rightly guided one"), who will come out from his hiding place to bring about global justice in the end of days. In case you are not familiar with the history, origin, and development of the Shi'ite branch of Islam, this idea is basically a Messianic concept stolen from the Judeo-Christian belief system. It is a forfeited version of the biblical prophecy, attesting that Jesus will come back in a millennial reign to bring about justice and righteousness on the earth.

WHAT KIND OF ATTITUDE SHOULD YOU HAVE WHEN APPROACHING MUSLIMS WITH THE GOSPEL?

The way one presents the Gospel message has an effect on its impact. Its presentation is not dissociated from the content, and the nobility of the content does not give us permission to present it sloppily, thinking that the content should take care of everything and so we shouldn't worry. We have to realize that Muslims are people whose lives are built and centered on their belief system(s). Islam, to them, is the core of *everything*...yes, *everything*. So, when speaking with them about religion, whether you realize it or not, know that you are touching their central nerve, if not shaking the foundations of their very beings. They are going to be sensitive, and perhaps a bit defensive if not offensive.

Miracles happen, however, and more and more Muslim peoples are opening themselves to the Gospel. This, in fact, is happening in unprecedented numbers today. Something of a revival is sweeping through Islamic lands, with reports of miraculous conversions coming in by the droves.

Still, barring supernatural intervention—which, once again, is happening—helping Muslims see the light of Christ's cross may take time...a rather *long* time. Why? With the centrality that their faith has in their lives, a turnaround can be very difficult and time consuming. Conversion bids them to reexamine their entire personal and corporate past, look squarely and boldly at the present, and consider the kind of future they will have under a new faith, one that will prompt dissociation from kinship and social networks. Each one of these is a major undertaking, with less-than-desirable social ramifications. It takes great courage for a Muslim to differentiate from his or her tribal traditions! Accordingly, any attempt of accelerating the process or exercising some sort of pressure may result in permanent damage to the person and to your relationship with him or her.

Acceptance: As a rule of thumb, rejection builds walls—and moderate and secular Muslims know they are on the other side of the wall. It is a matter of fact that the rejection of Muslims, in general, has especially escalated since 9/11, for understandable reasons. They feel it.

Mindful now that there are various types of Muslims, we can more readily realize that not every Muslim is a potential terrorist. In more practical terms, preconceived judgment is always felt by the target, and in a way that can jeopardize bridge-building endeavors. Know that *most of your Muslim friends, neighbors, and co-workers will let their guard down once they feel accepted and are assured that they are not perceived in a negative way.*

Humility: Those who embrace Yeshua (Jesus) have the assurance of the Holy Spirit within, and have abiding conviction that what they believe in is absolute truth and that there is no way to God except through the blood of Israel's Messiah. Muslims, on the contrary, really do not have this kind of assurance. The negative side of this assurance is the human temptation to behave arrogantly while communicating the message of the Gospel—something Christians can be all too guilty of. On the other hand, worth noting is that humility here does not mean subordination. There is a fine balance between confidence and humility, as Jesus demonstrated in His life and ministry; we do well to prayerfully consider how to balance this in our own lives and presentation.

Sensitivity: We do well to prayerfully and carefully approach discussions of spiritual things sensitively, mindful that Muslims feel defensive about their lifelong belief system—Islam. Mocking their belief system or any of its components does not usually bring any positive results. In fact, it is provocative, if not vexing, to them. By way of application, our one-on-one conversations should avoid harsh criticism or piercing words. Treating people with respect is always a good rule; we believe the Gospel will get more mileage out of those minded to remember the principle.

WHAT ARE SOME AVAILABLE
BRIDGE-BUILDING METHODS?

While discussing this part, we recommend that you exercise discernment and prayer before deciding which one you should use. God may even guide you to use a method not listed here.

Using media: All media-related tools—especially *The Jesus Film* and *The Passion of the Christ*—are very powerful evangelistic tools for many reasons. First, the message is communicated in a moving picture, which in itself is a penetrating method because of its visual component. Second, one can watch these movies in the privacy of his or her own home, which does not expose the audience to any sort of public embarrassment. Third, it is a mono-communicative way with no anticipation of participation by the audience, which alleviates any possible tension. Fourth, there is no argumentation, which practically means folks can "let their guard down!"

Healing crusades: Jesus, we are told, drew an inordinate amount of initial interest and support on the heels of His various healing and miracle campaigns. *Miracles captured the imagination—then as now—and tended to galvanize support for the miracle-worker who showed Himself personally unbounded by the conventional laws of nature.* Sheer infatuation with mysterious and unexplained phenomena draws peoples' energies toward the Gospel—today as yesterday—rendering one miracle to, in certain respects, be better than one hundred sermons.[78]

The Bible: Never forget that the Bible is God's dynamite for salvation, as it is written: "So shall My word be that goeth forth out of My mouth; it shall not return unto Me void, but it shall accomplish that which I please, and it shall prosper in the thing whereto I sent it" (Isa. 55:11). Many lives of Muslim converts were unshackled just by merely reading the Bible. Without prior exposure to a preacher, teacher, sermon, or Sunday school class, or by using any aiding materials, God is reaching into Muslims' hearts through Bible reading. Hand them Bibles in their own language, and see what God will do!

One-on-one conversation: We prefer to call this "conversation" rather than "evangelism." By this we mean that it is preferable to let the conversation come naturally, without forcing it. When you befriend a Muslim and he or she feels secure, religious discussion will open up spontaneously as the topic of most interest to them.

Your lifestyle: Muslims believe that Christianity is not only corrupt, but that it is also corrupting. They are wired to believe that Christians and Jews are more or less immoral, decadent, idolaters, and that Christians are "pig eaters," which simply means they are "defiled." Your blameless lifestyle can refute this idea without much debating. It is your lived-out testimony that can speak better than a thousand words.

Invite Muslims to the church—or Messianic synagogue:[79] Many Muslims believe that New Testament congregations are "brothels," where Christians drink "wine" (of the communion) and have illicit sex. This misconception can be challenged by a simple invitation to the congregation or to a Bible study group. With all this misconception in the background, you never know the kind of response or result of this simple invitation. You may be reluctant, understandably concerned about a turndown. But believe it or not, many Muslims have come to faith based on a simple invitation like this. I (Ihab Griess) can recall a story of an Iranian Shiite who fled from Iran to the USA. A few months after arriving in America, he somehow responded positively to an invitation to attend a meeting in a Baptist church. As he narrated to me personally, he accepted Christ upon listening to the very first song that night. It was his first time to attend a church ever, and it was his last time to attend as a Muslim.

Satellite programs: This technology is matchless in reaching the curtained countries with the Gospel through Christian programs. Preaching the Gospel via physical presence is very dangerous in most of the Middle Eastern countries like Iran, Saudi Arabia, Libya, Algeria, Morocco, etc. The best, safest, and most effective way is through Christian satellite programs. So, you can do them a favor by guiding them to these programs. One must keep in mind, however, that, unlike cultures where ideas are regulated and not freely expressed, Christian television is so diverse that not every program should be construed as being representative of what it means to be authentically Christian.

Christian websites: These function as effectively as Christian TV, if the targeted people have Internet access—as many do.

Miraculous appearances: That God is moving in a supernatural way and miraculously getting into the hearts of Muslim peoples is attested the world over. Seems that God is doing something man can't: Reaching His children who are hard to reach. As much as Jewish people are coming to faith, Muslims are coming en masse—an extension of the love of a miracle-working God.

WHY SHOULD MUSLIM PEOPLE—AND ALL PEOPLE, AS A RULE—CHOOSE JESUS?

You may have already asked this question if you are still a follower of Judaism or Islam, or even a secular person: *Why should I believe in Jesus?* Let us respond to you with the following points:

1. Jesus—"Yeshua" in Hebrew, as is our preference—is the only One born with a prophecy pointing to Him. ("Therefore the Lord Himself shall give you a sign; Behold, the virgin shall conceive, and bear a Son, and shall call His name Immanuel," according to Isaiah 7:14.)
2. He is the only One born to a virgin.
3. He is the only One who could debate theology scholars at the age of twelve and confound them (according to Luke 2:41–50).
4. He is the only One who lived out a completely blameless life with not one sin or mistake held against Him ("holy, harmless, undefiled, separate from sinners," according to Hebrews 7:26).

5. He is the only One who performed matchless miracles that made His enemies admit that He came from above. ("Rabbi, we know that Thou art a teacher come from God; for no man can do these miracles that Thou doest, except God be with Him," according to John 3:2.)

6. He is the only One who dared to open His mouth and say, "Which one of you convicteth Me of sin?" (John 8:46) without a hint of arrogance or false pretense.

7. He is the only One who dared to speak of Himself, saying, "I Am the way, the truth, and the life" (John 14:6).

8. He is the only One who yielded Himself to death and gave His life by His own choice. ("Therefore doth My Father love me, because I lay down My life, that I might take it again. No man taketh it from Me, but I lay it down of Myself. I have power to lay it down, and I have power to take it again," according to John 10:17–18.)

9. He is the only One with a vivid picture of His crucifixion depicted seven hundred years before the event, according to Isaiah 53.

10. He is the only One who predicted His resurrection and set the time for it. ("For as Jonah was three days and three nights in the belly of the great fish, so shall the Son of man be three days and three nights in the heart of the earth," according to Matthew 12:40.)

11. He is the only One who conquered His own grave and raised Himself from the dead. ("Destroy this temple, and in three days I will raise it up," according to John 2:19.)

12. He is the only One who maintained presence on the earth for forty days after His resurrection. ("To whom

He also showed Himself alive after His passion by many infallible proofs, being seen by them forty days, and speaking of things pertaining to the kingdom of God," according to Acts 1:3.)

13. He is the only One who promised to come back from the dead. ("I go to prepare a place for you. And if I go and prepare a place for you, I will come again, and receive you unto Myself, that where I am, there ye may be also," according to John 14:2b–3.)

As James Allan Francis once noted in his poem "One Solitary Life," Jesus never wrote a book with His own hand. He never held a political or religious office. He fathered no family. He owned no home. He did not go to college. He never visited an enormous city. He never traveled more than two hundred miles from the place where He was born. He did none of the things that usually accompany greatness. He had no real human credentials to speak of. He was only thirty-three when the tide of public opinion turned against Him. His friends ran away from Him. One of them denied Him outright. He was turned over to His enemies and went through the mockery of an unjust trial. He was nailed to a cross between two thieves. While He was dying, His executioners gambled for His garments, the only property He had after thirty-three years of living. When He was dead, He was laid in a borrowed grave through the pity of a friend. Twenty centuries have come and gone, and today *He is the central figure of the human race.* All the armies that ever marched, all the navies that ever sailed, all the parliaments that ever sat, all the kings that ever reigned, combined, have not affected the life of man on this earth as much as this one solitary, special life.

Jesus never held a sword or led an army. He never so much

as raised His voice against the Roman occupiers of His country. He never marshaled the power of government to enforce social changes. Most renowned leaders have been wealthy, but Jesus owned little and lived with the poor. Lastly, all great world leaders were famous during their lifetime, but are dead now. Jesus, by contrast, died as a criminal and was executed on a cross, but His inglorious death was the birth of the Messianic Jewish movement—what we call Christianity today.

Jesus of Nazareth is by far the greatest person in all of history. He did not pursue the agendas that made others great, but He still towers above them all. He turned the world upside down as no one had done before or has done after Him. Now one-third of the world population calls themselves His followers, Christians, and even those who do not follow Him still experience the impact He had, has, and will have on the world. *This observation alone sets Him aside from all others*[80]—and on a plain well distinguished from the Islamic platform with its sullied and extremely abusive history.

TESTIMONIES FROM THE SONS OF ISAAC AND FROM THE SONS OF ISHMAEL

As much as the Messianic Jewish movement—called "Christianity"—historically and chronologically comes between Judaism and Islam, Jesus stands between the sons of Isaac and the sons of Ishmael. If we hear His voice correctly, we believe that He is calling them—us!—into a family reunion, and that God wants to bring both right between His loving arms. In the past, the Messiah alone was able to break down the walls of hostility that separated the Jews from the pagan world. Today, it is also the Messiah alone who is capable of bringing all the sons of Abraham together, tearing down the walls of hatred and hostility. It is not a matter of politics! Politics and politicians have failed to do it—and will fail. The true answer is in the hand of the One born from the seed of Abraham, yet who existed before him.

In closing this chapter, and just before closing the book, we would like to present to you three real-life testimonies. The first is of one of the sons of Isaac, the second is of one of the sons of Ishmael, and the third combines a so-called Palestinian and a Jew who, together, give an extraordinary testimony.

I. Avi Mizrachi—A Jewish Son of Isaac

My name is Avi Mizrachi from Tel Aviv. I was born in Joppa from a Sephardic Jewish family that came to Israel from Bulgaria. I was raised on Jewish tradition, but was not really very religious. We ate kosher food, celebrated all the biblical Jewish feasts, observed all holidays, studied the Hebrew language and the Hebrew Bible, took the matriculation exam, etc. We did not think much about God. Yes, we believed in Him, His existence, and His created order, but had no relationship to speak of.

I graduated from school and served for four years in the Israeli army. Then, I decided to come to America in 1984. At that time, I was not thinking about anything except having fun, making money, and living my life. But God had a different plan for my life.

While in America in 1984, I stopped by Florida to visit my sister only to find out that she had become a Christian. On my first Sunday in America, my sister challenged me to go and visit her church. I responded positively only because she had challenged me, but I did not really want to go. "What would I do in a church anyway?" I wondered, "for I am a Jew." I had seen Christians in Israel—monks and nuns in monasteries; so, I decided to check out how different it was in the States, only to be shocked.

I did not expect what I saw—many young people singing and worshipping. They were singing with all their hearts. I realized that they really meant what they were doing. They had something I did not have. The pastor delivered a very simple message that day. The content was that God was a loving God and He wanted to be in relationship with us. Despite the simplicity of the message, I was shocked. God is a loving Father. What? Only then did I realize that I did not really know God, and that I was a sinner. I started crying. I realized my need for forgiveness, and for the Messiah who took the sins of the world. Right there and then, I made a decision to follow Jesus. For the first time in my life, I cried: "Abba, Father, change my life." I felt an instantaneous change in my heart, as so many others have before me.

From that point on, I realized that *that* was what I was looking and searching for. I, a nice Jewish boy, started reading the New Testament—of all things—and, to my surprise, realized that it really was a good Jewish book, written by Jewish disciples. A few days later, I was baptized. Then I decided to come back home, to Israel, after which I started sharing the Gospel with my friends and family. All of that happened within six months.

In Israel, I started meeting together with Jewish and Arab believers. We embraced each other as brothers and worshipped together. Only Jesus could tear down those walls that separated us, and He did!

Today, we have about twenty thousand Messianic Jewish believers in Israel, from all ethnic backgrounds. I believe all of that is because of the faithful Christians from all over the world praying for the peace of Jerusalem. Jesus is the *only* hope for Israel and for the entire Middle East. This is what is happening today in the Middle East. God is bringing Jews and Muslims—the sons of Isaac and the sons of Ishmael—to Yeshua, the Lord Jesus.

II. An Awakening Dream: Mohammad, a Muslim from Saudi Arabia

I was born to a Saudi family, in Saudi Arabia, and lived very close to Mecca. I was raised up under the strict principles and traditions of Islam within the Arab culture. As a teenager, I went to the mosque five times a day in obedience to my parents. One night while I was asleep, I had a horrible dream of being taken down to hell. What I saw there terrified me and brought me real fear. Unfortunately for me, those dreams kept coming back to me almost every night. At one point, I began wondering why I was seeing hell in this manner. Suddenly one day, Jesus appeared to me and said: "Son, I am the way, the truth and the life. And if you would give your life to Me, and follow Me, I would save you from the hell that you have seen."

This came to me as a total surprise, for I did not know who this Jesus was. Of course, He is mentioned in the Koran, in the Sura of Mariam [Mary]. He is stated as one of the prophets, but not as a Savior who could save us from hell. So I started looking out for a Christian who could give me some advice about this Jesus whom I have seen, and possibly give me one of the Christian Holy Books, which I now know as the Bible. But it was a difficult task to get any Christian to speak to me—a Muslim Arab—about Jesus. Christianity is totally banned in Saudi Arabia, and if a Christian is caught witnessing to a Muslim, he could almost be sure that he would be beheaded.

But the Lord led me to an Egyptian Christian who was sick. I prayed for this man's healing and he gave me a Bible. Then I, by myself, started reading the Bible. By this time, Jesus had become a close friend to me. Soon, I started witnessing about my experience that I had with all my family members and friends. The religious authorities were informed that I had converted to Christianity. I was reported by one of my family members.

It is stated in the Koran, if someone would turn away from Islam, he is a traitor to the faith and he should be executed. So I was taken into custody and tortured. They told me that I would be beheaded if I would not turn back to Islam. But I had already made [up] my mind that I would never turn back. So, I told the authorities that I was willing to die for Jesus and that I would never come back to Islam. After much torture and imprisonment, I was sentenced to be beheaded. They appointed a date and time. I responded: "Go ahead and execute me; I am going to heaven to see Jesus. But I pray that what you would do to me would stay in your minds and not give you rest until you come to Jesus."

The appointed day and time for my execution came, and I was waiting with much anticipation with strong faith in Jesus. Generally, executions are carried out on the appointed time and date. But to my amazement, no one showed up to attend to it. One hour lapsed, two hours went by, three hours, and then the whole day passed by and no one showed up. Then two days later, the religious authorities showed up and opened the door and told me: "You demon! Get out from this place!" I noticed that the person who was determined to get me executed was not present when they came to release me. I asked them about him. After much hesitation, they replied that his son had died on the same day they planned to execute me.

Although I continue to go through much persecution, one thing I know is that the Lord's hand is upon me.

III. The Forbidden Peace: Making the Impossible, Possible

The protagonists of this particular amazing, real-life story are Roosevelt (a Jew) and Taiseer (a "Palestinian" Muslim).

Roosevelt was raised on the Kibbutz in a secular Jewish home. As a rebellious teen, he never relented to Jewish orthodoxy. He led an average lifestyle until he joined the Israeli army. Ever since then, one memory remained alive in his heart and mind—suicide bombers are everywhere. In one incident, twenty-three Israeli soldiers from his unit died, some of whom were his very close friends. As a result—for understandable reasons—anger, hatred, and a general and understandable mistrust of all Arabs filled his heart. He dealt with the pain of losing friends in such treacherous ways by consuming large amounts of alcoholic beverages. Feeling hopeless, Roosevelt eventually left his homeland for the USA.

Taiseer arrived to the American mainland too, but twenty years earlier. His position was that the Jews stole his land from him, and he hated Jews deeply for so doing. Taiseer joined the PLO (Palestine Liberation Organization) when he was young in order to fight under the leadership of Arafat. After serving for a few years, he left active PLO service and the Middle East, and made his way to the USA. Though removed from his homeland, his anger and hatred never left him. Despite succeeding in the hospitality business as a restaurant owner and manager, he lived an empty life from the inside. One of his regular customers by the name of Charlie once asked Taiseer if he'd like to go for a short walk and talk. It was then that Charlie tried to introduce Taiseer to Jesus. "Do you want to tell me that a man was the 'Son of God'?" he asked. He continued: "Charlie, I do not believe in this stuff…and I do not even want to go this route."

Taiseer had been a devout Muslim, was raised in a Muslim home by devout Muslim parents, and made several pilgrimage trips to Mecca. But on March 14, 1993, this Muslim man unexpectedly started another journey. Charlie brought his Bible and insisted on putting the Bible between both of them. Taiseer was shaken up, scared, and he literally jumped away. When asked why, Taiseer said: "I cannot touch that…. It is the Word of God!" He never could explain why he said that the Bible was the "Word of God," but somehow he knew it to be the case, despite the fact that modern Muslims are wholeheartedly indoctrinated into believing that it is corrupt. Just placing the Bible in front of him was revelatory enough to unshackle him and lift the heavy burden off his shoulders instantly—one of the many miracles that happens when Muslims hear about Jesus.

Taiseer started reading the Bible, both the Old and New Testaments. He had already realized that he was a descendant of Ishmael. But he was about to find out what we have just been saying throughout this book—*Ishmael was also blessed.*

Without reading *Making Our Peace with the Warriors of the Sand,* he said: "This revelation of Ishmael's blessedness blew me away. Wow! God had already included us in His plan of salvation as well." Later, he commented: "God put on my heart to pray for the Jewish people, even before my own people. I was stunned myself. I used to hate the Jews with passion to the point of going after them to kill them. But soon I started to pray: 'Lord, help the Jews to see you and bring them back to the Promised Land.' Although as a Palestinian I realized what I was saying, it was strongly bubbling within me."

Taiseer added that if Jesus on the cross could forgive so much, He could forgive so little. "Jesus is the model for me," adds Taiseer—as for all of us. Our Jewish friend Roosevelt was destined to come to the same conclusion, but five years later.

A Christian friend invited him to church, and he went. But he came out agitated, filled with questions about what the Bible and God said about the Jews. In seeking answers to his questions, Roosevelt was challenged to read the Bible for himself. It was his first time to come to grips with the abundance of God's love for His people, Israel, as represented therein.

Though distanced by five years, it took a month for each man—Taiseer and Roosevelt—to take the risk and break out of their traditional boundaries to seek after someone else: the One who was forbidden to both, by both families and cultures—Jesus, the Messiah.

Roosevelt commented: "Coming to know Jesus filled my heart with tremendous love, peace, and joy." But could that love displace years of hatred and anger? This was his question. It was hard enough to accept the principle, "love your enemies," in theory alone. Could he do it in practice?

In 2001, Taiseer was invited to share his testimony at an Arab-Jewish Conference in Los Angeles. There at the podium, Roosevelt was slated to share his testimony as well. It was there that both Taiseer, the former Muslim-Palestinian and now Christian, and Roosevelt, the Messianic Jew from Israel, met for the first time. How it would turn out was anyone's guess.

The conference leader asked the audience to divide into groups for prayer. They wept together and prayed for mutual forgiveness and the release of the past pain. From that day on, Taiseer and Roosevelt became very close friends on the personal and familial levels. No one could bring these two formerly fierce enemies into loving relationship and restore the essence of their former brotherhood except the Messiah—the Prince of Peace.

We offer these testimonies up as evidence that a miracle-working God is at work in the world, bringing wholeness and reconciling enemies. His healing estranged parties is a testimony to His Word, as is the emergence of Israel in the modern world.

As with the above, *Israel's emergence as a state among men, and its doing so against all odds, itself, testifies to God's saving[81] power in and for the world.* Scripture states—and in no uncertain terms—that the God of Israel has a love for Israel and that He will watch over His Word to perform it on Israel's behalf. This He will do, however, not simply because He loves Israel—His "chosen" earthly nation among men—but because, by virtue of what He does with Israel, He can show Himself strong in the world on behalf of all men—and this includes Arab men (and women, of course). As much as Israel's rise among men (and women) is deemed providential, so too is the emergence of her adversaries. That friends are emerging like Taiseer, however—and know there are many like him—similarly attests to God's watching over His Word to perform it and His world to heal it.

Today's battle lines are *not* between the European "West" and the Arabic "East," as is often misconstrued. The principal parties to the dispute, Jews and Arabs, are both from the "East." Both are kindred peoples, descended—by their respective philosophical and historical reckonings—from the same father: Abraham. Furthermore, the problem is not as much a contest between *civilizations* as it is between *revelations*.

As we have seen, Mohammed borrowed from Judaism and Christianity and—to his credit at one level—created a hybrid religion that lifted the aspirations and lot of the Arab peoples. Thus construed, the mutant form of Judaism and Christianity developed in Arabia under Mohammed's tutelage. It successfully took hold among peoples of Arab descent, making them the better for it materially in their own estimation. It spread from there. Known as the religion of Islam, this particular strain of religion evolved over time. Save for those who pride themselves as "jihadists," *I wonder if, given the chance, many within the Islamic world today would just as soon come to terms with modern culture than forever rage against it for lack of ability to gain entrance to it.* That the number of Taiseer is growing argues that they would.

Of the 1.92 billion people who are Muslims, only 7 percent would claim to embrace the radical edge of Islam. Though still a sizeable number (and formidable foe if activated), a recent Georgetown-based, systematic study of Muslim peoples turned up that of the 7 percent who pay lip service to martyrdom and the like, the lion's share do just that: pay lip service, and no more. Of those, relatively few are given to performing the dastardly deeds that they ostensibly support, and few raise pom-poms and cheer on homicide bombers as they do it.

Frankly, most shudder—as do we.

Could it be that most Muslims are brainwashed and/or simply "pistol-whipped" into submission by their religious and civil tyrants? Were the floodgates able to swing wide open, and were Muslim peoples given the option of abandoning their religion, hefty segments of the population would likely defect en masse.

If recent Middle East wars are any indicator, where Iraqi soldiers made haste to surrender to US soldiers—their principal objective being to survive the conflict and get out of it with their lives and with their dignity, over any expectation of defeating us—it may well be that, disconcerting saber-rattling aside, *there is reason to approach Islamic peoples with optimism and enthusiasm.*

A recent article from Aaron Klein of WorldNetDaily (taken from the Israeli newspaper *Haaretz*) buttresses the point. It is entitled: "Son of Top Hamas Leader Converts to Christianity" and reproduced in full below.

JERUSALEM—The son of one of the most popular leaders in the Hamas terrorist organization has moved to the U.S. and converted to Christianity, it has emerged.

In an exclusive interview with Israel's *Haaretz* newspaper, Musaab Yousuf, son of West Bank Hamas leader Sheik Hassan Yousef, slammed Hamas, praised Israel, and said he hoped his terrorist father will open his eyes to Jesus and to Christianity.

"I know that I'm endangering my life and am even liable to lose my father, but I hope that he'll understand this and that God will give him and my family patience and willingness to open their eyes to Jesus and to Christianity. Maybe one day I'll be able to return to Palestine and to Ramallah with Jesus, in the Kingdom of God," Musaab said.

Musaab said he previously aided his father with Hamas activities, but he now has affection for Israel and laments Hamas.

"Send regards to Israel, I miss it. I respect Israel and admire it as a country," he says.

"You Jews should be aware: You will never, but never, have peace with Hamas. Islam, as the ideology that guides them, will not allow them to achieve a peace agreement with the Jews. They believe that tradition says that the Prophet Muhammed fought against the Jews and that therefore they must continue to fight them to the death."

Musaab slammed Palestinian society as "an entire society [that] sanctifies death and the suicide terrorists. In Palestinian culture a suicide terrorist becomes a hero, a martyr. Sheiks tell their students about the 'heroism of the shaheeds.'"

Musaab's father is considered the most popular Hamas figure in the West Bank. He is serving a sentence in Israel for planning or involvement in multiple terror attacks, including an infamous 2002 suicide bombing in the school cafeteria of Jerusalem's Hebrew University in which nine students and staff members were killed.

In a statement to the Palestinian Maan news agency, Musaab's brother, Suhaib, strongly denied that Masab Musaab converted to Christianity. But Haaretz stood by its story. The newspaper said it sent a correspondent to the U.S., who met with Musaab for a detailed, in-person interview.

This is but one example—and a high-profile one at that. The aforementioned ones aren't headliner stories but, in truth, they are just as significant and amazing. Truth is, reports are circulating about many thousands upon thousands of individuals of Islamic persuasion miraculously coming to faith, as with Jewish people in Israel, in the States, and around the world. Needless to say, this gives cause for great rejoicing, much as the future promises for the Arab peoples give pause for some much-needed reflection and reassessment by those presently holding to biblical affinities.

CONCLUSION

Coming to Terms with the
Warriors of the Sand

D erived from the Greek word *soteria*, the word "soteriology" in theological nomenclature denotes the doctrine of
salvation. In today's parlance, "evangelical" Christians usually—
and appropriately—speak of salvation in the sense of an individual "making a decision for Christ" and being "born again."
Though attested above and supremely important in its own right,
personal and private religious decisions carried less weight in this
book than do the things that folks on earth will confront later.[82]
Though, for the most part, focus here has been on a broader
view of soteriology—in the global sense and in light of the coming eschatological tomorrow—know that there is nothing in the
authors that wants to diminish the importance of individuals
making decisions for the Lord today. We are wondering, though,
if *the Gospel's interests would be well-served were the church to do a
better job of capturing the imaginations of a generation* by offering
a salvation-telling of the day's news over incessantly pressing for
individuals' privatized concerns while ignoring and/or misinter-
preting the larger picture.

Mindful of the threat that Islamic imperialism imposes upon the world (and not just Israel) on the one hand, and the Gospel's exhortation that we endeavor to be peacemakers in the world on the other, the need to come to terms with ourselves in relation to Muslims and Arabs is a pressing question for our distressing times—as is the time and means by which these problems will finally be solved. So, how can we make our personal peace with the people of the sand—the Arab peoples?

At the outset, it was argued that the Arab-Israeli conflict dates backward to the dawn of biblical revelation and extends forward in time to the oft-anticipated but much-dreaded, futuristic Battle of Armageddon. Mindful that the present in-between times are indeed trying times, and that Arab and Israeli actors factor significantly into trying political dramas with global implications at this time, this book colored today's world news with yesterday's biblical hues in the interest of offering an answer to the question of how Jews and Christians might come to better terms with our Arab cousins.

First, *Making Our Peace with the Warriors of the Sand* countered the incorrect perspective that God uncritically loves the Jewish and Christian peoples and disavows and categorically condemns Arab peoples outright. *Making Our Peace with the Warriors of the Sand* drew upon a variety of biblical narratives to underscore the wonderful and mysterious interplay between Arab and Hebrew cousins in the Jewish and Christian Bibles to make clear that *there is no anti-Arab bias in biblical literature*. It simply does not exist in the Sacred Text, and we prefer that it not lodge in our hearts. While nation-states around Israel draw prophetic fire, the invective focused that way pales in comparison to denunciations of Judeans. As much as God judges both, He is minded to save both, too.

Thinking that we'd do well to counter the disconnectedness and affirm the interconnectedness between the various Arabian and Hebraic families, the authors of *Making Our Peace with the Warriors of the Sand* went back to the early biblical narratives to underscore how Jewish and Arabian peoples come from the very same genetic stock, and how both enjoy God's nuanced "blessings." Similarly, the authors were pleased to show Arabia as something of a favorable place in the New Testament's drama.

After noting how Jewish, Christian, and Arabian cousins interacted in biblical times and dwelt in proximity through the passage of time, this book then considered how *Mohammed's religion and politics left an indelible mark on space and time, and radically altered the interrelationship between the respective groups*—not to mention the world at large.

Worth noting, in our estimation, is the fact that past and present Middle East tensions are *not* rooted in race—given that Jews and Arabs are in effect from the same genetic material; rather, the chasm is philosophical, theological, and/or spiritual—and not material, at all. Since the problems are religious and spiritual in nature, and since the cessation of those problems is presaged in Israel's religious literature, we think it is particularly prudent to examine what the Judeo-Christian religious literature says about it—thus the Bible.

What does it say?

Scripture says that yesterday, sin made its entrance onto the stage of the human drama and, at the start of time, emerged in a place called Eden, from where it defiled humankind. Located in the Middle East, Eden was the place from which sin raised its hoary head yesterday, much as it will again tomorrow—and more precisely at the ragged edge of time. Biblical prophets predicted that forces will be unleashed from the very same region that will facilitate history's all-time most dreaded final conflict: Armageddon. As much as the biblical world focused on the Fertile Crescent at the dawn of human history, it similarly focuses upon it at the dusk—in advance of the Redeemer's reemergence onto the stage of the human drama. This is the Bible's testimony.

Until such time as He comes, Bible readers do well to not cast aspersions on Arab peoples. Let people rise and fall on the basis of their actions, and let's deal with them accordingly from that basis. We are not to discriminate against anyone, period. Because, like Jews, Arabs have promises vouchsafed to them in biblical literature, promises that should be respected—as with the people themselves—we do well to be constrained against the tendency to vilify Arabs as a people. We, of course, have both the right and the mandate to suppress criminals, but we are legitimized in so doing because they are criminals—not because some of the criminals may happen to be Arabs.

While Christian and Jewish people do well to be respectful of Arab peoples, and while we Americans do well to be tolerant of other religions generally (or individuals having no religion at all), we still needn't deceive ourselves and surrender our prerogatives to be suspicious of those who embrace a traditional Islamic worldview. Bible readers are keenly aware that trouble is to emerge in the Middle East at day's end. Driven arguably by a religious vision—one that looks like it's coming in a package called "Islam"—Scripture says that forces will be mobilized that will press against Israel and draw the world into their furies. The requirement to somehow "love" these and other peoples and yet be "on guard" is indeed perplexing, and is a question for our times.

How does one do that? Perhaps Moses can help.

Prior to the initial Israelite conquest of Canaan, a not-so-sheepish Moses gave the following exhortation, which is recorded in Numbers 33:52–53: "Drive out all the inhabitants of the land…destroy all their stone idols…demolish all their high places…dispossess the inhabitants of the land, and dwell therein; for I have given you the land to possess." Sounds aggressive, does it not? Moses' firm words could well be employed as an exhortation to fulfill what was promised to Abraham years prior, when He said: "Unto thy seed descendants I have given this land… the Kenites, and the Kenezzites, and the Kadmonites, And the Hittites, and the Perizzites, and the Rephaim, And the Amorites, and the Canaanites, and the Girgashites and the Jebusites" (Gen. 15:18–21). The absence of any mention of Arabs in this list is worthy of note, as is the fact that when approaching the land of Israel prior to the initial conquest, the children of Israel were instructed to avoid their north Arabian cousins outright. Moses went out of his way to underscore this. *The people of the sand, of the East, were not to be provoked into contention,* being that they, themselves, were related to Israel and that the God of Israel had no "bone to pick" with them. This seems the preferred scenario. Peace seems to be the overriding interest. If rejected, then we go to "Plan B" and contend.

In Deuteronomy 2:9, Moses noted: "The LORD said to me, 'Distress not the Moabites, neither contend with them in battle; for I will not give thee of their land for a possession, because I have given [it] unto the children of Lot for a possession'" (remember that Lot was Abraham's nephew). Similarly, in verses 19–20, He said, "When thou comest near over against the children of Ammon, distress them not, nor meddle with them; for I will not give thee of the land of the children of Ammon any possession." The people of the eastern sands were not to be molested and their land claims were to be respected.

Instructed as he was to avoid such skirmishes, Moses sought peaceful passage in verses 26–30, but was denied in verse 30 and then challenged in verses 32–33. Though the undesired battle went to the Israelites, in verses 34–35 (and they took spoils, in v. 37), Moses accentuated that they did not engage the Ammonites: "Only unto the land of the children of Ammon thou camest not...the LORD our God forbade us"—itself a reminder that the fight was undesirable in the first place. *Were he here today, Moses might well encourage that we would do well to keep our swords in our sheaths till provoked, if provoked.* If it comes to a fight, so be it. The point is that it was not preferred that we wrangle with our north Arabian kinfolk.

While dwelling peacefully with neighbors is the preferred scenario, biblical writers were keenly aware that it was still necessary to bear arms in defense of home and hearth, and that similarly, on the basis of the fact that not all peoples within Israelite society would perform well, a criminal justice system was established to deal with criminal elements. Various crimes met with various punishments—the death sentence being one. While we can and should endeavor to make our peace with Arabian peoples, we are not required to accept belligerence and let criminal conduct go unchecked—from them or anyone. The exhortation to be loving in this world does not necessarily require that every individual in all circumstances surrender his or her prerogative to offer a spirited defense and not ask for redress for grievances. Biblical justice affords individuals these rights, and thus provides a bulwark against the unbridled criminal forces of anarchy and oppression, irrespective of whether they come in secular or religious dress— Jewish, Christian, or Muslim.

While we should be willing to bear petty insults and "turn the other cheek" every now and again, we have no personal reli-

gious qualms about bearing arms when necessary. Being particularly struck by the requirement to—for as much as possible—be
kindly disposed toward Arab peoples, as with all peoples generally, is thus not born out of any sheepishness that we know of,
much as it is out of a biblically-based theological conviction.

*Should kinder gestures and peaceful people meet with resistance
and aggression, we have no problem adjusting our posture to meet the
challenges imposed by the less-than-hoped-for response(s).* Still, we
think it better that we stay our hand and keep our swords in our
sheaths until such time as situations require something else from
us. Should exigent circumstances require our going to war, we
say attend to that business with gusto—undesirable as it is. We
commend doing so decisively and with all verve, and can advocate for so doing with no pangs of religious conscience. "Peace
first" should always be our mantra; if someone makes it something else, so be it. Necessary preemptive strikes do not offend
our sensibilities.

In Scripture, the Israelites were given claim to the real estate
in Canaan and were exhorted to contend for it and to "drive out,"
"destroy," "demolish," and "divide." They were commanded to
be disciplined, and not to pick fights with the descendants of
Esau their brother—as with other Arabian peoples dwelling east
of Canaan. Though moderns are given to lumping every "-ite"
in Canaan-land together—as with Moabite, Ammonite, Hittite,
Amorite, Canaanite, and the rest—the children of Israel were bid-
den to be more discriminating and to not harangue Arab peoples.
In looking at problems in and around Israel today, might we do
well to be discriminating and discerning as well? We think so.

Speaking of discerning, when one considers both the nature
of the Islamic movement itself and the movement's history in the
Holy Land—as elsewhere—the notion that one can carve up the

Jews' God-given homeland piece by piece and give it to ambitious Muslims to secure a peace belongs to the realm of fanciful imagination—period. *It has no basis in biblical theology, none in history, and none in reality!* What will become of this is anyone's guess. It is worth noting, though, that Scripture condemns the practice.

Politicians bent on carving up Israel in exchange for some scraps of short-term security will be considered heroes by those with eyes for the moment only. Anyone with a view of history will note that they are fools, much as those with an understanding of theology will note the utter folly and the fact that short-term benefits will not bring about long-term solutions.

God's gifting Israel to the Jewish people in perpetuity is so ubiquitously attested in biblical literature that for Bible readers to disavow it dwarfs any and all approaches to reason and can only be seen as a satanic blindness imposed upon the mind's eye of readers unable to comprehend the Scriptures they are endeavoring to master. Preachers who advocate for so doing should be sued for malpractice!

The cowardly virtue-deficit that manifests with the irresolute dealing with the impulses of radical Islamic expansionism announces to belligerent sorts that we are dying and/or dead. When the lack of will to defend what's just is normalized, what we're left with is a coward's world and, with it, the end of the time-honored struggle for human betterment. The death of civilization will soon follow. When the coward suffers the loss of a captivating vision worth dying for, he likewise suffers the diminution of a life worth living. Those of us with a Bible in hand and some innate moral fiber on the other would do well to resist the petitions of those who have neither, despite the fact that they parade their worthless sheepishness around in the dress of Christian virtue.

If and when Judeo-Christian sorts give away our future for a parcel of false security in the present, we not only sell our own children down the river, but we give away part of our own humanity in the process. Because some fear the religion of Islam—what we intentionally misname the "religion of peace"—and because we disclaim biblical principles and promises in order to service our fear, we wind up serving the god of Islam with the prospect that the very thing we fear will come upon us. Byzantine Christians, as you may recall from the above, tried assuaging Islamic militants many years ago, but appeasement did not serve them well: The Islamic hordes overran them when the opportunity presented. If we give "pieces" for "peace," we'll only have to pick up the "pieces" again later. This is a lesson from yesterday. Would that we learn it today.

NOTES

1. Because I believe the Messiah has come and that His name is Jesus ("Yeshua" in the Hebrew), I know many of my Jewish friends do *not* appreciate me at this time. I don't take it personally, however, and understand the chagrin to be one of the hazards of my vocation. *C'est la vie.* Dr. Griess has his share of critics as well.

2. My love for the Arab people will come across so strongly that I expect to be marginalized by some of my associates in response to it. Frankly, I couldn't care less. Though my Arab-friendly inclinations will raise a few eyebrows, I trust that those with better temperaments and Judeo-Christian resolutions among us will appreciate that *we simply are not to be given to lumping all people together, to pre-judging and vilifying the innocent, and/or to be hating anyone.* It's simply not the Judeo-Christian way. If I have my way, readers will more readily appreciate that.

3. Lest some mistakenly think me a sheepish "pacifist" for my interest, know that I keep an active reserve police commission in the patrol and criminal investigations divisions of a reasonably big city, in the context of which I am called upon to pull out a gun every now and again and take a belligerent into custody. I serve about sixteen to twenty hours per month as a cop and, frankly, I love it, even after all these years. If I were afraid to use a gun, I'd be well-served to surrender my commission. I won't though, because—unpleasant though it indeed is—I do not construe the appropriate use of force (when necessary) to be an affront to my religious faith and virtue. To the contrary, for me

an abiding sense of justice propels me to offer my services in order to preserve our way of life and to defend home and hearth when necessary. Furthermore, I personally construe imposing "due process" upon dastardly belligerents—through soldiering and policing—to be a noble endeavor, a vocation akin to that of the honorable knights of a bygone era.

4. My wife and I are avid ballroom dancers. We've been taking private lessons for years, and we typically attend one dance every week. A few months ago, I was at a formal dance with her and observed a Muslim family make their entrance. The women were decked out with their religious garb, and the men who were with them had the facial characteristics that pointed to their being Muslims from the Middle East. I have been to many dance studios and dance floors, and have never seen the likes of them there. After securing permission from my wife, I went over to the Muslim ladies and asked if any would like to dance. They were caught a bit off-guard, as you might well imagine. Much as they all looked very Islamic, for my part, I looked very Jewish. One of the young women gathered her composure and answered affirmatively, save the fact that she admitted to not knowing how to dance. I told her to follow me. I took her in my arms (appropriately) and off we went. In the process of dancing with her, I couldn't help but deeply like her. I knew she was breaking with tradition simply by being at that Friday evening dance. Her willingness to respond to a Jewish stranger's overture to dance, in like manner, must have raised an eyebrow or two, as it surely flew in the face of one of her cultural moorings. She didn't seem to care, though. She surely possessed an intrepid and bold spirit; I couldn't help but appreciate her for that. I not only developed a godly and appropriate spiritual affection for her, but it prompted me to feel more kindly disposed to the people she represented. Similarly, a few months ago, while I was jogging around the Arab section of old Jerusalem early one morning, a young Arab boy came alongside me and motioned that he wanted to listen to the iPod he noticed I was using. Distracted by him as I was, I took the earphones out of my ears and placed them in his. He greatly enjoyed the sounds, though I doubt he understood the English lyrics. Running beside him was a highlight of the trip for me. As we ran along—guys separated by generations, cultures, and religions—I couldn't help but fall in love with him, as with those represented by him. While with him, I mused: I don't hate this boy; I love him, in fact, as with the people represented to me by him.

5. "Protological," in biblical theology, speaks of "first things" (as per the Genesis narrative), whereas "eschatological," in theological vocabulary, speaks of "last things" (as per the book of Revelation).

6. This book concerns itself with the question of how we might be loving toward the people of the sands on the one hand, while protecting ourselves from their way of life on the other. Try as we may to be objective and keep an open mind, with clear head and heart, when I open up the Bible to offer a telling of the Sacred Text's mysteries that have bearing upon this world, I present to the task with my own limited experiences, faulty assumptions, and theological preconditioning—all of which leave an invariable mark upon my particular understanding and intellectual end-product. Of one hundred percent Jewish extract myself, and a conservative theologian on top, I discern reality with certain, previously wired inclinations that favor worldviews associated with these inclinations. Though I have been to Israel many, many times, my experience with the broader peoples and places in the region is limited, a realization that prompts me to walk ever so humbly when endeavoring to give an accounting for peoples and events beyond my direct personal webs of experience. These weaknesses do not cause me to shrink back from the task, however, as much as they force me to approach it with more caution.

7. To use a term borrowed from Professor Tony Maalouf, a professor at Southwestern Baptist Theological Seminary, Fort Worth, TX.

8. I similarly construe an analysis of providence's role to make for a powerful defense of the Christian worldview. *Making Our Peace with the Warriors of the Sand* wonders whether advocating for the will and ways of the coming "Prince of Peace" is limited to preachers hammering away at hearers' interior worlds and focusing on individuals' quests for equilibrium and "inner peace." Believing that "advocating" for Him can likewise entail offering a reasoned telling of what a heavenly God is "up to" in the world that exists beyond the borders of our own typically self-centered noses, I am interested in providence's role in history and prophecy—as much as I am in "soul winning." Though pressing "sinners" to repent indeed has its place, this book operates with the belief that it also has its limits. I want to impress readers with the notion that Bible teaching should both address the question of "What on earth is going on?"—beyond our immediate sphere of interests and circumstances—while being "down to earth" in the way it answers that question. This will translate into decisions Christ-ward.

9. Herein, I consider how, through the Islamic religion that began with Semites in Arabia, Islam spread beyond Arabia and morphed into forms that spoke to the nuanced interests of adherents in the host cultures of its conquered peoples. Given that Islam has long ceased to be simply an Arabian experience, I believe modern Bible readers would do well to differentiate between Arabs, Arabia, and the religion of Islam itself, and be freshly exposed to what the Bible says about Arabs apart from Islam. Presently only 17 percent of Muslims are descended from Arabian extract. That, coupled with the fact that larger and somewhat differently nuanced Muslim populations exist in Indonesia, Pakistan, India, and Bangladesh than in Arabia proper, presses the need to differentiate and expand our thinking.

10. I found Professor H. L. Willmington's list of key events to be particularly helpful to me here, much as the *Bible Knowledge Commentary,* edited by professors Walvoord and Zuck of the Dallas Theological Seminary, proved particularly helpful as an aid to unpack some of early Genesis. *Both helped me organize my thinking and writing, in addition to providing me with further insights into the biblical and historical dramas.* The history of Jerusalem by lauded archaeologist Dr. Eilat Mazar likewise was invaluable in helping me offer a brief telling of the city's history.

11. I, in effect, invented the word "arabiology." To my knowledge, there is no specific, discernable category for the study of Arabs in modern, Christian theology. I couldn't find one, so I invented "arabiology" to refer to it. "Protology," by contrast, is a theological term harking back to humankind's early history. It's basically unknown outside of the theological academy, where it has no major circulation to my knowledge. "Heterology," however, is borrowed from the natural sciences, though it has employment in theology, too—as you'll see. "Soteriology" is a theological term that reflects upon the various senses of "salvation," and is a well-known category in systematic theology, studied by all serious Bible students.

12. I have taught college-level theology, Bible, and ministry courses for twenty years. Throughout, I have heard more than one student "complain" about my "heady" vocabulary. Thinking that it's not unreasonable to require folks to develop their vocabulary, I made light of their critiques—and still do. After all, I reason, all disciplines in "higher education" have their special, esoteric language: law, medicine, chemistry, physics, engineering, and more. Not wanting to "dumb

down" my area, I was pleased to foist the language on those wishing to "cut their teeth" on formal theological studies. As a rule, however, I used existing vocabulary. In this case, though, I am inventing it, not because I want to impress—or depress—you, but because here, at the borders of traditional knowledge, there just isn't much vocabulary to give voice to what needs to be said.

13. Books with titles like *Eurabia* and *Londonistan* have come out recently, giving Westerners a discomforting "warning shot across the bow" while raising concerns associated with Islam's rise in Europe and the threat its emergence poses to the "West." I raised this issue myself in a TV series entitled *Bad Moon Rising* previously, and am *not* minded to do so here. (Go to www.levitt.com if you'd like to see the archived television series.) For its part, this book is not a "warning shot" of the Arabs' coming as much as it is a "wake-up call" for Jews and Christians to come to terms with the manifold ways and means that Arabs are commended in Sacred Scripture—"warring" sorts being but one.

14. After hearing assurances that an heir from his body would indeed be forthcoming, in verse 4, Abraham went outside and turned his gaze heavenward. While thus inclined, God said, in essence, "Count the stars if you are able to number them" (v. 5), after which He affirmed, "so shall your descendants be." Abraham's turning and "believing" in God's Word to him, in verse 6, over and against his own perennial frustrations and circumstances, attested to an abiding faith within him, registered a place for him in the Bible's faith-based "Hall of Fame" (Hebrews 11:8–12), and entitled him to the name, "father of faith."

15. Cf. Ihab J. Griess, *Syntactical Comparisons between Classical Hebrew and Classical Arabic: A Study Based on the Translation of Mohammad ʿId's Arabic Grammar* (Lewiston, NY: E. Mellen, 2008), 247ff.

16. J. H. Charlesworth, ed., *The Old Testament Pseudepigrapha* (New York: Doubleday, 1985), 2:35.

17. Some say he married two different women.

18. The Messiah is attributed directly to David in Matthew 22:42, "What think ye of Christ? Whose son is he? They say unto him, 'The Son of David.'"

19. Josephus, *The Jewish War* (6.8.3).

20. Henry Barclay Swete, *An Introduction to the Old Testament in Greek* (New York: KTAV, 1968), 571.

21. In all fairness, however, it should be added that the cruel Assyrians were not easy for Israelites to love.

22. *The Writings of Justin Martyr* (Nashville, TN: Broadman & Holman, 1998), 9–10.

23. In 12:42, Matthew, who started us off here by noting that Arabians from the East came bearing gifts for the Messianic King, quotes Jesus corroborating this: "the queen of the South," the Queen of Sheba "came from the ends of the earth to hear Solomon"—from Arabia, particularly.

24. Those interested in my read on Paul would be well-served to get my 2008 book entitled *In the Footsteps of the Rabbi from Tarsus* (Dallas: Zola Levitt Ministries, 2008) and/or go to www.levitt.com and view the twelve-part television series we produced by that name.

25. Aryeh Kasher, *Jews, Idumaeans, and Ancient Arabs: Relations of the Jews in Eretz-Israel with the Nations of the Frontier and the Desert during the Hellenistic and Roman Era (332 BCE–70 CE)* (Tübingen, Germany: J. C. B. Mohr, 1988), 6.

26. "Nabat," *Encyclopedia of Islam* (Leiden: E. J. Brill, 1984), 7:834–35. In fact, a stele in the Damascus Museum bears Nabataeans inscriptions with the following written on it: "King of the Nabataeans." This archaeological evidence documents not only their presence in Syria, but also their control over it for some time.

27. Herodotus was a Greek historian (490–431 BC) who travelled extensively throughout the Mediterranean Sea, and whose work survived under the title *Histories*. Strabo was a Greek historian and geographer (63 BC–AD 23 AD). Although his historical writings were entirely lost, his seventeen-volume *Geography* work survived.

28. Cf. Israel Eph'al, *The Ancient Arabs: Nomads on the Borders of the Fertile Crescent, 9th–5th Centuries BC* (Jerusalem: Magnes Press, 1982), 193.

29. Dr. Griess favors the traditional site, with Dr. Seif favoring the Arabian location.

30. The Artapanus references, as with the *Jubilees* text (below), are culled from James Charlesworth's *Old Testament Pseudepigrapha II* (Garden City: Doubleday, 1985).

31. As per n. 30, above.

32. In 1:1, Deuteronomy refers to it with: "These are the words which Moses spoke unto all Israel on this side of the Jordan in the wilderness, in the Arabah opposite Suph, between Paran, and Tophel, and Laban, and Hazeroth, and Dizahab."

33. My principle source is Professor Allen Ross' assessment of Genesis in Dr. John Walvoord and Dr. Roy Zuck's *The Bible Knowledge Commentary* (Wheaton: Victor, 1985), 42–44.

34. This is Dr. Griess' position. I, however, am inclined to favor Israel as the proper the site.

35. Griess argues that there was once one huge continent and one huge ocean until the Flood of Noah. He sees that, in effect, the African Horn (Africa) and Yemen (Asia) were one part with no water divide in between. Three of the rivers of Genesis 2 (with the exception of the ambiguous Euphrates) form three-quarters of a circle that circumvents Egypt and Ethiopia from the west, Yemen from the south, and Iraq from the northeast. If we provide the fourth part of the circle, this makes the entire Middle East (including Israel) as the place of the garden with contemporary Saudi Arabia right in the middle! This may explain the subterranean ocean of petroleum under the vast Saudi desert, which argues that there was a huge garden/forest there one day that was eventually buried in the belly of the earth in order to form all that oil. Could it be that Arabia—the homeland of Arabs—was the actual place of the Garden of Eden?

36. As noted previously, for this I am appreciative of Professor H. L. Willmington's outline and summary of nations.

37. For that which follows immediately below, I am indebted to Dr. H. L. Willmington for his historical summaries in *Willmington's Guide to the Bible* (Wheaton: Tyndale House, 1984).

38. Should my abbreviated treatment not satisfy your interest in my read on eschatology, generally, and Iran's place in it, particularly, please go to www.levitt.com and pick up a copy of my *Iranian Menace in Jewish History and Prophecy*, where you'll get more.

39. Fifty-one of Jesus' sixty-three statements are contained in those two chapters, to be exact. Instructing through angelic intermediaries, Jesus is on record there giving seven very brief messages to seven distinct churches: beginning with that at Ephesus (2:1–7) and then Smyrna (2:8–11), Pergamos (2:12–17), Thyatira (2:18–29), Sardis (3:1–6), Philadelphia (3:7–13), and, lastly, Laodicea (3:14–22).

40. Jesus' exhortation to the Ephesian church to return to its "first love" in 2:5 is a telling and timeless revelation. That the church at Smyrna was enduring persecution, in v. 9, reveals that Christ doesn't always prescribe an easy road for His people. The church at Pergamos buckling under pressure prompted the Lord to call them to "repent," as per v. 16, which reveals that believers must keep on guard, lest we fall through our indolence. That the whore "Jezebel" is tolerated at Thyatira (v. 20), with the net result that some of the Lord's people are "commit[ting] sexual immorality" with her, is particularly revealing and appropriate in today's licentious world, where pornography is a $57 billion-dollar-per-year industry, earning more income than of all the major league sports teams combined. Is Jesus not here revealing and warning that we must keep ourselves undefiled? So it would seem. That the church at Sardis carries the name of being alive but it is dead (3:1b), with only a few authentic believers still resident therein noted in v. 4a, reveals that many will carry the name "Christian" who have long since lost the vision of what it means to be what the name implies. The exhortation to "be watchful, and strengthen the things which remain" in v. 2, to "remember" Christ's instructions and to "repent" in v. 3 are striking and revealing, and have bearing upon us today. That the church at Philadelphia is infiltrated by outsiders, in v. 9, is likewise telling and revealing, and underscores the importance of believers being individually faithful to the Lord, given that not all is as it might seem in the churches. The "lukewarm" Laodicean church's being "neither cold nor hot" (vv. 15–16), with the result that the Messiah will "vomit" it out, reveals the need for sincere believers to keep on guard against tendencies toward sloth and indifference.

41. Those interested in my further take on these matters should acquire my *Iranian Menace in Jewish History and Prophecy* (Dallas: Zola Levitt Ministries, 2007), available through www.levitt.com.

42. China has been suggested as a possibility.

43. My eight-part TV series launched in 2008 entitled *Ezekiel and the Mid East "Piece" Process* took this up some, as did my eight-part, 2007 series entitled *Bad Moon Rising*. Those interested should visit www.levitt.com and view them in the program archives.

44. My 2006–2007 series, *Daniel and the Last Days Battle for Planet Earth*, unpacked my understanding of these issues, and is available at the website above.

45. And, that being so, being exclusively responsible for this subsection, I have here applied myself to offer a rendering of that unhappy history.

46. See Bernard Lewis, *The Crisis of Islam* (New York: Random House, 2004), 6ff.

47. H. E. Wilkie Young, "Notes on the City of Mosul," enclosed with dispatch no. 4, Mosul, January 28, 1909, in F.O. 195/2308; published in *Middle Eastern Studies* 7 (1971): 232; culled from *The Political Traditions of Mohammed: The Hadith for the Unbelievers* (CSPI Publishing), 69.

48. http://history.club.fatih.edu.tr/103%20Huntington%20Clash%20of%20Civilizations%20full%20text.htm.

49. Vol. 266, September 1990, 60.

50. The late Professor Benjamin Mazar is lauded as having been one of Jerusalem's greatest archaeologists. His granddaughter, Dr. Eilat Mazar, has carried on his work and continues to make striking contributions to the field. I summarized her brief sketch of Jerusalem's history in her *Complete Guide to the Temple Mount Excavations* (Jerusalem: Shohan Academic Research and Publication, 2002), which I then presented at a class I conducted for a regional conference of the Messianic Jewish Alliance of America. Those notes constitute this subsection on Jerusalem's history.

51. The development of the "acropolis" in Jerusalem (i.e., the "upper house of the king," is noted in Neh. 3:25 [cf. 2 Ki. 5:24]), as is this "Ophel's" significance during Jotham's reign in 2 Chron. 27:3.

52. *Cf. Antiquities* XIII: 6:7.

53. See Andrew G. Boston, *The Legacy of Jihad: Islamic Holy War and the Fate of Non-Muslims* (Amherst, NY: Promethus, 2005) 43–51.

54. See Dr. Walter Emil Kaegi, *Byzantium and the Early Islamic Conquests* (Cambridge: Cambridge University, 1995), 88.

55. Adrian Morgan, "Winston Churchill on Islamis," *IslamWatch* April 10, 2007, http://www.islam-watch.org/AdrianMorgan/Winston-Churchill-Islamism.htm.

56. Boston.

57. *Cf.* Ihab J. Griess, *Syntactical Comparisons between Classical Hebrew and Classical Arabic: A Study Based on the Translation of Mohammad ʿId's Arabic Grammar* (Edwin Mellen, 2008), 1–2.

58. Norman A. Stillman, *The Language and Culture of the Jews of Sefrou, Morocco: An Ethnolinguistic Study* (Manchester: University of Manchester, 1988), 3–4.

59. C. J. Gadd, "The Haran Inscriptions of Nabonidus," *Anatolian Studies* 8 (1958), 87.

60. Griess, *Syntactical Comparisons,* 12–13.

61. Griess, *Syntactical Comparisons,* 13.

62. Ibid.

63. W. Bacher, "Grammar, Hebrew," in *The Jewish Encyclopedia* (New York: Funk and Wagnalls, 1902), 6:67.

64. Hartwig Hirschfeld, *Literary History of Hebrew Grammarians and Lexicographers* (London: Oxford University, 1926), 7.

65. Philip S. Alexander, "How Did the Rabbis Learn Hebrew?" in *Hebrew Study from Ezra to Ben-Yehuda,* ed. William Horbury (Edinburgh: T&T Clark, 1999), 77.

66. Joshua Blau, *The Emergence and Linguistic Background of Judeo-Arabic* (London: Oxford University 1965), 21.

67. *Cf.* Griess, *Syntactical Comparisons,* 16–18.

68. Abdelwahab Meddeb, *La Maladie De L'islam* (pub. is unknown, 2002), 129–130.

69. Fatima Mernissi, *Islam and Democracy: Fear of the Modern World* (Cambridge, MA: Perseus, 2002).

70. That made clear, in 50:1–51:64, Jeremiah moves closer to home and offers a lengthy treatment of Babylon—modern Iraq. Jeremiah proffers a "word of the Lord against Babylon" in 50:1. In v. 13, he notes that "every one that goeth by Babylon shall be appalled" and will "hiss" at her, given the waste and utter destruction noted by him in v. 21. Jeremiah sees that "the Lord hath opened His armory, and hath brought forth the [very fierce] weapons of His indignation," in v. 25. "Archers" will encamp around her and permit "none" "escape" their mark in v. 29. "Her young men [shall] fall in the streets," in v. 30, as will the "men of war...in that day." Many will fall, and "none shall raise him up," for God will "kindle a fire in his cities, and it shall devour all round about him," says the Lord (v. 32), whose "purpose is against Babylon, to

destroy it," 51:11, given "all their evil that they have done," in v. 24, in
molesting "all the earth," in v. 25. Babylon's fighting men have become
"like [distraught] women," in v. 30, and are left "devoured," "crushed,"
"empty" and as if "swallowed...up by a monster" in v. 34. In v. 58,
Jeremiah wraps up saying: "The broad walls of Babylon shall be utterly
broken, and her high gates shall be burned with fire, And the people
shall labor in vain, and the folk in the fire, and they shall be weary." He
finally finishes up in v. 64, noting: "Babylon shall sink, and shall not
rise from the evil that I will bring upon her; and they shall be weary."

71. Isaiah uses the term "Holy One of Israel" twenty-five times in his
    book(s), in 1:4; 5:19, 24; 10:20; 12:6; 17:7; 29:19; 30:11, 15; 31:1;
    37:23; 41:14, 16, 20; 43:3, 14; 45:11; 47:4; 48:17; 49:7; 54:5; 55:5;
    60:9, 14. That it is employed only six other times in the entire Old
    Testament (cf. 2 Kings. 19:22 [which is attributed to Isaiah]; Jer. 50:29;
    51:5; Ps. 71:22; 78:41; 89:18) argues for its unique importance for
    Isaiah, and begs the following question: why? The expression "Holy
    One of Israel" has no long-standing tradition of employment before
    Isaiah, and the premium placed upon it may well hark back to Isaiah's
    seminal religious experience, during which time he received his one
    and only vision in conjunction with his "call" to the ministry (cf.
    6:1–7, esp. v. 3b). As for its origin, the word "holy"—as in "Holy
    One"—comes from the Hebrew *kadosh* which denotes "set apart" and/
    or "separate," and harks to being "set apart" for the Lord's work. When
    initially confronted with this "Holy One," Isaiah, for his part—and
    by way of contrast with Uzziah (cf. 2 Chron. 26:1ff.)—felt personally
    unworthy and "unclean" (6:5), and said "I dwell in the midst of a
    people with unclean lips" (6:5)—itself but one of many problems they
    had. In what follows, we will consider how Isaiah's "Holy" God had an
    indictment against an "unholy" people, in the process of which we will
    pay attention to particulars.

72. Isaiah was an eighth-century BC, Jerusalem-based court prophet,
    known to have ministered successfully under the administrations of
    Judean kings Uzziah, Jotham, Ahaz, and Hezekiah (Isa. 1:1), and
    arguably unsuccessfully under one: Manasseh. A contemporary of the
    lesser-known prophets Amos, Hosea, and Micah, Isaiah seems to have
    towered above them in influence, owing perhaps to his being both a
    cousin to King Uzziah (as per *Meg.* 10b) and also the royal chronicler of
    Uzziah's administration (2 Chron. 26:22). With royal blood in his veins
    and administrative responsibilities, Isaiah had easy access to Judean

rulers (cf. 7:3; 8:2), a dynamic that both earned him the honorific title "Court Prophet/Preacher" and later cost him his life—given Manasseh's particular disdain for him (as per the *Assumption of Isaiah*).

73. It is likely that the unknown author of Hebrews was referring to Isaiah's horrific and tortuous demise when surveying the Old Testament's "Hall of Fame" of martyrs in 11:1–40. That he was referring to the persecution of individuals of faith is clear from the context (cf. 11:1ff.). What is less evident, however, is the reason the religious personalities incurred monarchs' displeasure. Given that Christian expositors are preoccupied with how Isaiah—and all the Old Testament prophets (by association)—spoke prophetically of the coming Messiah, many do not take the time to become acquainted with the context of the prophets' ministries, and thus they have trouble understanding their messages. Isaiah did not incur the wrath of the king because he uttered predictions of the coming Messiah—of Jesus Christ who would come later; rather, he incurred the wrath of Judean monarchs because he challenged their personal indifference and their political policies, exposing both as being incongruent with God's will for Judah. To illustrate, one needs only consider the book's introduction.

74. To give but one example, compare Isa. 53:1 and John 12:37–38; 53:2 and Luke 2:40; 53:3–4 and John 1:11; 7:47–48; 53:5–6 and John 1:29, 11:49–52, 1 Cor. 15:3, 2 Cor. 5:21, 1 Pet. 2:24–25; 53:7 and Matt. 26:59–62, 27:12–14, Mark 15:3–5, Luke 23:8–9; 53:8 and Matt. 27:1–2, Luke 23:1–25; 53:9 and Matt. 27:57–60, Mark 15:42–47, Luke 23:50–52; 53:10 and Heb. 2:10; 53:11 and Rom. 3:22–24, Eph. 2:8–9; 53:12 and Luke 23:32–33, Heb. 9:26, 28, 1 Pet. 3:18.

75. Al-Tabari, *The Book of Religion and Empire* (New York: Longmans, 1922), 51.

76. Jacques Jomier, *Jesus, the Life of the Messiah* (Madras, C. L. S., 1974), 216.

77. Gerhard Nehls, *Dear Abdullah*, Letter 2, http://www.answering.org/Nehls/Abdallah/abdal12.htm.

78. Our drawing attention to the power of miracles here should not be construed as our looking to advocate for the supernatural, or for the doctrine of churches given to accentuating the miraculous. We like to "play my cards close to my chest" on this score, so there's little to be gained in trying to second-guess where we stand on this issue personally. Here, we raise the matter because *I believe that there exists*

a great and under-reported miracle in the world today, one that has the power to galvanize a public support and draw individuals' attention to the fact that there is a great and powerful God who, being above all, is working in and through all for His expressed purposes. He transcends the typical bounds of human experience and has His own way of showing Himself real and strong in the world. What is that miracle? Modern Israel's emergence is significant—an undisputable proof for the veracity of Scripture. But, more on this later.

79. A Messianic Jew is someone who is wrestling with the question of what it means to be a Jew and walk in the footsteps of Israel's Messiah, all the while. A Messianic synagogue, by association, is a congregation where people are working this out.

80. http://www.abcarticledirectory. com/Article/The-Great-Men-of-History/129048.

81. Soul-sickened humanity is weakened by sin, hungry for meaning and purpose, and in need of an intoxicating vision to bring the best out in man by prompting him to transcend his otherwise unbridled base tendencies. Afflicted mortals can turn to this great and awesome God, find help, health, healing, and fresh opportunities to start all over again in life—and be "saved." In short, folk who have not made much out of being "born" can turn around and be "born again," in the wake of which they can become acquainted with God's plan and discover how what's happening in this precarious world is lining up in accordance with it. In this sense, "eschatology" marries and kisses "soteriology," serving each other's purposes as they do.

82. The fact is that fewer and fewer people are getting saved today. That we are not in a "revival era" has long been noticed. What has been kept from view, though, is the consequence of the lack of spiritual vitality. The closure of church properties is on the rise in some stalwart, conservative "evangelical" circles, evidence that all is not well. Epidemic levels of ministry-work-related dissatisfaction is attested in survey after survey. In fact, a reasonably recent longitudinal study designed to ascertain what becomes of individuals after they have taken a "Master of Divinity" degree—the standard academic "prep" degree for the ministerial vocation—has turned up that nearly half of all seminary graduates quit ministry ten years after their first assignment. The reasons for this are many and each is rather complex.

ABOUT THE AUTHORS

 Dr. Jeffrey L. Seif took a master's degree and doctorate from Southern Methodist University, and is a proud graduate of the North Texas Regional Police Academy. He serves as a Bible college and seminary professor, in addition to which he is the face and voice of *Zola Levitt Presents*, a nationally syndicated television concern that teaches on the Jewish roots of the Christian faith, Israel and prophecy, and more.

 Dr. Ihab Griess took a bachelor's degree in pharmaceutical studies in Egypt and came to the United States, where he earned a master's degree from Regent University and a doctorate from Southern Baptist Theological Seminary. He is an author and theology instructor, serving as an adjunct professor at Liberty University.